English as a Foreign or
Second Language

English as a Foreign or Second Language

Selected Topics in the Areas of Language Learning, Teaching, and Testing

Mohammed S. Assiri

PARTRIDGE
A Penguin Random House Company

To order additional copies of this book, contact
Toll Free 800 101 2657 (Singapore)
Toll Free 1 800 81 7340 (Malaysia)
orders.singapore@partridgepublishing.com

www.partridgepublishing.com/singapore

Contents

List of Figures

To my parents, my wife Fatimah, and my three sons Abdullah, Shuaib, and Alwaleed.

Preface

The fields of English language learning, teaching, and testing have been evolving over decades of practice and research. Specialists in these areas have gained insights from their practical experiences about how to advance their practices and dealings with the various aspects of their professions. Like the other areas in physical and social sciences, research in the fields of English language teaching, learning, and testing has continued to inform the decisions as to the adequacy of applying certain procedures or techniques in actual practice.

A vast amount of theory and research has been injected into the fields of English language teaching, learning, and testing, which goes so much far beyond the scope of a single book. Hence, this book offers a brief review of the theoretical views and empirical findings that have shaped our understanding of salient facets of English language teaching, learning, and testing. Besides its genuine goal of informing the reader of the current state of the literature on these areas, this book communicates my personal views in regard to certain issues. The review here assumes background knowledge of the terminology that is commonly used in the field of applied linguistics. Wherever it shows in this book, EL2 refers to English as an L2, intended to refrain from any specifics that arise from the distinction between EFL and ESL (i.e., English as a foreign language and English as a second language).

The book is divided into five chapters that range in their foci from theory to practice in the fields of English language learning, teaching, and testing. Chapter one presents the most influential theoretical perspectives that have sought to account for the processes involved in second language acquisition and the roles of the so many variables that affect how a learner acquires a second language. A unique element of this chapter is a whole section that offers a framework for an alternative theory by Michel Long, an often-overlooked vision. The second chapter discusses several methods and practices commonly used in EL2 teaching. It illustrates with specific examples how certain language skills can be taught at specific levels, including teaching an interpersonal communication strategy to novice learners. Chapter three highlights the differences between Basic Interpersonal Communication Skills and Cognitive Academic Language Proficiency (or BICS vs. CALP) as well as the various categories of language learning and use strategies. In the fourth chapter, the presentation centers on EL2 testing and assessment. It provides the reader with illustrations of how the four language skills (namely listening, speaking, reading, and writing) can be tested at two upper levels of proficiency (i.e., intermediate and advanced). Chapter five is wholly devoted to my personal views on EL2 learning, teaching, and testing. Such views have had their inspiration and support from my experiences both as a learner and as a teacher.

Embedded in the content of this book are views of a number of my former university instructors, colleagues, and friends, as expressed in meetings and seminars, over the years. I acknowledge their constructive ideas and opinions that have been of special import in informing the presentation and discussion all through this publication.

Chapter 1

Views and Considerations Underlying L2 Acquisition

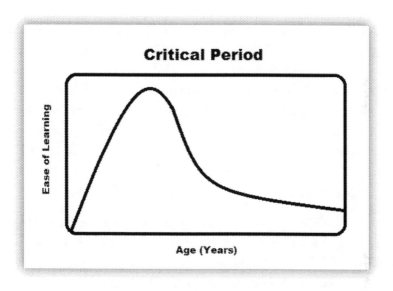

☐ Is L2 Learning Similar to L1 Acquisition?
☐ The Critical Period Hypothesis
☐ The Monitor Model and Its Five Hypotheses
☐ Communicative Competence
☐ An Alternative Theory
☐ Factors that Affect L2 Learning in Adulthood

+ *Native Language*
+ *Age*
+ *Anxiety*
+ *Motivation*

Is L2 learning similar to L1 acquisition?

The fact that L2 learning among adults is qualitatively different from L1 learning is evident across various language learning contexts and explainable in terms of a number of factors. However, there are several aspects that characterize both adult L2 learning and child L1 learning: First, both L2 and L1 develop in similar predictable stages e.g., the order of acquisition of morphemes (Devillers & Devillers, 1973; Dulay & Burt, 1974), negative and interrogative forms (Ellis, 1986). Second, both L2 and L1 spoken languages show shorter utterances, high-frequency vocabulary, and frequent use of gestures (Richard-Amato, 1987). Third, both L2 and L1 are constructed from prior conceptual knowledge. Fourth, both L2 and L1 learner groups go through a silent period before being able to produce meaningful utterances (Asher, 1972). Fifth, both L2 and L1 learning processes have developmental errors, use cognitive strategies, and require practice and comprehensible input.

In contrast, there are several aspects that set adult L2 learning and child L1 learning apart. Besides the fact that L1 is acquired subconsciously in natural settings, whereas L2 is acquired or learned consciously in natural or artificial (classroom) settings, the *Fundamental Difference Hypothesis* (Bley-Vroman, 1989, Schachter, 1988) claims that learning of an L1 is different from learning of an L2 in a number of ways:

1) L1 learners have the mental facility to acquire any language whereas adult L2 learners do not (e.g., access to universal grammar).
2) L1 learners and adult L2 learners vary in the degree of language attainment since L1 learners have access to universal grammar that adults do not.

3) L1 learners can reach a level of complete and complex knowledge of their L1 that adult L2 learners cannot (Schachter, 1988).

4) L1 learners are endowed with a domain-specific module that guarantees them success that adult L2 learners lack (Bley-Vroman, 1989).

5) Adult L2 learners may reach a plateau (i.e., cease to improve), whereas L1 learners do not.

6) L1 learners can use their L1 grammar more intuitively than adult L2 learners can with respect to L2 grammar.

7) L1 learning does not require formal instruction or lessons, whereas adult L2 learning calls for formal classes especially in non-L2 contexts.

8) L1 learning is not influenced by factors such as personality, motivation, attitude, and aptitude as is adult L2 acquisition.

9) The differences between L1 learning and adult L2 learning manifests itself in different aspects that include internal (cognitive state of adults and children), linguistic (caused by a change in the language faculty), and qualitative (affected by availability of the domain-specific acquisition system).

10) Maturational constraints, including neurological (effect of the critical period) and affective (much of the input for adults is filtered out "depending on levels of motivation, self-confidence, and anxiety." (Krashen, 1982; MacIntyre & Charos, 1996).

11) Affective constraints including negative attitudes or beliefs about L2 or its culture or ego boundaries and low or lack of motivation (Gardner and Lambert, 1972).

12) Linguistic constraints, including L1 interference (adult L2 learners transfer patterns from their L1 that lead to an L2 non-target-like usage) and L2 avoidance (adult L2 learners avoid using L2 patterns that are not part of their L1).

L1 transfer that he claims can be positive facilitating L2 learning, negative interfering with L2 learning, or takes the form of avoidance. Lado (1957) claims the positive L1 transfer (facilitation) occurs when the learner transfers patterns or forms of his or her L1 that can help him or her learn L2, whereas the negative L1 transfer occurs when such transferred patterns or forms interfere with L2 learning (interference).

Nevertheless, there are differences between child L1 learning and adult L2 learning that favor the latter to the former: 1) Adult L2 learners can benefit from L1 positive transfer (facilitation). 2) Adult L2 learners can make use of appropriate learning styles and strategies. 3) Adult L2 learners have more background knowledge of the world. 4) Adult L2 learners have more control of L2 input (e.g., ask for repetition, negotiate meaning, and change the topic). Therefore, when comparing L1 acquisition and L2 learning, we usually compare/contrast L1 child acquisition and L2 adult learning. Although there are some similarities between L1 child acquisition and L2 adult learning (Ervin-Tripp, 1974; Ellis, 1986), the important differences must be taken into account.

L1 and L2 learners develop language in similar, predictable stages. In reference to Krashen's (1973) *Natural Order Hypothesis.* Bailey, Madden, and Krashen (1973) found that adults and children followed similar order in learning a second language; Dulay and Burt (1974) found a universal order in L2 morpheme acquisition, and R. Brown (1973) and Devillers and Devillers (1973) reached the same conclusion in regard to L1 morpheme acquisition; and Cazden (1972) and Ellis (1986) noticed that L1 order of the acquisition of the transitional forms of negative and interrogatives is similar to the case of L2 acquisition. Also, Henzl (1973), Long (1981), and Richard-Amato (1987) discovered shared aspects in L1 and L2 speech: shorter sentences, high-frequency vocabulary, indirect correction, frequent gesture, and lack of over attention to formL1 and L2 constructed from prior conceptual knowledge. L1 acquirers benefit from a silent period before they begin to produce meaningful utterances (Krashen, 1973); however, Asher (1972), Gary (1975), and Postovsky (1977) also observed that if L2 speakers experience the silent period they also benefit from it.

According to Krashen's (1973) *Acquisition-learning Hypothesis*, children are not taught to learn a language. They acquire a language naturally and subconsciously whereas adults have two different ways: to acquire and to learn. The former is similar to L1 child acquisition and the second is through learning in formal classes. The two forms of adult L2 development are not overlapped. Schachter (1988) upholds the view that children are capable of learning any language. Given exposure to language (or linguistic input), a child will learn it. No language is easier to learn than another, and all languages are equally learnable by all children. This is, however, not the case for adult L2 learners. The *Fundamental Difference Hypothesis* argues that what happens in child language acquisition is not the same as what happens in adult second language acquisition. This hypothesis starts from the belief that with regard to language learning, children and adults are different in many important ways. For instance, the ultimate attainment reached by children and adults differs. In normal situations, children always reach a state of "complex" knowledge of their native language. In second language acquisition, at least in adult second language acquisition, not only is "complete" knowledge not always attained, it is rarely, if ever, attained.

Fossilization representing a non-target language stage is frequently observed with L2 adult learners. Thus, the major difference between childhood L1 acquisition and adulthood L2 acquisition is the lack of "general guaranteed success" (Bley-Vroman, 1989, p.43) on the part of L2 learners. All children achieve perfect mastery of L1; however, the same cannot be stated about L2 learners. In spite of years of classroom instruction, exposure to L2 input, and motivation, many adults L2 learners are not able to acquire the target language. If universal grammar were operative during the process of L2 learning, such a lack of guaranteed success would not occur. This lack supports Bley-Vroman's (1989) claim that L2 acquisition is guided by "general human cognitive learning capacities rather than by the same domain-specific module which guarantees child success in first language acquisition" (p. 44). There is also substantial variation in "degree of attainment, in course of learning, and in strategies of learning" (Bley-Vroman, 1989, p. 45). Such a degree of variation in the ultimate attainment of the L2 further supports Bley-Vroman's contentions that universal grammar is not available to adult L2 learners and that no domain-specific cognitive mechanisms are utilized by these learners.

Unlike children, L2 adult learners set up different goals as to their desired level of L2 mastery. For instance, some adult learners may be satisfied with a basic level of L2 proficiency that allows them to survive in the target language culture; others may wish to acquire an L2 only to be able to read in the target language. Children do not experience this type of flexibility because their goals are not under control. Adult L2 learners also differ from children acquiring an L1 in terms of "fossilization". Adult learners may reach a certain plateau that cannot be surpassed no matter how hard the individual tries to overcome. Also, adult L2 learners at the very advanced level of proficiency do not exhibit the same level of intuition about grammaticality of sentences that native speakers do. Children, unlike adults, do not require formal grammar lessons to acquire native language. They simply need exposure to linguistic input. Children's success in L1 development is not affected by such factors as personality, motivation, attitude, and aptitude, which play important roles in adult L2 acquisition.

The *Fundamental Difference Hypothesis* not only described differences between child and adult language acquisition, but also asserts that these differences are internal (cognitive states of adults and children), linguistic (caused by a change in the language faculty), and qualitative (the domain-specific acquisition system is not just attenuated).

Long (1999) gives an account of maturational constraints that affect language acquisition process, combining neurological and affective aspects: 1) L2 learners lose some of their earlier abilities, such as speaking native-like according to the *Critical Period Hypothesis* which proposes that language learning needs to take place before puberty; otherwise, it will become difficult later and a foreign accent will emerge. (Lenneberg, 1967). 2) L2 learners exhibit increased inhibitions and anxiety, and are afraid of making errors (MacIntyre & Charos, 1996). 3) L2 learners may also have poor attitude and lack of motivation (Gardner & Lambert; Deci). 4) Interference may occur with structures that are different from L1 to L2 (Newmark, 1983; Lado, 1957), 5) L2 learners may try to avoid using certain structures because they are not part of their L1 repertoire (Schachter, 1974; Kleinman, 1977).

Nonetheless, because learners are usually older when acquiring an L2, they are more cognitively developed when compared to L1 learners. In fact, they have advantages in several areas: 1) L2 learners have an L1 from which they can transfer strategies and linguistics; 2) Knowledge of more than one culture gives them advanced information about expectations, discourse in general, and how to get things done with language. 3) L2 learners typically have more background knowledge of the world than their L1 counterparts; 4) L2 learners have more control over the input they receive (e.g., ask for repetition, renegotiate meaning, change the topic ... etc.); 5) L2 learners can learn, comprehend, apply rules, and so tend to learn more quickly; and 6) L2 learners have their own personal variables, such as their learning styles and strategies, and motivation that may produce remarkable language learning results. Due to these considerations, older learners demonstrate much greater variation in their rate of acquisition and in their degree of ultimate proficiency than do young learners (Richard-Amato, 2003).

Mohammed S. Assiri

Because language development involves learning processes, be it L1, L2 ...or L3, adult L2 learning and child L1 learning share a number of aspects some of which have empirically been confirmed. First, both L1 and L2 develop through similar stages in that some grammatical aspects have shown to be learned in the same order in both L1 and L2 learning (e.g., the rate of acquiring grammatical morphemes) (Devillers & Devillers, 1974; Dulay & Bert, 1973), and the acquisition of negatives and interrogatives (Ellis, 1991). Second, similar aspects tend to characterize both L1 and L2 speech, for example, high-frequency vocabulary and frequent use of gestures. Third, both L1 and L2 benefit from conceptual knowledge about the world (Amato-Carlos, 1986). Fourth, both L1 and L2 exhibit what is called the silent period—a period during which a child or a learner does not speak until she is ready for meaningful utterances (Asher, 1972). Finally, there are similar processes that have been observed in both L1 and L2 such as developmental errors, cognitive strategies, and need for practice and comprehensible input.

However, despite the above-mentioned similarities, there are a variety of aspects that favor child L1 learning to adult L2 learning. First, L1 is acquired subconsciously in a natural setting, whereas L2 is acquired or learned consciously in a formal or artificial setting. The majority of scholars agree that children are endowed with a mental ability or facility that enables them to acquire any language; however, adults learning an L2 lack this facility and so some of them end up with native-like speech and some do not. It is this language facility that also enables children to achieve higher level of L1 attainment than do adults learning an L2. This language facility is sometimes equated with universal grammar to which children have fuller access than that allowed for adults. Children can also achieve a high level of mastery and knowledge of their L1s that adults are unable to attain in an L2. Another advantage favoring children is that they have a domain-specific language module which promises children success in their L1 learning endeavor; such an aspect is almost lacking in the case of L2 adult learners. Children can use their L1 grammar intuitively without ever having to rely extensively on formal grammar instruction as is the case in adult L2 learners. L1 is not influenced by such factors as psychological, affective, and social as is L2.

In conclusion, it is obvious that when comparing child L1 learning to adult L2 learning, we have to consider not only the aspects that favor the first to the latter, but also the advantages that the later have over the former. This is important in order to keep the adult L2 learners motivated and encouraged in such a tremendous undertaking as language acquisition.

The Critical Period Hypothesis

The twofold aim of this section is to survey the literature on the *Critical Period Hypothesis* (CPH) and highlight its implications in second language acquisition (SLA). In order to achieve this purpose, this section is divided into four sub-sections. In the first section, the CPH's inception in the field of language acquisition as well as its assumptions are explained. The second section presents thought and research evidence supporting the CPH premises along with the underlying factors accounting for its role. The third section reviews several studies that sought to refute the CPH assumptions and proposed other sets of factors explaining the differences between adult and young learners in L2 attainment. And last but not least, section four is entirely devoted to elaborating on the CPH's implications in SLA.

The Canadian neurosurgeon Penfield (1963) proposes that the earlier a foreign language is learned the better, maintaining that a child's brain has a time-limited plasticity. This encouraged Lenneberg (1967), a psycholinguist and the originator of the CPH, to suggest that language acquisition should take place by puberty, otherwise it will become difficult and a foreign accent will appear at puberty for L2 learners. Supporting his view, Lenneberg (1967) maintains that this critical period (CP) concurs with the cerebral lateralization of the brain, or the process by which language functions become part of the left hemisphere. In an attempt to summarize Penfield and Lenneberg's perspectives, Scovel (1969) claims that the brain loses its plasticity after the cerebral lateralization is completed at the age of puberty and that affects speech in the case of post-puberty language acquirers more perceptibly than the other aspects of language. In his book, Lenneberg (1976) argues that habitual acquisition from the surrounding environment fades away after puberty; hence, language learning will then call for "a conscious and labored effort" and a foreign accent will become inevitable.

What follows is a synthesis of thought and research that advocate the CP's role in language acquisition. Most of this research has attempted to investigate the difference between young and adult L2 learners. Accordingly, in their study of child and adult L2 learners in an immersion setting, Herschensohn, Stevenson and Waltmunson (2005) found that children were more attentive to inflectional morphology details than adults. Also, Johnson and Newport (1989) conducted a study of ESL attainment among immigrants to the U.S. and found that for the participants aged from seven to seventeen years old, there was a noticeable decline in their performance in a grammaticality judgment task, whereas for the other participants up to seven years old, their performance was steady and promising. A similar study carried out earlier by Patkowski (1980) pointed out parallel findings.

Accounting for foreign accents, Diller (1981), Long (1990), Molfese (1977), Rubin (1997), and Seliger's (1987) propose that phonetic/phonological aspects are more constrained by the CP than the other linguistic aspects, including morphology, syntax, and semantics. Likewise, Scovel (1988) suggests that because of its neuromuscular basis" pronunciation is not as achievable for adult L2 learners as morphology, syntax, and vocabulary. Flege, Munro, and MacKay (1995) studied ESL sentence production by Italian immigrants to Canada and found that the participants' ratings for a native-like tone of voice declined steadily as their age of arrivals increased. As regards laterality effect, after synthesizing a number of studies, Neville and Bavelier (1998) and Newport, Bavelier, and Neville (2001) suggest that the left hemisphere is involved in language acquisition in bilinguals' L1 generally and young bilinguals' L2 specifically and that the neural systems for L1 and those for late L2 acquisition are apart. In a study of 34 English native speakers and 34 immigrants with different ages of arrival in the U.S., Patkowski (2003) argues that his findings agreed with the CPH "of increased right hemisphere involvement in multilingual (immigrants) during speech production."

According to Singleton (2005), the most oft-cited principal causes of the CP are the decrease of cerebral plasticity with age (Penfield & Roberts, 1959), the cerebral lateralization (Lenneberg, 1967; Molfese, 1977), ego boundaries or language ego in adult individuals (Guiora, Brannon & Dull, 1972; Guiora, Beit-Hallahmi, Brannon, Dull & Scovel, 1972), the optimal distance between an L2 acquirer and the L2 context and culture (Schumann, 1978), the localization of certain language functions in the dominant hemisphere (Seliger, 1978), the different developmental timetables of different neurons (Diller, 1981), the affective filter which is seen high in adult L2 learners (Krashen, 1982), the myelination of neurons (Ioup, Boustagui, El Tigi, & Moselle, 1994), the different spatial representations of L1 and L2 in the brain (Kim, Relkin, Kyoung-Min & Hirsch, 1997; Wattendorf, Westermann, Zappatore, Franceschini, Lüdi, Radü, & Nitsch, 2001), and cognitive maturation accompanied by a diminution in language acquisition ability (Bialystok, 2002; DeKeyser, 2003). As seen so far, the research evidence for the CP's role in language acquisition suggests that the Penfieldian view "the earlier, the better" (Scovel, 2000) seems to typically apply to sound production and accent more than the other aspects of language including grammar and vocabulary.

On the other hand, substantial research evidence has been launched against the CPH's claims. The CPH proponents have noticeably come up with a variety of explanations for their views (Singleton, 2005). Thompson (2001) critiques these attempts as being complex concepts that make "it difficult, if not impossible, to identify the parameters of sensitive periods with appropriate specificity." In fact, Lenneberg (1967) himself maintains that "most individuals of average intelligence are able to learn a second language after the beginning of their second decade," despite the increasing "language-learning-blocks" with age. This obviously implies that the CP's claim is overinflated considering that language acquisition will occur sooner or later. Similarly, Abello-Contesse (2009) argued that the attainment of adequate command of a second language is possible for young and adult learners alike.

Snow and Hoefnagel-Höhle (1978) conducted a study of differently aged English speakers who were learning Dutch. The researchers found that subjects aged from twelve to fifteen showed more rapid acquisition when compared to younger subjects aged from three to five. In their study of Julie who acquired a native-like proficiency of Egyptian Arabic, Ioup et al. (1994) attributes this success to, among other learning habits, her flourishing manipulation of grammatical aspects through conscious attention to both form and function. Birdsong (1999) reported that among twenty adult learners of French, fifteen showed a native-like performance on a grammaticality judgment task; however, their performance was nearly predictable by their age of arrival in France. More recently, Karen, Eleonore, Wolfgang, Inge, Marko (2011) observed that the bilateral superior temporal gyri was centrally activated with age, which augmented the functionality of the language comprehension network.

While some research suggests that the CP has an undeniable effect on pronunciation or accent, a number of studies have shown that adults still have a chance to attain a native-like pronunciation. Moyer (1999) had a sample of 24 English-speaking, proficient learners of German of whom one was judged by an expert to be a native speaker of German. Olson and Samuels (1973) found evidence that stands against the CP and supports adults' superiority to children with regard to the achievement of L2 native-speakers' accent. In fact, their adult subjects scored better than the young ones in pronunciation accuracy. The explanatory power of the CP counter-evidence stems from multiple factors that can be classified as either psychological or societal. According to Patkowski (1980), who was critical of this approach, Gardner et al., (1976) and Brown (1980) maintain that success or failure (in language acquisition) depends more on motivational and attitudinal factors which are more affected by socio-cultural factors than by age.

Snow and Hoefnagel-Höhle (1978) see that L2 learners have advantages that will facilitate their future tasks of acquiring a language irrespective of their age. That is, they have already learned a language and their dominant hemisphere is already specialized for language acquisition. Other researchers see other factors better explain the difference between children and adults than do neural or physiological factors. For example, Rosansky (1975), Felix (1981), Krashen (1975), and Elkind (1970) establish a connection between personality and environmental factors and L2 learning, suggesting that these factors tend to favor children to adults in terms of eventual attainment. Krashen (1982) also held this position in his notion of affective filter which, he believes, is stronger in adults than in children; and so, much of the input for adults is filtered out "depending on levels of motivation, self-confidence, and anxiety."

In summarizing the research and thought on the differences between young and adult L2 learners, Singleton (1989) maintains that the only abilities that disadvantage old learners have to do with affect and aspects of phonetic coding. He suggested, however, that there are some aspects of affect that favor adult learners. Birdsong (1999) considers such factors as type and amount of L2 input, motivation, attitude, and amount of L2 use as contributing to native-likeness. The latter, he notes, affects the degree of foreign accent. Therefore, for this realm of thought and research, as Marinova-Todd, Marshall, and Snow (2000) put it "age does influence language learning, but primarily because it is associated with social, psychological, educational, and other factors that can affect L2 proficiency, not because of any critical period that limits the possibility of language learning by adults".

Regarding the connection between the CPH and actual practice, Singleton (2005) suggests "... there are differing views on the practical implications of the notion of CP as far as language teaching is concerned." Marinova-Todd et al. (2000) recommends that a model of L2 instruction be a motivating, well-designed and -structured program (Singleton, 1995) that adds to prior learning (Singleton, 1997) over a number of years. In response to the effect of the CP on accent, the *Total Physical Response* method and the *Natural Approach* emerged (Scovel, 2000). According to Singleton (1989), some researchers preferred 'andragogy' as opposed to 'pedagogy' in adult L2 learning settings in which learners' needs, self-directedness, self-analysis, and self-assessment are emphasized (Allman, 1983; Knowles, 1970; Mezirow, 1981). Singleton (1989) also points out that other researchers recommend the use of individualized classes in which learners use materials and activities of interest to them and progress at their own pace (Stern, 1983), classroom logistics be made appropriate to adults (Joiner, 1981; Brandle, 1986), and learners be engaged in meaningful learning (Wingfield & Byrnes, 1981).

Stern (1983) especially notes that Penfield's "a proto-CP theorist" idea of "the younger, the better" in the 1950s and 1960s advocates that foreign language instruction starts from elementary school. In the same fashion, Singleton (1989) maintains that in order to achieve higher levels of L2 proficiency, L2 learning should occur in childhood. Based on their study of Julie, Ioup et al. (1994) agreed to the suggestion of many researchers that adults be made consciously attentive to form from the beginning of their L2 learning. In fact, they view conscious attention to form, associative memory, and mastery of new codes as abilities that distinguish talented adult learners. Therefore, L2 teachers may need to give more attention to the abilities that are associated with successful learning and incorporate such abilities in the activities they offer to their students.

From other perspectives, Carroll (1969, 1975) and Burstall et al. (1974) assert that the most important determinant of L2 learning success was the amount of instruction or exposure, which Krashen (1985) highlighted later in his *Input Hypothesis*. Hatch (1983) stresses the importance of the amount of exposure, practice, and interaction regardless of age effect. Titone (1986) recommends that L2 be used to teach other subjects. This is clearly in line with the 'exercise hypothesis' which, according to Bever (1981), suggests that speech perception and production should work jointly in order for acquisition to occur. Birdsong (1999) cites research findings (e.g., Bradlow et al., 1996; Yamada et al., 1996) indicating that training in L2 phonetic contrast can make L2 learners' production more accurate. Furthermore, Bongaerts (1999) notes that successful adult learners have high motivation, constant exposure to immense L2 input (Klein, 1995), and intensive training in L2 sound perception and production. Therefore, in brief, L2 learning should occur at an early stage, be tailored to learners' needs and interests, benefit from the insights brought up by the *Communicative Approach*, namely learner-centered and meaningful learning.

The Monitor Model and its Five Hypotheses

Krashen's (1973) *Input Hypothesis* has tremendous impact on the fields of second language teaching and learning. His *Input Hypothesis* makes up a major component of his larger theoretical framework, namely the *Monitor Model* (see the diagram below), which attempts to account for the process of acquiring a second language. This model comprises the following five hypotheses:

I. *Acquisition-learning Hypothesis.* Adults have two ways of developing competence in a second language. The first way is through acquisition, that is, by using language for communication. This is a subconscious process and the acquired competence is also subconscious. The second way is by learning, which is a conscious process and results in formal knowledge of the language. Krashen holds that there is no overlap or interference between acquisition and learning.

II. *Natural Order Hypothesis.* It states that second language acquisition proceeds in well-defined order. That is, L2 is acquired in a predetermined way; it unfolds along a natural path of development that cannot be altered. This hypothesis sets the stage for an information-processing view of second language acquisition. Accordingly, if there is a natural order of acquisition, there must be a mechanism that processes the incoming information according to an innate, universal, and rule-governed system.

III. *Monitor Hypothesis.* Learning can function as a monitor. The overall model explains the existence and operation of learned knowledge. For example, the ability to speak in another language comes from the acquired competence or subconscious knowledge. Learning, conscious knowledge, serves only as an editor, or monitor. It helps screen out utterances and is available only in production, not comprehension.

IV. *Input Hypothesis.* Second languages are acquired by understanding language that contains structures "a bit beyond the current level of competence (i + 1)", or by receiving "comprehensible input". When the input is understood and there is enough of it, the condition of i+1 will be met automatically. Here, the *natural order* and *input* hypotheses merge, because we move along the natural order of development by understanding the input that contains structures at the next level. The *Input Hypothesis* refers to acquisition, not learning. In other words, acquisition is the result of receiving comprehensible input. It is not taught directly.

V. *Affective Filter Hypothesis.* It is part of the internal processing system that subconsciously screens incoming language based on the learners' motives, needs, attitudes and emotional state. This filter is a mental block that prevents learners from fully using the comprehensible input they receive for language acquisition. If the affective filter is high, input is prevented from passing through; and so, there is no acquisition. The affective filter is responsible for individual variation in second language acquisition. It explains why some learners never acquire full competence.

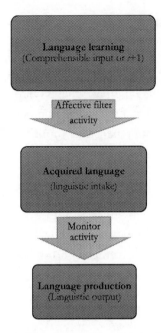

Figure 1: Stages of L2 Acquisition in the Monitor Model

Figure 1 demonstrates the stages of L2 acquisition according to Krashen's Monitor Model. Krashen considers the *Input Hypothesis* as the most important one among his five hypotheses since it relates directly to language teaching and explains how acquisition occurs. The *Input Hypothesis* claims that an important condition for language acquisition is that the learner understands, via hearing or reading, input language that contains structure a bit beyond the learner's current level of competence. In other words, an individual acquires a language in only one way—by understanding messages, or by receiving comprehensible input. Comprehensible input is interpreted as *i+1*. *i* represents the learner's current level of language competence, and *1* represents the next level of competence in the natural order of development. In this regard, the language to which learners are exposed should neither be so far beyond reach that learners are overwhelmed (i+ 2), nor so close to their current stage that they are not challenged at all (i + 0).

Thus, the comprehensible input must be just far enough beyond learners' current competence that they can understand most of it but still are challenged. Input will then turn into intake, which indicates that the input is actually understood by the listeners. This suggests that speaking is not to be taught directly or very soon in the language classroom. Rather, speech will merge once the learner has built up enough comprehensible input (*i+1*); further, if there is enough comprehensible input, "the necessary grammar is automatically provided". Therefore, there is no need to teach grammar deliberately because it can be acquired subconsciously with the assistance of the internal language processes (or Chomsky's Language Acquisition Device).

Thus, the main characteristics of the comprehensible input are as follows:

- The input must be comprehensible or understandable to the learner.
- The input must not be too simple or too difficult; rather, it needs to be a bit beyond the learner's current level.
- Nonverbal language (such as gestures, eye contacts) as well as prior knowledge may be used to help the learner understand.
- Speaking is the result, not the cause, of acquisition; it takes longer and emerges much later than listening skills.

Until recently, the applicability of the Monitor Model along with its five hypotheses has been checked in a number of EFL contexts like China (Li, 2013), Libya (Abukhattala, 2013), and Saudi Arabia (Gulzar, Gulnaz & Ijaz, 2014).

Communicative Competence

The term *communicative competence* was coined by Hymes (1967, 1972) as a response to perceived limitations in Chomsky's competence and performance model of language. It refers to the aspect of our competence that enables us to convey and interpret messages and to negotiate meanings interpersonally within specific contexts. *Communicative Competence* takes into account the social and functional rules of language. A speaker with communicative competence should understand the immediate conversational content, and the overall broad social-cultural context. In the 1970s, research on communicative competence distinguished between linguistic and communicative knowledge (Hymes, 1967; Paulston, 1974). This move aimed to highlight the difference between the knowledge about language forms and the knowledge to communicate functionally and interactively. Similarly, Cummins (1979, 1984) proposes a distinction between cognitive academic language proficiency and basic interpersonal communication skills. The former is more context-reduced and the latter is more context-embedded. A good share of classroom- oriented language is context-reduced while face-to-face communication is context-embedded.

Communicative Competence was further developed by Canale and Swain (1980). They define four components that make up the construct of *communicative competence*:

1) *Grammatical competence* refers to the knowledge of lexical items, and the rules of morphology, syntax, phonology, semantics, and sentence-level grammar. It is the competence that we associate with mastering of the linguistic code of a language.

2) *iscourse competence* is the ability to connect sentences to form a meaningful whole out of the series of utterances. Discourse means everything from simple conversations to lengthy texts.

3) *Sociolinguistic competence* is the knowledge of the socio-cultural rules of language and discourse. It requires the understanding of the social context in which language is used.

4) *Strategic competence* includes both verbal and nonverbal communication. It either enhances the effectiveness of communication or compensates for the breakdown in communication, due to performance variables or insufficient competence.

According to Richards and Rodgers (1986), *Communicative Language Teaching* (CLT) started with a theory of language communication. The goal of classroom instruction focuses on the development of learners' communicative competence. Thus, learners are encouraged to communicate in the target language from the beginning of the course of study. In CLT, meaning is most important. Larsen-Freeman (1986) maintains that "almost everything that is done is done with a communicative intent" (p.132). Accordingly, the process of meaning negotiation is essential in CLT (Paulston, 1974). In order to encourage learners to communicate better, errors are tolerated and little explicit instruction on language rules is provided (Larsen-Freeman, 1986). Naturally, CLT favors small group activities so as to maximize the time each student has to negotiate meaning. CLT employs information-gap activities, problem-solving tasks, roleplays by pair and group work (Larsen-Freeman, 1986). Another feature of CLT is its "learner-centered" view. According to Savignon (1991), every individual student has unique interests, needs, and goals. Teachers develop materials based on students' demonstrated needs of particular class. Also, CLT emphasizes the use of authentic materials in teaching language (Widdowson, 1996). It also encourages giving learners opportunities to respond to genuine communicative needs in real-life situations.

Paired interactions are an excellent way to develop communicative competence (Porter, 1986) for several reasons. First, pairing students of different proficiency levels increases negotiation between them as well as their use of strategic competence. Second, information-exchange activities (e.g. students interview one another about what they did at the weekend, discuss whether the activities are active or sedentary, and compare their discussion with the rest of the class). There are also other ideas for classroom activities (Taron, 1984). For example, students may see a picture of an object for which they do not know the term (e.g. a windshield wiper, ceiling fan, blender ... etc.). The students then describe the object to the class. This can help develop strategic competence, as students would likely use approximation, word coinage, or circumlocution. In addition, the instructor may give an idiomatic term to students (e.g. funny bone, punch line, laughing stock, deadbeat, bed head ... etc.). A student who understands the term can describe it to the class in the target language. As an example of an information-gap activity, a student gets a picture and then describes it to her partner who cannot see the picture. The partner then attempts to draw what the picture might look like based on the description.

Another way of implementing the communicative perspective is referred to as the *Task-based Approach.* As described by Willis and Willis (2001), task-based learning is actually a more resolutely communicative application. The task-based framework is an effective response to research that has shown that learners need opportunities for negotiated interaction in order to accelerate their comprehension and production (Kumaravadivelu, 1994). Therefore, task-based activities, such as simulations are helpful in developing communicative competence. They provide an atmosphere for authentic language use. Students must use aspects of communicative competence to interact with their groups (i.e., sociolinguistic and strategic competences), work together and come to terms. They can also use aspects of communicative competence to develop their writing assignments (i.e., grammatical and discourse competences). Therefore, developing communicative competence can best be achieved by encouraging learners to communicate (Richards & Rodgers, 1986). Communicative intent and meaning negotiation are essential (Larsen-Freeman, 1986; Paulston, 1974). Small-group activities are favored in order to maximize interaction among all students. Pair and group activities include information-gap, problem-solving, roleplay, and simulation activities (Larsen-Freeman, 1986). A "learner-centered" approach is implemented such that learners dominate most of the class interaction and use authentic materials in ways that fulfill communicative needs in real-life situations (Widdowson, 1986).

What follows are examples of activities that help develop communicative competence:

1) *Information-gap* to convey or to request information (pair or group). Simple: finding out from others their birthdays, addresses, favorite foods... etc. Moderate: pooling information about different occupations e.g., necessary qualifications, job conditions, salary levels ... etc. Complex: discussing a topic e.g., an author's message, thoughts on a certain issue, imaginary situations ... etc.

2) *Problem-solving* by providing a solution to a specific problem (pair or group). Simple: giving directions on a map. Moderate: working out an itinerary from train, plane, and bus schedules. Complex: solving a mystery or dealing with a social or moral dilemma.

3) *Roleplay* involves assigning a role to one or more members of a pair or group and specifying an objective the participants must accomplish (Example 1: student A is an employer; student B is a prospective employee; the objective is for student A to interview student B) (Example B: each student represents a particular political party or social group; the objective is to discuss an issue of common interest).

4) *Simulations* involve a group working through an imaginary situation as a social unit and trying to solve some specific problem (e.g., people shipwrecked on a desert island).

In spite of the so many practical suggestions of how to aid students in the development of their communicative competences, recent research (e.g., Zhang & Wang, 2012) has shown that teaching practices in a number of EFL contexts are not in line with the communicative approach. For example, teachers tend to abide by teacher books and manuals that involve ideas or suggestions not derived from the communicative uses of English. In addition, numerous programs continue to place undue emphasis on grammatical forms and structures that are isolated from any language functions or communicative uses.

An Alternative Theory

All human beings reach a minimal standard in at least one language and are capable of communication using it. In the case of second languages, however, there is variation in proficiency ranging from little knowledge to native-like ability. A central problem in the development of a theory of second language acquisition is to account for this. In order to discuss this topic, I intend to first highlight essential aspects of a second language theory, next discuss what a second language theory needs to be able to account for, and last address a number of implications of a second language theory. For the most part, this discussion benefits from Micheal Long's (1990) "the least a second language theory should explain".

In order for it to be successful and valid, as viewed by second language scholars and specialists, a second language theory needs to meet three essential conditions. First, a SL theory needs to be multi-dimensional in that it takes into account all factors relevant to the process of second language acquisition. Among such factors are learner- and environment- related variables that determine variation in language development. Second, a SL theory needs to be able to explain or account for some of the major accepted findings within its scope. Third, a SL theory needs to be interactionist in that it considers the role each of the learner- and environment- related factors has in language acquisition and development. Not only that, but also a SL theory needs to address how each of these factors affects one another, which ones interact, when and how.

Of the three essential conditions a SL theory must meet is that it needs to be able to account for some of the major accepted findings within its scope. Such findings are basically those the research has confirmed, and there is an overall consensus among SL scholars and researchers about their validity. Among these findings are those relevant to language learners that point out variation in SL attainment among language learners. For example, individual differences among learners represent one area of such variation in language attainment. Learners differ from one another in terms of their motivation and aptitude (Spolsky, 1989), for instance. Learners also achieve varying degrees of SL attainment depending on how old they were when they started their SL learning (Scovel, 1988). Affective factors are also seen as another explanation of variability in language attainment among SL learners (e.g., attitudes) (Skehan, 1989).

Another consideration is due to maturational constraints, and how age affects SL acquisition as is known from the assumptions of the *Critical Period Hypothesis* (Lenneberg, 1967). This hypothesis claims that language acquisition after puberty is difficult and a foreign accent will emerge in the case of adult SL learners. Another set of findings can be linked to the environment in which the SL is acquired. These findings also provides us with explanations for the varying degrees of attainment among SL learners. For example, the type and amount of input are determined by the relationship between L1 and L2 (Larsen-Freeman & Long, 1991), whether the input is comprehensible or not (White, 1987), and the role of noticing in converting this input into intake (Schmidt, 1992). Another environmental aspect that makes up a noticeable part of formal instruction is the amount of focus on form, which has been shown to correlate positively with SL acquisition (Long, 1989; Schachter, 1989).

The last set of findings comprises those concerned with interlanguage. A SL theory needs to propose one or more mechanisms to account for interlanguage change. According to Selinker (1972), interlanguage exhibits systematicity and variability at any point of time of its development. An example of interlanguage systematicity can be seen in the persistence of the same type of errors over a period of time (Sato, 1990). Interlanguage is variable when we look at the individual characteristics of language learners that differentiate among them (e.g., planning) (Crooks, 1989). When interlanguage is considered, adequate consideration needs to be given to the role of L1 in interlanguage development. The L1 effect manifests itself in either positive or negative transfer. L1 transfer has been shown to depend on the L1-L2 markedness relationship (e.g., Odlin, 1989). Furthermore, interlanguage exhibits non-linear progress or what is referred to as U-shaped learning. U-shaped learning is characterized by what is called backsliding, which suggests that at some point of his or her interlanguage development, the learner backslides or regresses to some previous stage (Gass & Selinker, 2001).

In this section, I elaborate on some of the major implications of a SL theory based on what Long (1990) points out in his article:

- Universals in language and cognition account for the common patterns among language learners.
- Environmental factors account for the differences associated with input.
- Different mechanisms or differential accesses to these mechanisms explain the differences between children and adults in the rate of language acquisition and proficiency.

- Affective factors need to be seen as facilitative conditions of language acquisition and not means or causes of acquisition.
- Awareness and/or attention to language form is needed for learning some aspects of L2.
- L2 mastery cannot be attained by simply exposure to sample of comprehensible input since learning some aspects of L2 from positive evidence alone is impossible.
- A strong cognitive contribution explains interlanguage systematicity.
- The gradualist, U-shaped course of interlanguage development entails unsteady acquisition.

Thus far, I have pointed out to the minimal conditions that a SL theory needs to meet in order to be valid and reliable. Such conditions as taking into account learner and environmental factors, explaining at least some of the well-established findings, and being an interactionist theory comprise indispensable aspects of a SL theory.

In a more recent article, Long (2012) has mentioned a number of criteria derived from historical as well as scientific perspectives that can be used to evaluate a theory of second language acquisition. From Long's viewpoint, such criteria

include internal consistency, non-tautologousness, systematicity, modularity, clarity, explanatory adequacy, predictive adequacy, scope, generality, lack of ad hocness, extendibility, fruitfulness, consistency with accepted theories in other fields, experimental testability, ability to make quantitative predictions, simplicity, falsifiability, fertility as a paradigm for puzzle-solving, explanatory power, ability to account for different kinds of data, ability to account for phenomena different from those for which the theory was invented to explain, novel predictive successes, ability to account for data a rival theory cannot handle, simplicity/

parsimony, consistency, generality, empirical adequacy, proven fertility, unproven fertility/generative potential, continuity/ rationality, a pragmatic ('get on with things') relationship with experiment, and ability to resolve fundamental conceptual difficulties (ibid., p. 141).

Factors that Affect L2 Learning in Adulthood

This section offers a review of important factors that determine success of second language acquisition among adults. Such factors make up the major headings of the discussion.

Native language

According to the behaviorists, language learning involves the establishment of new habits (Bloomfield, 1933) and the process of habit formation is affected by old habits. Lado (1957) points out learners' tendency to transfer their old habits to new tasks, and claims that learners tend to transfer their L1 forms and rules to their L2 when attempting to use their L2. He distinguishes two types of language transfer: positive (facilitation) and negative (interference). L1 transfer refers to the influence that the learner's L1 exerts on his L2 acquisition.

Contrastive Analysis (henceforth CA) (Fries, 1945) examines the role of L1 in L2 acquisition, and suggests that the study of the similarities and the differences between L1 and L2 can help predict the difficulties learners encounter in their L2 learning. By knowing the differences between L1 and L2, we can predict what errors L2 learners are likely to make. CA considers L1 interference (negative transfer) to be a major difficulty in L2 learning. In fact, L1 interference is seen as a major source of errors in L2 learning. For example, Chinese learners of English do not add the 's' at the end of the third verb singular (e.g., 'he speak good English'). The occurrence of these errors is due to the differences in language structures between Chinese and English. Another example is that in English [p] and [ph] are allophones of the same phoneme /p/, but in Hindi, [p] and [ph] are different phonemes.

L1 transfer can affect L2 acquisition or development in three ways:

1. *Facilitation* e.g., because French does not permit object pronouns in relative clauses whereas Arabic does, French learners do not have the same problem as do Arab learners when using these pronouns in English relative clauses.
2. *Interference* e.g., because the sound [p] is not part of Arabic phonemes whereas [b] is, Arab learners of English tend to pronounce [p] as [b].
3. *Avoidance* e.g., because Chinese does not have relative clauses, Chinese learners of English avoid using these structures.

However, a number of studies have shown that a small percentage of errors in L2 learning is due to L1 interference (e.g., Schumann, 1979), and that such errors tend to occur in the beginning stages. An analysis of the errors produced by Spanish learners of English, for example, indicates that less than 5% of errors is the result of L1 transfer (Schumann, 1979). Certainly, there are several other sources of errors than L1 interference (e.g., overgeneralization or intralingual transfer). Certain language forms may be used excessively due to L1 transfer (Ellis, 1995). For instance, some Chinese learners tend to overuse expressions of regrets when apologizing in English, in accordance with the norms of the Chinese language.

According to Kellerman (1986), L1 interference tends to show in pronunciation and word order more than in grammatical morphemes. There is also evidence that when L2 is very different from L1, learners are less likely to transfer (Ringborn, 1986). In his interlanguage theory, Selinker (1972) identifies L1 transfer as a mental process, rather than interference, L2 learners use to form interlanguage hypotheses. To sum up, recent research has shown that L1 effect is a subtle and evolving aspect of L2 development. Learners do not transfer all patterns from L1 to L2, and as their L2 acquisition proceeds, they become more aware of the similarities and differences between their L1 and L2.

Thus, L1 is not the only cause of negative interference with L2 learning. L2 learning difficulties depend on some other factors such as the learner's age, attitude, motivation, aptitude, and background knowledge of other languages. L1 transfer is regulated by the stage of L2 development as well as learners' perceptions about what is transferable. Linguists need to focus on the errors that learners make, or conduct error analysis, rather than compare L1 to L2. Unlike contrastive analysis, error analysis focuses on the errors that learners make. Error analysis provides a broader range of possible explanations of errors. However, some L2 learning phenomena cannot be captured by error analysis, and error analysis does not provide any insights into the course of the L2 learning process.

In spite of the rejection of contrastive analysis by some researchers, most teachers and researchers have remained convinced that learners draw on their knowledge of L1 when learning a new language. Current research shows that L1 influence is a subtle and evolving aspect of SL development. Learners do not simply transfer all patterns from L1 to L2. There are changes over time as learners come to know more about the L2, and thus, recognize similarities between L1 and L2 that were not evident in earlier stages of SL acquisition. There is evidence that suggests that when learning a language that is very different from their L1, learners are less likely to attempt transferring any linguistic aspects (Ringbom, 1986).

Age

L2 learners start their learning of L2 at different ages. This can serve as one possible explanation of the varying degrees of their L2 attainment. According to the assumptions of the *Critical Period Hypothesis* (Lenneberg, 1967), language learning should take place by puberty, otherwise it will become difficult after puberty, and a foreign accent will emerge in the case of L2 learners. However, ample evidence suggests that the critical period has a possible effect on the area of phonological competence. Nonetheless, the acquisition of L2 phonology is not as straightforward as it might appear to be. People who start learning before the age of seven will have native-like speech and those who start learning after fourteen will probably not demonstrate the same ability. Yet, the results for people who start learning between seven and fourteen vary; some end up with native accents and some do not (O'Grady, 2005).

Used to explain the critical period, brain lateralization is now thought to be of little predictive value in determining L2 ability. Current research suggests that adult L2 learners can reach a state in their mastery of L2 pronunciation (e.g., Moyer, 1999) and syntax (Ioup et al., 1994) indistinguishable from native speakers. The critical period now seeks to determine whether adults have access to universal grammar rather than neurological changes in the brain with maturity. It is postulated that adult L2 learners adopt hypotheses unendorsed by universal grammar, and therefore they perform less accurately than native speakers. For example, when adult learners of French study gender, they use problem-solving and hypothesis-forming ways to help them. Unfortunately, this tendency leads them to less accurate or even non-target-like usage.

Anxiety

Scovel (1978) defines anxiety as "a state of apprehension, a vague fear …". Since L2 learning requires the learner to go through new and complex tasks, language anxiety is one influential factor that has either a facilitating or debilitating effect depending on its severity. The research on anxiety suggests that, like self-esteem, anxiety can be experienced at various levels (MacIntyre &Gardner, 1991). At the deepest or global level, trait anxiety affects a person who is prone to be anxious. Some people are predictably and generally anxious about many things. However, at a more momentary, or situational level, state anxiety is experienced in relation to some particular event or act. Language anxiety has been shown to have a negative effect on L2 learning at the situational level (MacIntyre & Gardner, 1991). Horwitz et al. (1986) have identified three components of foreign language anxiety:

1. *Communication apprehension*: arises from the learner's inability to adequately express her thoughts and ideas
2. *Fear of negative social evaluation*: arises from the learner's fear to make negative social impressions about her
3. *Test anxiety*: arises from the learner's apprehension about academic assessment and testing

It is important to distinguish between two forms of foreign language anxiety: facilitative and debilitative. Facilitative anxiety enables the learner to become more aware of his performance, and so tries to make fewer mistakes (e.g., test anxiety). It also encourages the learner to work harder and compete with his peers (Bailey, 1983). The feeling of nervousness before giving a public speech, for experienced speakers, is often a sign of facilitative anxiety, that is, just enough tension to get the job done (Brown, 1994). Debilitative anxiety hinders the learner from his best language performance (e.g., communication anxiety). Subsequently, a moderate level of anxiety is appropriate in L2 learning (i.e., the level of anxiety that regulates the learners' performance and not hinders or weakens it. In Bailey's (1983) study of competitiveness and anxiety in L2 learning, facilitative anxiety was found to be a key to success, and closely related to competitiveness. In other words, anxiety can hinder one's progress, but at other times, it motivates the learner to study harder. Thus, both too much and too little anxiety may hinder the process of successful L2 learning, a little nervous tension, or low anxiety, in the process is normal.

Motivation

Motivation is commonly thought of as an inner drive or desire that moves one to a particular action. It refers to "the choices people make as to what experiences or goals they will approach or avoid and the degree of effort they will exert in that respect" (Keller1983, p. 389). Some psychologists define motivation in terms of certain needs or drives. In the L2 learning context, motivation involves the attitudes and affective states that influence the degree of effort that learners make to learn the language. Gardner and Lambert (1972) introduced the notion of instrumental and integrative motivation. Instrumental motivation refers to the learners' desire to learn a language for a utilitarian purpose such as a reward, payment, travel … etc. Integrative motivation indicates the desire to learn a language successfully in order to integrate into the target language community. In other words, learners choose to learn an L2 because they are interested in the language and the people who speak it.

Motivation, a goal-directed behavior, can also be separated into intrinsic motivation and extrinsic motivation. The former one is motivation in which the task is enjoyable or satisfying by itself; the latter one is induced by rewards or punishments, depending on the success or failure in a given task (Deci, 1975). Motivation is clearly a highly complex phenomenon. These four types of motivation should be seen as complementary rather than as distinct and oppositional. Learners can be both integratively and instrumentally motivated at the same time. Motivation can result from learning itself. Furthermore, motivation is dynamic in nature. It varies from one moment to another depending on, among several factors, the learning context or task.

Chapter 2

Methods and Practices of EL2 Teaching

- ☐ Notions of Approach, Design, and Procedure
- ☐ Popular Controversies in EL2 Pedagogy
- ☐ Communicative Language Teaching
- ☐ Schema Theory and Reading Comprehension
- ☐ Error Analysis and Correction
- ☐ The Debate on Whether or Not Grammar Should Be Taught
- ☐ Teaching English for Specific Purposes
- ☐ Key Aspects of a Post-method Pedagogy
- ☐ Using Read-aloud Technique with Child Learners
- ☐ Methods and Beginning EL2 Learners
- ☐ Teaching Pronunciation to High-level EL2 Learners
- ☐ Teaching Simple Past versus Present Perfect Tenses
- ☐ Contrastive Rhetoric and Teaching Advanced Writing
- ☐ Use of Media in EL2 Classrooms
- ☐ An Observation of a Composition Class

Mohammed S. Assiri

Notions of Approach, Design, and Procedure

Richards and Rogers (1986) have outlined a model for the systematic description and comparison of language teaching methods in the hope that such a model may make it easier to understand recent developments in methodology. Approach, design, and procedure have been derived from Edward Anthony's (1963) notions of approach, method, and technique. Ever since, these terms have been used to label three interrelated elements of organization upon which language teaching practices are founded.

All language teaching methods originated from theories about how languages are learned. Theories at the level of approach relate directly to level of design since they provide the basis for determining the goals and content of a language syllabus. They also relate to the level of procedure since they provide the linguistic and psycholinguistic rationale for the selection of particular teaching techniques. *Approach* can be defined as theoretical positions, assumptions and beliefs about the nature of language and language learning. *Approach* serves as the source of principles and practices that language teachers ultimately follow in language teaching. There are three theoretical views of language proficiency that inform current approaches and methods in language teaching:

I. *Structural view* (the traditional view): Language is a system of structurally related elements for the coding of meaning. The target of language learning is the mastery of language elements that are generally defined in terms of phonological units (e.g.; phonemes) grammatical units (e.g., clauses, phrases, sentences) and grammatical operations (e.g., adding, shifting, joining, and transformation), and lexical items (e.g., function words and structure words).

II. *Functional view*: Language is a vehicle for the expression of functional meaning. The communicative movement in language teaching subscribes to this view. It emphasizes the semantic and communicative dimensions rather than merely the grammatical aspects of language. It leads to the specification and organization of language teaching content by categories of meaning and function rather than by categories of form. For example, the movement of *English for specific purposes* begins from a functional account of learner needs.

III. *Interactional view*: Language is a vehicle for the realization of interpersonal relations and the performance of social transactions between individuals. Language is a tool for the creation and maintenance of social relations. Areas of inquiry in the development of interactional approaches to language teaching include interaction analysis, conversational analysis, and ethnography. Interactional theories focus on the patterns of moves, acts, and negotiations and exchanges in conversational exchanges. Language teaching content may be specified and organized by patterns of exchange, or may be left unspecified in order to be shaped by the learners as interactors.

Structural, functional, or interactional models of language provide theoretical frameworks that motivate particular teaching method. However, in themselves they are incomplete and need to be complemented by theories of language learning.

Design specifies the relationships of theories of language and learning to both the form and function of instructional materials and activities in instructional settings. As such, *design* includes the following specifications:

---

1) What the objectives of a method are (e.g., oral skill, writing skill; grammar, pronunciation)?

2) How language content is selected and organized (e.g., the syllabus, subject matter, linguistic matter (process-based method)?

3) The types of learning tasks and teaching activities (e.g., dialogues, pattern drills, and information-gap activities).

4) Learner roles (e.g., stimulus-response, repetitive practice, role-plays).

5) Teacher roles (e.g., primary source of language, facilitator, organizer),

6) Roles of instructional materials in connection with classroom techniques and practices.

Procedure involves the actual moment-to-moment techniques, practices, and behaviors that operate in teaching a language according to a particular method. It is the level at which we describe how a method realizes its approach and design in classroom behaviors. At the level of design, we saw that a method advocates the use of certain types of teaching activities as a result of its theoretical assumptions about language and learning. At the level of procedure, we are concerned with how these tasks and activities are integrated into lessons and used as the basis for teaching and learning. Essentially, *procedure* focuses on the way a method handles presentation of language content, practice of skills, and feedback of performance. *Procedure* may involve the use of teaching activities (e.g., drills, dialogues, information-gap activities), exercises and activities for practice, and resources (time, space, equipment … et cetera).

What follows is an illustration of use of *approach*, *design*, and *procedure* to describe two examples of teaching methods: Audio-lingual and Total Physical Response.

Audio-lingual Method (ALM)

Approach: ALM embodies the structural view of language. Traditional approaches to the study of language have linked the study of language to the mentalist approach of grammar. Language was viewed as a system of structurally related elements for the encoding of meaning, and the elements are phonemes, morphemes, words, structures, and sentences. The term structural refers to such features as: (1) elements in a language are linearly produced in a rule-governed way, (2) language samples could be described at any structural level (phonetic, phonemic, morphological ... etc.), (3) linguistic levels are systems that are pyramidally structured, for example, phonemic systems lead to morphemic systems that in turn lead to higher-level systems of phrases, clauses, and sentences. The most important tenet of structural linguistics was that the primary medium of language is oral, that is, speech is language, not writing. The early practice should focus on mastery of phonologicalcal and grammatical structures rather than lexis.

ALM was equipped with a powerful theory of the nature of language and language learning. It views learning as a process of mechanical, habit formation: 1) Good habits are formed by giving correct responses rather than by making mistakes. By memorizing dialogues and performing pattern drills the chances of producing mistakes are minimized. Language is verbal behavior, that is, automatic production and comprehension of utterances. 2) Language skills are learned more effectively in spoken form before they are used in written form. Aural-oral training is needed to provide the foundation for developing other language skills. 3) Analogy surpasses analysis in promoting language learning; therefore, the approach to the teaching of grammar is essentially inductive rather than deductive. 4) Word meanings can be learned only in a linguistic and cultural context, not in isolation.

Design: ALM advocates a return to speech-based instruction with the primary objective of oral proficiency, and dismisses the study of grammar or literature as the goal of foreign language teaching. The focus in the early stages is on oral skills, with gradual links to other skills as learning develops. The teaching of listening, comprehension, pronunciation, grammar, and vocabulary are all related to the development of oral proficiency. Reading and writing may be taught, but they remain dependent on prior oral skills. Language is primarily audio-lingual. Fluency involves the use of key grammatical patterns and knowledge of sufficient vocabulary to use with these patterns. In the design of the syllabus, key items of phonology, morphology, and syntax of the language are arranged according to their order of presentation. In addition, a syllabus of basic vocabulary items is usually specified in advance. The language skills are taught in the order of listening, speaking, reading, and writing. Listening is largely viewed as training in aural discrimination of basic sound patterns.

The language may be presented entirely orally at first, whereas written representations are usually withheld in early stages. Certain types of learning activities include dialogues and pattern drills. Dialogues are used for repetition and memorization. Correct pronunciation, stress, rhythm, and intonation are emphasized (via repetition, replacement, restatement, substitute, completion, transportation, expansion, transformation, integration, restoration ... etc.). Learners can be directly taught using skill-training techniques to produce correct responses. Learners react to stimuli, but are not encouraged to initiate interaction because this may lead to mistakes. They listen to and imitate their teacher accurately. They are assigned controlled tasks involving verbal behavior. The teacher's role is central and active. ALM is a teacher-dominant method. Teacher models the target language, controls the direction and pace of learning, and monitors and corrects the learners' performance. Examples of instructional materials used in ALM include tape recorders, audiovisual aids, textbooks, and language labs for listening practice.

Procedure: The process of teaching involves extensive oral instruction. The focus of the instruction is on immediate and accurate speech. There is little provision of grammatical explanations or talks about language forms. The native tongue is discouraged. A set of procedures is followed in a regular class session: (1) Students first hear a model dialogue, either by the teacher or in a recorded format, containing the key structures that are the focus of the lesson. (2) Students repeat each line of the dialogue individually and then in chorus. (3) The teacher pays close attention to pronunciation, intonation, and fluency and offers immediate corrective feedback. (4) Students memorize the dialogue line by line. The prevailing features of a language class in the ALM comprise what follows. The dialogue is adapted to students' interests or needs through changing certain key words or phrases. Certain key structures from the dialogue are selected and used as the basis for pattern drills. Such structures are first practiced in chorus and then individually. Some grammatical explanations may be offered at this point but this is kept to an absolute minimum. Students may refer to their textbook and complete reading, writing, or vocabulary activities based on the dialogue. Follow-up activities may be done in the language lab using further dialogues and drills.

Total Physical Response (TPR)

Approach: Asher (1969) perceives of language as implicit rather than explicit, but based on a formalistic, structural model of language with the primary focus being on the form of communication rather than the content. It uses a surface-level concept of grammatical system in which language is viewed as a code composed of structural elements that have to be mastered. Language is a vehicle for controlling the behaviors of others, or a manipulative instrument. The learning theory that underlines the TPR is based on the belief that language is learned through motor activities. In child language learning, there is an intimate relationship between language and the child's body. Language production with body movement is thought to promote success in learning.

Design: The TPR aimed to teach the spoken language to beginning level students. Comprehension precedes production. Specific objects are not elaborated. Because of the criteria for the selection of language items, common conversational forms are not selected. The syllabus is sentence-based, primarily lexical and grammatical. Items are selected according to the ease with which they may be used in imperative forms to initiate actions. Vocabulary must be concrete and situational. The verbs selected must be action verbs. The progression of items is from concrete to abstract. The syllabus items are presented in sentence patterns. Learners must perform actions in response to commands given by the teacher. At the advanced level, learners may also give commands to other learners in groups. Pair work is possible at late stages. Learners mainly learn from the teacher. The teacher is the initiator of activities and communication. The teacher may proceed without materials. Materials (e.g., charts, pictures, slides … etc.) mainly play a supplementary role.

Procedure: The activities used in the TPR are typically command-based drills. Meaning is communicated via gestures, demonstrations, or body language in general. Both individual and group activities are used. Errors are allowed and not corrected at once. Comprehensible input is emphasized before production.

Popular Controversies in EL2 Pedagogy

There are three controversies that have dominated the scholarly discussion in ESL pedagogy:

Teacher-centered versus Learner-centered Paradigms

(Norman, 2003)

Teacher-centered

- *Inception*: emerged from a post-positivism framework – prevalent from 1950s-1970s.
- *Aspects*: in a typical teacher-centered ESL classroom,
  - The teacher is an expert of specific knowledge.
  - The teacher's role is central and authoritative in all class activities.
  - The teacher's presence dominates the classroom.
  - The teacher develops the curriculum.
  - The teacher takes a particular teaching point, breaks it into segments, and teaches it to students.
  - Students study new language elements and practice the correct forms and discourse.
- *Research*:
  - Students with basic skills benefits from the teacher's segmenting and reducing content into comprehensible input (Smerdon et al., 2000).
  - Some students need structured curriculum and direct assistance from the teacher (Reyes, 1992).
- *Criticism*:
  - Too linear and restrictive in assumptions about language acquisition and writing (Chen, 1998)
  - Language is more dynamic, involving interaction and communication (Johns, 1997)
  - Students are held passive and their needs are not met.

Learner-centered

- *Inception*: stems from Vygotsky's (1978) constructivist theory on learning and language development - learners develop their knowledge through interaction with their environment.

- *Aspects*: in a typical learner-centered ESL classroom,
  o The learner's perspective is important.
  o Instruction is directed by what is meaningful to students.
  o The teacher acts as a facilitator of all class activities.
  o Language learning is an active process.
  o Students dominate most of the class talk.
  o Students choose their language learning materials.
- *Criticism*:
  o Only bright students tend to benefit from learner-centered classrooms (Johns, 1997).
  o Bilingual students need explicit instruction in how to use language (Cummins, 2000).

In connection to this topic, Lewis and Reinders (2007) have provided insightful, practical suggestions as to how to facilitate the adaptation of English language learners who are used to teacher-centered settings in their home countries to learner-centered environments in other countries. Other scholars (e.g., Sreehari, 2012) have proposed that teachers implement communicative practices in their classes in order to augment learner-centered atmosphere.

Native English-speaking Teachers versus Non-native English-speaking Teachers
(Medgyes, 1992)
A native English-speaking teacher
- *Characteristics*:
  o Represents the target language culture.
  o Has an ideal level of language competence or proficiency
  o Is more concerned with meaning and fluency
  o Uses an analytic approach (e.g., by establishing distinctions such as generalized semantic definitions and word-forms).

- *Criticisms*:
    - o May be monolingual and so does not have the experience of learning a language consciously.
    - o Tends to improvise and not follow the textbook so closely.

A non-native English-speaking teacher

- *Characteristics*:
    - o Uses a standard variety
    - o Serves as an imitable model of a successful language learner.
    - o Is more concerned with form and accuracy.
    - o Prepares their lessons more carefully to cope with any defective language proficiency.
    - o Uses a synthetic approach by aiming to integrate language into a situational or linguistic context.
    - o Teaches learning strategies more effectively.
    - o Better anticipates language learning difficulties.
    - o Is more empathetic about his students' needs and problems.
    - o Benefits from L1 sharing with his students when necessary.
- *Criticisms*:
    - o May have a linguistic insecurity using the language they teach.
    - o May adopt either one of two types of attitudes: pessimistic (obsessed with grammar, little attention to pronunciation or vocabulary, no attention to appropriateness) or aggressive (a prescriptive and intolerant attitude)
    - o May have weakness in pronunciation and/or lexicon.
    - o May use words not in their appropriate contexts.

Last, it is worth noting here that a number of scholars (e.g., Hayes, 2009) have expressed their concern about the assumption that nativeness suffices to make certain language teachers outbalance others in terms of teaching efficacy.

Teach or Not Teach Grammar in L2 Writing

According to Frodesen (2001), the role of grammar in L2 writing has remained a topic of controversy since the 1980s. The use of grammar in writing classes takes the form of explanations of rules and corrections of errors. Fluency and accuracy are unfortunately "inversely related. As attention to one goes up, attention to the other goes down" (Casanave, 2004). For Frodesen (2001), the role of grammar in L2 writing is controversial because of the following factors:

- The influence of L1 composition pedagogy and research on L2 writing practices.
- The widespread L2 teachers' adoption of Krashen's (1982) belief [noninterventionist position] that form-focused instruction is not only unnecessary but thwarts natural acquisition processes.
- The adoption of the communicative models of language learning that consider comprehensible input sufficient for language acquisition.
- Misconceptions about the meaning and scope of the term grammar.

Frodesen (2001) has also differentiated between the teaching of linguistic forms in context and out of context. While the former aims to help learners develop their ability to communicate meaningfully, the latter is concerned with the knowledge of the linguistic forms in isolation from communicative goals. Frodesen (2001) has summarized the different perspectives in this controversy as follows:

I. *Grammar is necessary in L2 writing*:

1) Meaning-focused instruction solely does not develop many linguistic features at target-like levels (Doughty & Williams, 1998)

2) The wholesale adoption of L1 composition theories and practices for L2 writing classes is misguided in light of the many differences between L1 and L2 writers, process, and products (Silva, 1993).

3) Form-focused instruction benefits learners who need advanced-level writing proficiency for academic work or careers (Scarcella, 1996).

4) Teaching grammar helps learners develop their linguistic knowledge to convey their ideas meaningfully and appropriately to their intended readers (Frodesen, 2001).

5) Incorporating both fluency- and accuracy-oriented work in heterogeneous ESL writing classes can lead to better academic language proficiency (Reid, 1993).

6) Indicating their grammatical errors can help learners make fewer errors in rewriting their compositions (Fathman & Whalley, 1990).

II. *Grammar is unnecessary in L2 writing*:

1) Formal grammar instruction has little or no effect on L1 writing improvement (Hillocks, 1986).

2) L2 writing research strongly follows English L1 writing research that does not include linguistic analyses (Grabe & Kaplan, 1996).

3) Corrective feedback on form was not helpful in either eliminating surface errors or encouraging higher-level writing performance (Kepner, 1991).

4) Lexicon, morphology, and syntax represent separate domains that are acquired through different processes and at different stages (Truscott, 1996).

5) If learners acquire grammar through exposure and interaction in L2, they can apply this knowledge to their writing (Hinkel, 2002).

Communicative Language Teaching

In a major departure from an old paradigm in which L2 classes were centered upon language formal and structural aspects, a new trend focusing on the communicative functions of language has emerged. Hymes (1972) introduced the notion of *Communicative Competence*, which involves those aspects of our competence that enable us to convey and interpret messages and to negotiate meanings interpersonally within specific contexts. This trend was associated with interactionism that emphasizes the dynamic nature of the interplay between L2 learners and speakers. Consequently, significant changes were brought about to teacher-student relationship and curriculum development in SLA.

Similarly, the constructivists have drawn attention to language as communication among individuals. They believe that "all human beings construct their own version of reality, and therefore multiple contrasting ways of knowing and describing are equally legitimate" (Brown, 2001, p.11). One of the most widely discussed social constructivist positions in the field is Long's (1985) *Interaction Hypothesis*. According to this hypothesis, comprehensive input is the result of modified interaction, which is defined as "the various modifications that native speakers and other interlocutors create in order to render their input comprehensible to learners" (p. 287). In other words, interaction and input are seen as two major players in the process of SLA; therefore, communication is the basis for the development of language competence or knowledge. L2 learning has started to be viewed not just as a predictable, developmental process, but also as the creation of meaning through interactive negotiation among learners (Brown, 2001).

Theoretical claims have been made by a number of researchers (e.g., Corder, 1978; Higgs & Clifford, 1982; Swain, 1985) that demands placed on learners to manipulate their current interlanguage system give learners the opportunities to develop their productive capacity in L2. There is empirical evidence showing that mutual understanding can be reached when learners and interlocutors modify and restructure their interaction because of their requests for clarification or confirmation of each other's input and checks on the comprehensibility of their own productions (Pica, Doughty, & Young, 1986). Therefore, a language is learned through internalization of its rules from comprehensible input within a context of social interaction rather than through memorization of such rules.

Following this new conceptualization of the learning process, there has been a gradual shift from teaching-centered classes to learning-centered classes, with special attention to learners at the individual level. In traditional classrooms, the teacher would judge whether the learner's performance is acceptable based on grammatical phonologicalcal accuracy (Brumfit, 1984). The current trend sees the language classroom not just as a place where learners of varying abilities and styles mingle, but as a place where the contexts for interaction are carefully designed. It focuses on creating the optimal environments for input and interaction so that the learners can be stimulated to create their learner language in a socially constructed process (Brown, 2000). Therefore, the teacher-learner relationship has been redefined.

Teacher intervention, according to Clark and Silberstein (1977), should be minimized in order to motivate the learners to use and develop their new language skills. This is because the unequal status between the teacher and the learners provides minimal opportunities for the restructuring of social interaction and inhabits successful learning. Clark and Silberstein (1977) propose a new paradigm where the teacher is seen as a coach when the class is trying to solve a problem, a participant in activities where knowledge and opinions of all people in the class are off equal weight, and as a facilitator when creating an environment in which learning can take place. This paradigm puts the responsibility for learning on the shoulders of learners. It is currently a popular notion that learners should be given an active role in shaping their L2 learning.

As a consequence, structurally or grammatically sequenced curricula are no longer a mainstream for language teaching. Instead, there is a tendency to develop and upgrade activities for comprehensible input and meaningful L2 use. Classroom activities now include discussion-oriented and problem solving. Learners are frequently asked to work in groups or pairs rather than in the more traditional teacher-centered arrangement. Learning a language is an interactive process not only between learners and the teacher, but also among the learners themselves. Overall, interactionist theory has had a profound impact on SLA research over the past couple of decades. It views language as a vehicle for the realization of interpersonal relations and the performance of social transactions among individuals. It maintains that language acquisition is achieved through interaction and comprehensible input. This has led to the current trend of creating a learning environment that involves the teacher and all learners in a cooperative mode. Language classroom has been treated as a locus of meaningful, authentic exchange among all L2 users (Brown, 2001).

Schema Theory and Reading Comprehension

Schema theory describes the process by which readers combine their own background or prior knowledge with the information in a text to comprehend the text. All readers carry different schemata and these are often culture-specific. Schema enables us to make inferences and interpretations of texts. This is an important concept in ESL teaching, and pre-reading tasks are often designed to build or activate the learners' schemata. Research on schema theory has shown the importance of background knowledge in a psycholinguistic model of reading based on the belief that "every act of comprehension involves one's knowledge of the world" (Anderson, Reynolds, Schallert, & Goetz, 1977, p. 369). Reading comprehension is an interactive process between the readers' background and the text, which requires the reader to relate the text to her knowledge. According to Nunan (2000), "[T]he process of reconstructing meaning is one of mapping the linguistic content onto extra-linguistic context in order to build background knowledge" (p. 71). Effective comprehension requires the ability to relate the textual material to one's own knowledge.

Schema can be divided into two categories: textual schema which involves knowledge about discourse conventions, organization, structures, and sequences of texts (Anderson, Pichert, & Shirey, 1983); and content schema which refers to knowledge of the world as obtained through experiences (Long, 1989). Conversely, James (1987) identifies three categories of schemata that a reader needs to know: linguistic (linguistic knowledge), content (extra-linguistic or topic knowledge), and formal (discourse or rhetoric knowledge). As Carrell and Eisterhold (1983) point out, one of the most obvious reasons why a particular content schema may fail to exist for a reader is that the schema is culturally specific and is not part of the reader's cultural background. Some key concepts may be absent in the schemata of some non-native readers or they may carry alternate interpretations (Stott, 2001). For instance, the concept of 'full moon' is linked to schemata that include 'horror stories' and 'madness' in Europe, but in China and Japan is linked to schemata for 'beauty' and 'family gathering'.

Schema-related research has found that reading problems can be linked to absent or alternate culture-specific schemata, non-activation of schemata, and overuse of background knowledge. Research also suggests that the structures of schematic knowledge can either facilitate or inhibit comprehension according to whether they are over- or under-utilized (Aslanian, 1985). If the appropriate schemata are not activated, comprehension will be affected negatively. Efficient readers use background knowledge to make predictions and check these predictions against the text (Goodman, 1998). Also, background knowledge is more important than grammatical complexity in determining comprehension of textual relationships (Nunan, 1985). A text on a familiar topic is better accessed and recalled than a similar text on an unfamiliar topic (Johnson, 1983; Swales, 1990).

An ESL reader's failure to activate an appropriate schema may impede comprehension wholly or partially. This can be due to either the reader not effectively utilizing his bottom-up processing mode to activate schemata or not having the appropriate schema anticipated by the author. In both instances, a mismatch exists between what the writer anticipates the reader can do to construct meaning from the text and what the reader is actually able to do. Differences between writer intention and reader comprehension are most obvious when the reader has had life experiences that diverge from the writer's model. Readers sometimes feel that they can comprehend a text, but may have interpretations different from those intended by the author (Hudson, 1988). When faced with such unfamiliar topics, some students may overcompensate for absent schemata by reading in a slow, text-bound manner, or wild guessing (Carrell, 1988a). Both strategies can bring about comprehension difficulties.

Therefore, 'narrow reading' or reading within the learner's area of knowledge or interest is recommended (Carrell, 1988b). Similarly, it would be useful to provide local texts or texts developed with the learner's experiences in mind. Carrell and Eisterhold (1983) also suggest that "every culture-specific interference problem dealt with in the classroom presents an opportunity to build new culture-specific schemata that will be available to the EFL/ESL students outside the classroom". Thus, rather than attempting to neutralize texts, it would seem more suitable to prepare learners by helping them build background knowledge on the topic prior to reading a text on it through appropriate pre-reading activities (Carrell, 1988b). Carrell (1988b) lists numerous ways in which relevant schemata may be constructed, including lectures, visual aids, demonstrations, real-life experiences, discussions, role-plays, besides text previewing and introduction of key vocabulary.

However, readers may have prior knowledge, but their schemata are not activated while reading. That is why pre-reading activities must accomplish both goals of activating the existing background knowledge and building on it (Carrell, 1988a). Particularly popular and useful are questioning and brainstorming where learners can generate information on the topic based on their own knowledge and experiences (Aebersold & Field, 1997). Another relevant point is that because lower level learners may have the necessary schemata, but their deficient L2 skills hold them back. If necessary, L1 can be used to access prior knowledge, but the teacher must introduce the relevant L2 vocabulary during the discussion; otherwise, a "schema has been activated but learning the L2 has not been facilitated" (Aebersold & Field, 1997). Carrell, Devine, and Eskey (1988) claim that schema theory has substantially benefitted L2 teaching and learning; and in reality, most current ESL textbooks attempt schema activation through pre-reading activities. However, there may be limits to the effectiveness of such activities and there may even have been over-emphasis of the schema perspective and neglect of other areas (McCarthy, 1991).

Nonetheless, schema applications do not always bring about improvements in comprehension, particularly when there is insufficient attention to textual details, or schema-interference or activation of negative schemata. There is also some evidence that the background information provided by the teacher may not always be utilized by the learners. Therefore, it may seem sensible to teachers that she should employ pre-reading activities, but not to blindly assume that the expected effect is actually occurring. In other words, teachers should take the time to verify the usefulness of the activities they want to use and pay attention to possible schema-interference or non-activation. L2 readers require training in the skill of rapid recognition of a group of words and structures in order to accomplish the objective of reading extensively enough to build and improve the schemata they need. Identifying the topic, genre, and formal structure of a text activates readers' schemata and allow them to comprehend (Swales, 1990).

Generally, ESL readers should read as much as possible in order to capture schemata as well as textual memory (Stott, 2001). ESL readers need massive receptive vocabulary that is rapidly, accurately and automatically accessed (Grabe, 1988). This motivates Carrell (1988b) to suggest that a "parallel" approach in which vocabulary and schemata are concomitantly pre-taught. In addition to training their students in extensive reading, teachers should not overlook basic bottom-up processing and lexico-grammatical focus (Stott, 2001).

Error Analysis and Correction

Language learning is essentially a process that involves the making of errors. An error is a noticeable deviation from the grammar of an adult native speaker (Brown, 2007). An error reflects the learner's competence, for example, "Does John can sing?" reflects a competence level at which all verbs require a preposed *do* auxiliary for question formation (Brown, 2007). The absence of errors is not always a sign of native-like competence because the learner may be avoiding the structures that pose difficulty for him. L2 researchers have realized that the mistakes made in the process of language learning need to be analyzed carefully. Just as Corder (1967) notes, a language learner's errors are significant because they provide evidence of how language is learned and what learning strategies are used. In a sense, errors are viewed as a window to the SLA process.

An L2 learner's performance can be analyzed by investigating ill- and well-formed language elements. L1 is an important determinant of L2 acquisition, simply because L2 learners are not in a linguistic vacuum, L1 is already in their minds. L1 can influence L2 learning both positively and negatively. Contrastive Analysis (CA) hypothesis, established by Fries (1945) and endorsed by Lado (1957), holds that language learners have the tendency to transfer their L1 linguistic and cultural features to their L2 learning. CA also maintains that L1 interference is the major source of L2 learner errors, and that all these errors can be predicted by identifying the differences between L1 and L2. Thus, errors in L2 are mainly caused by L1 transfer. This conclusion is based on the following assumptions:

- The prime cause of difficulties and errors in L2 learning is interference with the learners' L1.
- The difficulties are mainly due to the differences between the two languages. The greater these difficulties are, the more acute the learning difficulties will be.
- The results of a comparison between the two languages are needed to predict where the difficulties lie.

Error analysis sets off as an alternative to CA. It refers to the study of a learner's ill-formed production (spoken or written) to discover systematicity. Two error types in error analysis framework are interlingual and intralingual. Interlingual errors are those that can be attributed to L1 whereas intralingual errors are those that are due to the target language, independent from the native language.

Intralingual errors are also known as developmental errors. Error analysis follows three steps:

1) A model for identifying erroneous or idiosyncratic utterances in L2 (Corder, 1971): starts from whether an error is overt (sentence level) or covert (discourse level) to identifying the source of the error.

2) Categories for describing errors (Lennon, 1991): errors of addition, omission, substitution, and ordering. Levels of errors: phonology, morphology, syntax, semantics, and discourse. Global versus local errors: global (hinder communication) while local (do not hinder communication). Error dimensions: domain (the rank of the linguistic context) and extent (the rank of the erroneous form).

3) Identifying sources of errors: interlingual transfer (L1 interference), intralingual transfer (overgeneralization), context of learning (due to the learning context), and communication strategies (due to strategy use).

According to Selinker (1972), L2 learning appears to develop in variable stages through an interlanguage process. Interlanguage refers to the variable progression through which each language learner constructs a system of abstract linguistic rules. Corder (1973) claims that there are four stages of interlanguage development:

1) The first stage is *the pre-systematic stage*, which means learners make errors randomly. Learners are only vaguely aware that there is some systematic order to a particular class of items. Learning at the stage is experimental and overuses inaccurate guessing.

2) The second stage is the *emergent stage*. Learners consistently grow in linguistic production. The learners began to discern the system and internalize the rules. However, these rules may not be correct in the target language, but the learners

think they are correct. At this stage, learners are still unable to correct errors even though the errors are made clear to them.

3) The third stage is *the systematic stage*. Learners are able to manifest more consistency in producing the second language. Even though the rules are not well formed in learners' minds, the big difference between the second and the third stage is that learners can correct the errors when the errors are pointed out.

4) The fourth stage is *the post-systematic (or stabilization) stage*. The learners have mastered the L2 system to the point that fluency and intended meaning are not problematic. This stage is characterized by the learner's ability of self-correction. Yet, some errors slip by undetected.

Nonetheless, learners exhibit variation, sometimes within the parameters of accepted norms. Erring by itself may not be an adequate measurement of overall competence. Such factors as motivation, attitude, anxiety level, willingness to take risks, age, and cultural expectations should be considered.

Error correction

As the focus of language teaching has shifted from structural forms to functional uses, the question of the place of error correction becomes more and more important. On one hand, the meaningful language use pays attention to the message; on the other hand, without correct language forms, communication becomes futile. Sutherland (1967) argues that if accuracy is the main focus of language teaching, the end result will be limited proficiency in the target language. Researchers have found that increased, direct correction does not lead to great accuracy in the target language (Hendrickson, 1976; Semke, 1984), and such an emphasis on error correction can be overly directive and intimidating and can even lead to increased language anxiety (Young, 1991).

However, some studies have pointed out possible advantages of providing correction in context, sometimes coupled with explanation or focus on a rule (White, Spada, Lightbown, & Ranta, 1991; Carroll & Swain, 1993; Lyster & Ranta, 1997). Other researchers like (Lightbown & Spada, 1990; Long, 1989; Spada, 1997) suggest that form-focused instruction can increase the learner's level of attainment. Error treatment and focus on language forms appear to be most effective if implemented in a communicative learner-centered classroom. The teacher should be wary not to pay too much attention to, or overcorrect, learners' errors because the ultimate goal of L2 learning is the attainment of communicative fluency. Positive reinforcement of free communication is very vital. The teacher's emphasis should be on content rather than form. In this manner, learners will feel free in developing their language.

L2 teachers also need to correct errors, but effectively. Error correction should be subject-sensitive and non-threatening or -embarrassing. Moreover, students will sometimes reach a plateau. If not dealt with properly, learners' errors may become part of their interlanguages. The relatively permanent incorporation of incorrect linguistic forms into a learner's competence is referred to as fossilization (Selinker, 1972). Fossilization is unique to L2 learners and does not occur to L1 learners (Ellis, 1997). Vigil and Oller (1976) provided "[a formal] account of fossilization as a factor of positive and negative affective and cognitive feedback" (Brown, 1994, p. 217). Fossilization may be the result of too many 'green' lights when there should be some 'yellow' and 'red' lights. Too much positive feedback may reinforce the learner's errors; and, too much negative feedback can deter the learner from participation. Thus, feedback must be optimal in order to be effective. The teacher should discern the optimal tension between positive and negative feedback. This can be achieved by providing a reasonable amount of corrective feedback that treats errors but does not limit communication or interaction.

Generally, error correction can be performed by teachers, but with due consideration to the following points:

1. *Effect of feedback to errors*: Positive or neutral feedback by ignoring errors reinforces the ill-formed forms and leads to fossilization. Negative feedback that causes the learner to reformulate the ill-formed forms (Vigil & Oller, 1976) is punitive and so should be avoided.

2. *Cognitive feedback*: The teacher needs to discern the optimal tension between positive and negative feedback so as to be effective and supportive rather than suppressive.

3. *Local versus global errors*: Local errors need not be corrected so long as the message is clear. Global errors need to be corrected if the message is unclear (Hendrickson, 1980).

4. *Form-focused instruction*: Types of feedback: *recast* (a reformulation or expansion of the form used incorrectly by the student e.g., S: I goed to home. T: I see, you went home.), *repetition* (the teacher repeats using a corrected form with a change in intonation e.g., S: When I have 12 years old … T: When I was 12 years old …), *clarification request* (an elicitation of a reformulation or repetition from a student e.g., S: I pencil. T: I'm sorry?), *metalinguistic feedback* (the teacher provides comments, information, or questions related to the well-formedness of the student's utterance e.g., S: I am here since July. T: Ok, but you remember when we said when to use the present perfect tense?), *elicitation* (a request of the student to self-correct e.g., S: [to another student] What this word means? T: Uh, Ali, how do you say that, again? What does …? S: Ah, what does this word mean?), *explicit correction* (a clear indication that the form

is incorrect and provision of a corrected form e.g., S: When I have 12 years old ... T: No, not have. You mean, when I was 12 years old ...), and *peer correction* (the teacher elicits the corrected form from the whole class or a specific student e.g., S1: I buyed a bicycle. T: Uh, Ahmed said what, "He .... S2: bought a bicycle).

5. *Error treatment*: Preferred when incorporated into a communicative, learner-centered curriculum. It depends on the context and benefits from focus on form. It works better when involving a progression of noticing and repair.

Teachers can have their students do self-correction or any similar activities that are self-initiated. In oral tasks, the teacher should try to extend the wait-time between hearing the student and correcting the error(s) he has made. The teacher may also want to leave the time for the student in anticipation that he may correct his error(s). Learners self-correct 50% to 90% of their own errors if they are given time as well as encouragement (Walz, 1982). Weak learners may not be able to correct their errors by themselves; therefore, teachers can correct their errors indirectly by recasting and modeling correct utterances. Another way of non-threatening correction is that the teacher can point out correct forms to the whole class rather than single out individual students. Edge (1994) gives innovative suggestions of peer correction, whole-class correction, and correction competitions. Conferencing is another way to personalize corrective feedback on writing, in which the students meet with the teacher to know of common errors in their writings.

Yorio (1980) suggests that teachers keep notes of the errors their students make in order to determine which errors are systematic (occur with regularity) and which are random (caused by memory lapses, inattention, unawareness of the required rule, or overgeneralization). He also recommends that teachers not mark students' papers in red ink, but rather discuss their errors in a meaningful way in accordance to the following scheme:

- Hold sessions with students who seem to be making the same kinds of errors.
- Give students chances to find their own errors and correct them.
- Focus on meaning, especially in oral tasks, as opposed to form.
- Model or repeat what the learner said erroneously but in the correct form.
- Explain errors as often as possible.

Learners want to know the nature of the errors they tend to make. And, providing them with explanations of their errors can aid them to relearn the related rules. Hedgcock and Lefkowitz (1994) found that the English learners in their study welcomed the teacher's focus on accuracy and valued functional and content-oriented correction. Kaufmann (1993) found that ESL students preferred explicit to implicit corrections of their oral errors.

Many teachers are keenly aware that their students make numerous errors; some teachers feel the need to correct all of these errors; while others permit a flood of mistakes in the interest of free expression. Students whose every mistake is corrected may feel language learning is hopeless; but on the other hand, students who make many errors may find out that they cannot communicate adequately. Consequently, teachers should aim for the objectives of the language course and tailor error correction in a way that best matches these objectives. Further research may enable teachers to establish an appropriate hierarchy of errors in the various tasks and activities of their classes. Such hierarchy can help teachers determine priorities for error correction either during regular classes or on testing tasks. Teachers may opt to correct those errors for which native speakers have the least tolerance rather than attempting to correct all errors or only a few errors in some random fashion.

U-shaped learning: Error making and correction

U-shaped learning can be defined as "the phenomenon of moving from a correct form to an incorrect form and then back to correctness" (Brown, 2007, p. 392). U-shaped learning characterizes the three-stage process in which a language learner produces a correct form in one instance; produces the same form incorrectly in another instance; and in a third instance, produces the form correctly (Gass & Selinker, 2001). Brown (2007) refers to this process as backsliding because the learner has acquired the rule or principle that governs such a linguistic form, but then retroverts to a previous state. At this stage, the leaner cannot make use of error correction or corrective feedback and may exhibit avoidance of using structures (Brown, 2007).

As an implication, teachers ought to keep in mind that learners make mistakes not because they have not acquired the relevant rule; rather, the learners are going through a process in which they are naturally inclined to err. Teachers are advised to show more tolerance of mistakes that are not frequent from a given student. That is, teachers can use frequency of a mistake as a criterion on the basis of which they decide how to provide corrective feedback.

The Debate on Whether or Not Grammar Should Be Taught

Since about the early 1980s, there has been an ongoing controversy about whether to teach or not to teach grammar explicitly in the ESL classroom. In other words, scholars have argued the merits and demerits of *focus on form* instruction in L2 teaching, particularly in the context of the communicative language teaching. The term *focus on form* was originated by Long (1991) to refer to any teaching technique that "overtly draws students' attention to linguistic elements as they arise incidentally in lessons whose overriding focus is on meaning or communication" (pp. 45-46). To address this topic, I intend to first review the literature on the 'teach-or-not-teach-grammar' debate, offering the theoretical account that has given rise to this debate. Then, I will discuss some other relevant considerations as well as important findings drawn from empirical research. After that, I will focus on pedagogical insights of how to combine between focus on form and communicative goals of language teaching methodology as informed by the latest developments in the field. Finally, I will conclude by taking a stand on the role of grammar instruction in the teaching of ESL.

A careful look at the history of the debate about whether grammar should be taught explicitly will reveal that such a debate has existed since the time when the direct method was first used in the 1890s (Macaro & Masterman, 2006). According to Ellis (2002a), this debate has been even getting sharper over the last three decades. Ellis (2002a) sees that grammar was a prominent aspect in the methods that relied on a structural syllabus. Then, such a status of grammar was downplayed later in the natural approach and the communicative language teaching when more emphasis was placed on a notional-functional syllabus. In the recent years, several arguments have been made about whether grammar should become part of the language syllabus. These arguments differ in whether form should be taught (or the so-called *focus on form*); and if taught, should it be implicit or explicit? From another perspective, Hood (1994) suggests that the debate primarily evolves about three questions: "a) what grammar is; b) who it should be taught to; and c) whether it should involve overt use of terminology or merely the establishment of patterns" (p. 28).

Before discussing the theoretical framework of the debate, it is worthwhile to know how form is defined so that we can establish a better understanding of why it is debatable. In contrast to the initial perception of what form implies, Ellis (2001) maintains that the term form "is intended to include phonological, lexical, grammatical, and pragmalinguistic aspects of language" (p. 2). Hence, *focus on form* can be defined "as the incidental attention that teachers and L2 learners pay to form in the context of meaning-focused instruction" (Ellis, Basturkmen, & Loewen, 2001, p. 1). Subsequent to their definition, Ellis and his colleagues note that this meaning has been expanded by Long (1991) who suggests that focus on form can be proactive, intensive, or repetitive instruction of a single linguistic element. In any case, *focus on form* distinguishes itself from decontextualized grammar instruction that is isolated from meaningful or communicative language use (Lyster, 2004).

We can relate the implication above to Celce-Murcia's (1992) description of formal grammar instruction and Terrell's (1991) definition of explicit grammar instruction in that the learner's attention is focused on the form as conveyed by a message. Terrell's (1991) use of the term *explicit grammar instruction* leads us to an important distinction between implicit and explicit instruction. While the former aims to have learners learn grammatical rules inductively, the latter adopts a deductive approach in teaching such rules (DeKeyser, 1995). Housen and Pierrard (2005) contrast aspects of implicit versus explicit modes of form-focused instruction, suggesting that while the implicit mode is conducted spontaneously, encourages fluent production, and contextualizes target forms, the explicit mode is prepared for in advance, encourages accurate production, decontextualizes target forms. DeKeyser (1995) proposes that the amount of awareness learners have of the forms being taught determines if these forms will become part of the learners' explicit or implicit knowledge. In fact, it is this dichotomy between implicit and explicit knowledge that further provoked the debate revolving around the teaching of grammar, as Lyster (2004) maintains that whether or not explicit knowledge can ultimately become part of an

L2 learner's implicit knowledge, and so can be used in unplanned oral performance "is still an open question" (p. 321).

The facets of L2 pedagogy that have given rise to the teach-or-not-teach-grammar debate become more evident when we consider the change from the structural syllabus to the notional-functional syllabus in the early 1980s. It is central to the discussion of this debate to shed some light on the place of grammar in the era of the communicative approach. A number of scholars (e.g., Brumfit & Johnson, 1979; Widdowson, 1978; Wilkins, 1976) have attempted to apply Hymes's (1967) *communicative competence*, suggesting that language instruction should aim to enable learners to communicate in the target language. They also suggest that the language teaching syllabus should be focused on notional and functional aspects rather than structural aspects. Another influential strand is that led by Krashen (1981) and influenced by his *monitor model* along with its underlying hypotheses. Krashen (1981) claims that a low affective filter and comprehensible input at an "i + 1" level through meaning-focused instruction are sufficient conditions for the acquisition of the rule system and that explicit grammar instruction is needless (Macaro & Masterman, 2006).

In the same vein, Prabhu (1987) proposes that teaching language with a focus on a descriptive grammar is prone to hinder learners' interlanguage development. He holds that the learner's internal grammar is too complicated to be paralleled to the way in which a descriptive grammar can be taught. Prabhu (1987) believes that "[g]rammar-construction by the learner is an unconscious process which is best facilitated by bringing about in the learner a preoccupation with meaning, saying or doing" (as cited in Willis, 1997, p. 114). Obviously, as Lyster (2004) notes, Krashen (1981) and Prabhu (1987) favor implicit or what came to be called incidental learning to explicit learning. Nonetheless, some other scholars believe that *form-focused instruction* contributes to the development of explicit knowledge, but not implicit knowledge, and as such, it does not aid the learner's spontaneous oral performance (Ellis, 2002a).

Krashen (1992) sees explicit or conscious knowledge of rules as a monitor, and argues that when three conditions of monitor use (i.e., knowledge of the rule, enough time to apply the rule, and focus on form) are met, grammar can lead to improved accuracy. Pica (1994) and other scholars understate the role of accuracy in negotiation, suggesting that "[l]earners and their interlocutors find ways to communicate messages through negotiation, but not necessarily with target-like forms" (as cited in Lyster, 2004, p. 323). In general, as Wright (1999) puts it, the opponents of *form-focused instruction* are motivated by the fact that L2 acquisition can be assimilated to L1 acquisition in that language learning can occur naturally by simply exposing the learner to comprehensible input through interaction in meaningful context "with learners receiving little or no formal instruction in grammar" (p. 33).

On the other hand, the scholars who support the *form-focused instruction* consider it indispensable for the ultimate attainment of language proficiency. For this realm of thought and research, "explicit teaching of grammar rules may be viewed as a necessary 'short cut' to learning the rules and structures that limited classroom language input can never hope to cover sufficiently for them to be acquired" (Wright, 1999, p. 34). One important claim that represents this view is that post-pubescent L2 learners lack full access to the underlying mechanisms that support child L1 acquisition; therefore, they need to rely on mechanisms of inductive learning that utilize negative evidence (Felix, 1985; Schachter, 1989, as cited in Ellis et al., 2001). Beeching (1989) defends this position clearly when he asks "[i]s not a grasp of underlying grammar essential if learners are to generate their own meanings?" (As cited in Wright, 1999, p. 35). Although Long (1996) opts for the use of implicit or incidental learning as does Krashen (1992), Long (1991) subscribes to the dominion that considers drawing learners' attention to form necessary. He distinguishes focus on forms as being more concerned with the systematic and intensive teaching of isolated forms in accordance with a structural syllabus.

The proponents of the *form-focused instruction* point out two important outcomes of such an instructional mode. First, as Ellis (1997) notes, it can help learners ward off premature fossilization and promote their consciousness in order to acquire explicit knowledge. This is seen especially vital for post-pubescent learners; or else, they will not develop interlanguage systems free from errors of various sources (Celce-Murcia, 1992). In connection with consciousness, Schmidt (1994) believes that noticing is "the necessary and sufficient condition for the conversion of input to intake for learning" (p. 17), suggesting that learners must consciously notice language forms in order to acquire them (Ellis, 2001). Endorsed by research from the field of cognitive psychology, noticing serves to make learners aware of the input they are receiving, which results in the learners' internalizing the input (Schmidt, 1990). It is also crucial to Schmidt's noticing hypothesis (1990) that the effect of noticing may not be instantaneous; in fact, it can be an outcome of an interaction between what is being noticed and what is already part of the intake (Long & Robinson, 1998).

On the whole, the above discussion brings to mind the distinction between two models of language learning: skill-building versus input-processing models. While the former upholds that "learners acquire forms by proceduralizing explicit knowledge through production practice", the latter sees that "learners acquire forms by consciously attending to them and the meanings they encode in the input" (Ellis, 2001, p. 36). There are other noteworthy considerations pertinent to the debate. For example, Lyster (2004) summarizes three facets of grammar pedagogy that are still controversial as "the extent to which form-focused instruction must be integrated into communicative activities…", the differential effects of form-focused instructional options that vary in degrees of explicitness, as well as the types of L2 features that can most benefit from form-focused instruction …" (p. 324). Ellis (2002a) attempts to answer the question as to why such doubts as those mentioned above have been raised about the *form-focused instruction*. He suggests that, first, there is notable distinction between the grammar being taught and the learner's implicit knowledge; second, the manner in which a structural element is taught may deform the input; and third, it is not yet clear if intensive instruction can result in the development of implicit knowledge.

Counter to Krashen's (1981) view, a number of scholars have expressed their skepticism about the sufficiency of comprehensible input, isolated from any focus on form, in the attainment of language proficiency. Citing research evidence, Lightbown and Pienemann (1993) maintain that the *form-focused instruction* proved effective in causing developmental changes in interlanguage and promoting language acquisition. More to the point, Ellis (2002b) points out that mere exposure to positive input does not guarantee the acquisition of all grammatical structures and that negative feedback is extremely needed in order for learners to achieve grammatical competence. Another problem with Krashen's (1981) position is that he limits the role of explicit grammar knowledge to that of a monitor that adult learners use under certain conditions (Terrell, 1991). To the contrary, Terrell (1991) details three ways in which explicit grammar instruction affects acquisition: "1) as an "advance organizer" to aid in comprehending and segmenting the input; 2) as a meaning-form focuser that aids the learner in establishing a meaning-form relationship for morphologically complex forms; and 3) by providing forms for monitoring, which in turn will be available for acquisition in the output" (p. 58).

Indeed, Krashen himself (1993) admits Lightbown's (1991) finding regarding the long-term effect of focus on form. A fact often overlooked in this debate is that learners like to be taught grammar explicitly and that is the only way they can be helped to form their hypotheses about language (Wright, 1999). Many learners as well as teachers believe that grammar teaching aids language acquisition (Terrell, 1991). Referring to numerous studies he has reviewed, Ellis (2001) states that "[i]n general, however, these experimental studies did show that grammatical form was amenable to instruction, especially if the learners were developmentally ready to acquire the targeted structure, and also that these effects were often durable" (p. 4). In their meta-analysis of 49 studies, Norris and Ortega (2000) concluded that explicit instruction results in more positive and lasting outcomes than implicit instruction; the same applies to explicit feedback versus negative feedback.

From six studies investigating the role of comprehensible input among Canadian French immersion students, Hammerly (1991) found that the results turned out dissatisfactory in terms of both language competency and accuracy (as cited in Wright, 1999). Likewise, Ellis et al. (2001) report a number of studies that have indicated that learners who are taught through intensive meaning-focused instruction fail to achieve acceptable levels of grammatical and communicative competence. In a study that aimed to develop a rating scale for elementary-level EFL writing, Assiri (2015) identified grammatical accuracy as one major factor that significantly differentiated among five scoring levels, which attests to the importance of focusing on form in writing instruction and assessment. Generally, Ellis (2002a) maintains that ample research provides us with positive evidence regarding the effect of formal instruction on the development of explicit knowledge. Despite the limitations they identify in their study, Housen, Pierrard, and Van Daele (2005) found explicit grammar instruction to be conducive to the learners' acquisition and mastery of two grammatical structures in spontaneous speech. Nevertheless, Macaro and Masterman (2006) caution that it remains unconvincing as to whether explicit grammar instruction can result in the grammatical rules being internalized and become part of the learner's implicit knowledge.

Evidently, a considerable body of research evidence points to the efficacy of explicit instruction of grammar or *focus on form*. This is especially the case if it is implemented in conjunction with meaning-focused instruction and tailored to learners' current level of language competency. However, as Ellis et al. (2001) mention, the question remains as to how this can be accomplished. The bitter fact is that, as Celec-Murcia (1992) comments, this poses a challenge that language teachers need to confront in order "to develop effective ways of focusing learner attention on form at critical moments while learners are using the second language for purposeful communication" (p. 408). In an attempt to tie these two types of instruction together; that is, form-focused and meaning-focused, Ellis (2002b) offers us two options: integrated and parallel. He suggests that the integrated option can be implemented through one of two approaches:

1. *A proactive approach* or "focused communicative tasks" (p. 24): the curriculum content involves communicative tasks that focus on specific forms.
2. *A reactive approach*: the method of instruction involves the teacher's feedback with a focus on specific errors during or after learners' performance of communicative tasks.

Whereas for the parallel option, Ellis (2002b) says that
[h]ere no attempt is made to integrate a focus on code and message; instead, these are entirely separate components. In such a syllabus, the main component would consist of communicative tasks, designed to engage learners in receptive and productive processes involved in using language to convey messages. A second, similar component would consist of a list of grammatical structures to be systematically taught. There would be no attempt to create any links between the two components. (p. 25)

Thus, a vast amount of thought and research defies any doubts about the efficacy of explicit grammar instruction or *focus on form* in the growth of explicit knowledge and the development of interlanguage. The current argument, however, should not be over teach-or-not-teach-grammar; rather, it should aim to address such questions as where, when, and how to teach grammar effectively (Ellis et al., 2001). This fact has recently brought about a shift in research from examining whether grammar teaching can help to how different types of *form-focused instruction* can be carried out in a variety of language learning settings (Ellis, 2001). This form of teaching is needed if we seek to help learners, especially adults, develop their communicative competence, knowing that grammatical competence is an integral component of communicative competence. On the other hand, there is a lack of empirical evidence regarding the reverse effect of explicit grammar teaching. In fact, the opponents of this form of instruction tend to base their arguments on theoretical aspects using abstract terms to defend hypotheses whose premises are disputable. For example, Lightbown and Pienemann (1993) maintain that "Krashen ... seems ready to make strong claims about pedagogical implications of his hypotheses" (p. 720).

In this era of language teaching, we need to create "a mixture of opportunities both for acquisition through communicative interaction and for form-focused instruction, in a balance which takes account of individual learner and classroom environment variables" (Wright, 1999, p. 38). In so doing, we need to consider learners' needs and learning objectives; for example, do the learners need to accomplish academic or non-academic goals?, and to what extent should we focus on form? We also need to keep in mind that adult learners benefit from *form-focused instruction* more than youngsters do; especially, if it is aimed at areas that pose problems to the learners, as Ellis (2002b) suggests.

Mohammed S. Assiri

Teaching English for Specific Purposes

Teaching English for Specific Purposes (TESP) is another trend of learner-centered teaching. According to Savignon (1991), every learner has unique characteristics, needs, and interests. It is recommended that teachers develop materials based on learners' needs of a particular class. TESP is thus intended to meet learners' needs and interests in today's academia or business. TESP embraces a great diversity of language teaching settings around the world. A common means of identifying ESP groups is in terms of their specialist area of work or study. Various branches of ESP are identified, including EOP (English for occupational purposes), EAP (English for academic purposes), and EBP (English for business purposes).

The goal-directed ESP teaching has become a vital and innovative move especially in EFL settings. In ESP programs, courses are designed for classes that are homogeneous in terms of fields of study or work. Essentials to the course design are the analysis of learners' needs and the adjustment of the design to fit these needs. A task-based, communicative approach seems most appropriate for ESP classes. The ESP teacher is often the designer, material writer, and evaluator. It is necessary that the ESP teacher be familiar with the specific area of study or work of the learners. ESP learners are typically adults and highly motivated. The rationale for ESP has always been that it is motivating for learners to be in study- or work-related classes, taking courses relevant to their academic or vocational needs. The assumption is that ESP programs produce more efficient and effective language learning when compared to general English programs. ESP programs may be provided by private schools or institutes, or public institutions of education. ESP courses may be intensive or extensive. Some EOP courses are conducted at the workplace, for example, courses which combine language and job training for immigrant workers.

Needs analysis can be seen as crucial to an ESP course of study especially in intensive programs. Needs analysis attempts to answer questions as follows: what are the setting features?, what are the learners' current abilities?, what should the learners be able to do at the end of the course? The teacher, or course designer, has to make the ESP course so specific to the learners' needs. In a general course of business English, for instance, all the structural patterns of English ought to be taught. Genres, such as the different types of letters, functions such as describing processes, checking facts and figures, requesting information should be practiced. A more specific business course can focus on finance, importing and exporting, or management. In this case, a particular types of document and communicative routine should be utilized, which may favor certain structural patterns over others. A very specific course may focus on the work and products of one particular company, taking into account its stylistic preferences in speaking and writing.

ESP courses thus vary in terms of how language is actually presented and where the focus is placed. Some learners may be required to learn a large amount of terminology, in which case a lexical syllabus and CALL may be appropriate. In EAP, one expects a considerable use of long and complex texts, with more attention paid to features of textual organization than structural accuracy. Each ESP course can make use of custom-made and authentic materials. The ESP teachers may build up expertise in the subject and in the culture of the discipline. They may also manage to develop good contacts with experts in the field. Recent trends in TESP are motivated by three views that are themselves driven by societal factors (Belcher, 2004). According to Belcher (2004), such views represent socio-discoursal, socio-cultural, and socio-political facets that can be understood on the basis of genre-based pedagogy, situational learning, and critical pedagogy respectively.

Key Aspects of a Post-method Pedagogy

In this section, Kumaravadievelu's (2001) proposal of a post-method pedagogy is outlined.

I. A *post-method pedagogy must*:

    ▪ Facilitate the advancement of a context-sensitive language education based on a true understanding of local linguistic, sociocultural, and political particularities.

    ▪ Rupture the reified relationship between theorists and practitioners by enabling teachers to construct their own theory of practice.

    ▪ Tap the sociopolitical consciousness that participants bring with them in order to aid their quest for identity formation and social transformation.

II. *A post-method pedagogy*: A three-dimension system comprising the following pedagogic parameters:

    ▪ *Particularity*: Language pedagogy needs to be sensitive to a particular group of teachers teaching a particular group of learners pursuing a particular set of goals within a particular institutional context embedded in a particular sociocultural milieu.

    ▪ *Practicality*: Language pedagogy seeks to overcome the deficiencies inherent in the theory-versus-practice, theorists'-theory-versus-teachers'-theory dichotomies by encouraging and enabling teachers themselves to theorize from their practice and practice what they theorize.

    ▪ *Possibility*: Language pedagogy empowers participants and calls for developing theories, forms of knowledge, and social practices that work with the experiences that people bring to the pedagogical setting, and provides them with challenges and opportunities for a continual quest for subjectivity and self-identity.

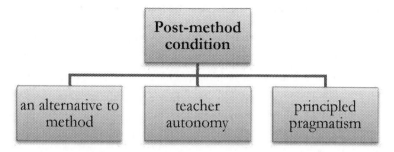

Figure 2: Requirements of a post-method condition

III. A strategic framework for L2 teaching under the *post-method* condition comprises ten macro-strategies that are both theory and method neutral:

- Maximize learners' creation of opportunities for their learning.
- Facilitate negotiated interaction through activities.
- Minimize perceptual mismatches between teacher's intentions and learner's interpretations.
- Activate intuitive heuristics for learners to learn (e.g., grammar through inductive learning).
- Foster language awareness by drawing learners' attention to language form and function.
- Contextualize linguistic input by using meaningful and context-based activities.
- Integrate language skills.
- Promote learner autonomy or self-directed learning.
- Raise cultural consciousness by creating a synthesis between the learner's home culture and the target culture.
- Ensure relevance to social, political, and educational L2 learning environment.

IV. *Post-method pedagogy* demands the following roles:

- The learner has academic autonomy (to be an effective learner), social autonomy (to be a collaborative partner), and liberatory autonomy (to be a critical thinker).
- The teacher has self-autonomy (entails competence and confidence), self-direction (controls teaching and learning tasks), and self-development (through teacher training and research).
- The teacher educator has dialogic interaction and responsive understanding, knowledge-sharing, and research-undertaking.

Using Read-aloud Technique with Child Learners (moviemaking)

One specific strategy that has been found to improve reading skills is what is called read-aloud. This strategy has proved to be useful by general population comprising beginning readers, adults, teachers, daycare providers, book clubs, and reading volunteers. It is generally recommended that learners be assigned read-aloud tasks on a regular basis in order to encourage them to read before class, and also have their classmates become part of these tasks (Hurst, Scales, Frecks & Lewis, 2011). In the same vein, Rasinski (2006) states that "[h]aving students take turns reading aloud is beneficial to cultivating a literate classroom environment, providing for ownership of classroom activities, and allowing for social learning" (p. 705). The goal of this section is to demonstrate how to make a movie of a read-aloud activity.

Audience

The audience for the movie intended consists of teachers of early grades, daycare providers, reading volunteers, book clubs, and adults involved in reading and its development. In general, people who deal with beginning readers, teach reading, or enjoy reading to people can be considered part of the audience. In this regard, the audience can be said to be diverse in nature and not limited to a particular group. The major commonality among the audience is a shared interest in developing reading skills for themselves, others, or maybe both. As such, the audience is expected to have at least some basic knowledge about the importance of reading. However, not all members of the audience are expected to be familiar with read-aloud.

Treatment

An adult and a child are sitting comfortably on a sofa indoor. The adult is modeling a technique called read-aloud to teach the child how to read. The adult asks the child to choose a storybook. Then, she asks the child why he chose the book. The child responds. The adult asks the child to predict what the story might be about from the illustration on the front cover of the book. The child responds. The adult and the child do a picture walk through the book. The adult asks questions and the child responds.

Afterwards, the adult starts reading the story and involves the child by asking about what he predicts to happen next. She reads at a pace fitting both the story style and the child's age, altering her expression and tone. The adult involves the child also by asking him to say repetitive phrases as they occur. At the end of the story, the adult closes the book and asks the child to comment on it.

Script

Int.
Developing Reading Using the Read Aloud Strategy
Afternoon

An ADULT and a CHILD are in casual clothing are sitting comfortably in a sofa in a room. The ADULT is holding a number of picture storybooks, engaging her CHILD who is sitting to her right side. The ADULT asks the CHILD to choose a book.

CUT TO:

ADULT

What story do you want to hear today? Why
don't you choose one of these?

The CHILD leans over to pick a book.

CHILD

OK. I like this one.

ADULT

Why did you pick this one?

CHILD

Because ....

CUT TO:

The CHILD hands the book to the ADULT and snuggles up to her. Both look at the illustration on the cover of the book.

ADULT

Let's look at the picture here! What do you
think this story is going to be about?

CHILD

It's going to be about ....

ADULT

What makes you think so?

CHILD

Because ....

CUT TO:

The ADULT opens the book.

ADULT

Before I read, let's look at the pictures in the book! Let's
start with this first picture! What do you see?

CHILD

I can see ....

The ADULT and the CHILD go through the pictures.

CUT TO:

ADULT

Now, we're ready to read.

The ADULT reads a few pages and stops to ask about the CHILD's earlier prediction.

ADULT

Do you think you guessed right about what the story is about?

CHILD

....

ADULT

OK! Now, let's continue!

CUT TO:

The ADULT continues reading the rest of the story, pausing every now and then to ask the CHILD about his predictions.

The ADULT closes the book and asks the CHILD to make a comment about the story.

ADULT

And, that's the end of "…....". What do you think about this story?

CHILD

Methods and Beginning EL2 Learners

One method that is appropriate for a beginning ESL class is *Total Physical Response*.

Total Physical Response (TPR)

In 1960s, Asher's TPR involves instructors' giving a series of commends to which students respond physically. It is a very communicative method of language learning and it is appropriate for beginning learners including children and adults based on research findings (Asher, 1972). It is a comprehension-based approach.

Students act out commands and they do not need to speak at first until they are ready for oral production. Thus, students share a low-anxiety learning environment, and will gradually develop their speaking skills. TPR brings the target language alive by making it comprehensible, and at the same time, fun. TPR does not focus on grammar, but on meaning. It is also a good way of teaching listening skills, basic vocabulary (e.g., color, number, position). Students' actions range from single performances to double performances, and gradually, commands become more complicated. They progress from silent comprehension of language to full participation in a few weeks of instruction.

TPR is a good method for teaching beginning level ESL/EFL students, especially listening. Asher's (1972) study indicated that children and adults alike could improve their language proficiency through TPR. Asher's study indicated that a group of adult learners of German with whom TPR was used for only 32 hours outperformed two groups of learners who had traditional instruction. One control group had 40 hours, and the other 80 hours. The two control groups had 35% more class hours' exposure to German than the TPR group, and had much more emphasis on reading and writing. The TPR group also did better than the control groups on a listening test. However, the TPR and control groups performed equally on reading comprehension test. According to the current theory, TPR works because it is an excellent way of providing students with comprehensible input. The teacher's movements provide the background knowledge that makes commands understandable. As students become more comfortable and capable in the target language, they can begin producing the language and participating in role-plays, presentations, and conversational activities. Stress is kept low because students are not forced to produce the language until they are ready.

TPR activities are designed to be fun and interesting for learners (e.g., learning a dance step or a martial art technique, cooking instructions, wonderful tricks ... etc.). Relevant real-life situations can be simulated in the classroom, with more focus on meaning over form. Learners are not corrected in the beginning, but later when they are more advanced and can better benefit from correction. While of obvious value for language beginning learners, aspects of TPR can be used with more advanced learners in teaching various facets of daily life (e.g., auto maintenance, computer fix, auction sale, game play ... etc.). Because a TPR class is free of focus on grammar, class activities can be expanded. However, TPR has some limitations: 1) It is hard to teach abstract concepts or verb tenses through TPR, 2) TPR is a teacher-dominant method, 3) The lack of meaningful sequencing. To delimit the weaknesses associated with TPR, Kalivoda, Morain, and Elkins (1971) suggested that commands be combined in meaningful ways and used in more contextualized situations. Conroy (1999) proposed adjustments to TPR so that it can be useful with SL learners who suffer some kind of visual impairment.

In brief, TPR is based on a number of principles: psychomotor associations (use of physical activity to strengthen L2 learning), child L1 acquisition (listening associated with physical responses before speaking), and motor activity (a function of the right brain before L2 processing by the left hemisphere). TPR involves teachers giving a series of commands and interrogatives to which learners respond physically. They do not have to speak until they are ready for oral production. Students can develop their L2 gradually in a low anxiety or stress environment. L2 learning activities can be made more interesting and enjoyable. Real-life situations can be simulated in the L2 classrooms. Corrective feedback is used less initially to stimulate students' active participation. TPR is very communicative, comprehension-based, and appropriate for beginners (Asher, 1972), invigorates L2 learning experience, makes L2 learning more enjoyable and comprehensible, provides more comprehensible input, and focuses on meaning rather than form, useful in teaching listening and vocabulary. Research by Asher (1972) indicated that TPR was useful in teaching listening to beginning level students both children and adults and helping them improve their L2 proficiency.

The two methods that are not appropriate for beginning ESL classes are the *Grammar Translation Method* (GTM) and the *Audio-lingual Method* (ALM).

Grammar Translation (GT)

GT, also known as the "Prussian Method", was the most popular method of foreign language teaching in Europe and America from about the mid-1800s to the mid-1900s. It still exists today in many countries around the world. GT embraces a wide range of approaches. The foreign language study is viewed as a mental discipline, the goal of which is to read literature in its original form or simply to be a form of intellectual development. The basic approach of GT is to analyze and study the grammar rules of the language in an order roughly matching the traditional order of the grammar of Latin, and then to practice manipulating grammatical structures by means of translation both into and form the mother tongue. The method emphasizes the reading and writing aspects of the foreign language. Language is taught without paying much attention to speaking and listening. Grammar rules are introduced at the beginning, followed by written exercises and bilingual vocabulary list, and translation. Accurate use of language forms is central to this approach.

According to Richards and Rodgers (1986), there is no attention given to listening and speaking, so learners often finish the course with no communicative competence in the language. New learners may quickly feel bored and find this instruction to have little relevant to the outside world. The target language is not used for instruction, only the native language, so learners have no actual exposure to meaningful input in the classroom. Attention and priority are given to translating passages and doing grammar exercises in isolation. Learners may find little meaning in doing such activities, since there is little relevance to learners' actual lives. This method has its own downsides. First, focusing only on form does not enhance communicative skills. Second, it is less motivating with authentic practice. Third, it pays little attention to oral production; and thus, it subdues fluency and meaningful language use. Fourth, formal grammar instruction does not necessarily contribute to the development of acquired knowledge. In fact, knowledge needs to be employed in authentic communication (Krashen, 1982).

In short, GT focuses on grammar rules as the basis for translating from L2 to L1. L2 is taught using L1 with little exposure to meaningful L2 input, isolated-word lists of vocabulary, elaborate explanations of grammar, form-based, reading of classical texts, grammatical analysis, and L2-L1 translation exercises. L2 learning becomes boring and irrelevant to the outside world. Little attention to pronunciation, speaking, and listening severely limits any chances of developing L2 communicative competence (Celce-Murcia & McIntosh, 1979). A serious limitation of GT is that it is not justified or rationalized by theory or research (Brown, 2001).

Audiolingualism (ALM)

ALM was the new oral method that was developed to replace the *Grammar Translation* method. It was introduced as component of the "army method", used during World War II. It was recognized as the "audio-lingual method" when it began to gain favor in teaching English as a second/foreign language in the 1950s. It is based on a combination of linguistic and psychological theories. It emphasizes the use of drill practice and rote learning. It holds that enough memory will help build language sense. Nonetheless, meaningful communicative activities are not used by ALM.

Some characteristics of ALM:

- Dependence on mimicry and memorization of phrases
- No grammatical explanations.
- No use of the mother tongue.
- Extensive oral practice in the form of role-plays and dialogues.
- Learning vocabulary in context.
- Use of audio-visual aids.
- Immediate reinforcement of correct responses and negative feedback for incorrect responses.

Language is learned based on the basis of the behaviorist paradigm; and so, imitation is all that is necessary to learn a language. Chomsky (1957) challenges this view, suggesting that language is creative, not simply imitative. ALM pays undue attention to rote learning and practice drills, while downgrading the role of context and world knowledge in language learning. Subsequent research has shown that the language is not acquired through a process of habit formation and that mistakes are not necessarily bad or hurtful. Also, mimicry and rote learning lay aside the fact that language learning involves affective and interpersonal factors, and that learners can produce novel language forms. Besides, learners are unable to transfer the skills they learned in ALM classes to the outside world. Overall, ALM procedures were considered boring, repetitious, and dissatisfying (Richards & Rodgers, 1986).

In a nutshell, the ALM began to gain favor in ESL/EFL settings in the 1950s. It is firmly grounded in structural linguistics (descriptive analysis) and behaviorism (conditioning and habit formation). It emphasizes imitation, practice, error-free utterances, and memorization. It makes extensive use of oral drills, language labs, and audio-visual aids. It teaches grammar inductively, and vocabulary in context. ALM's weaknesses are apparent in that imitation and rote learning minify creative L2 learning and usage (Richards & Rodgers, 1986). ALM also failed to teach long-term communicative proficiency (Rivers, 1964). L2 is not acquired through a process of habit formation, and errors should not necessarily be avoided at all costs. Beginning in the early 1990s, as Moore (1996) put it, almost few language teachers can claim to be using a single method of teaching in their classes.

Teaching Pronunciation to High-level EL2 Learners

The communicative perspectives on SLA over the last past few decades have brought profound impact on every facet of second language study. There has been a change from the focus on language as simply a formal system to the use of language to serve communicative functions. This seems to have resulted on a gradual trend reversal from earlier movement toward eliminating or downplaying pronunciation instruction. Beginning in the early 1980s and gathering momentum into the 1990s, a renewed interest has been in the pronunciation component of ESL curricula, and a growing trend toward communicative approaches to teaching pronunciation. SLA research has been concerned with pronunciation with a proper place in a large communicative framework. Increasing attention has been paid to techniques for developing intelligible pronunciation, with the aim of enabling L2 learners to communicate and negotiate their educational, occupational, and social interests and needs (Morley, 1991).

Figure 3: Pronunciation and L2 teaching

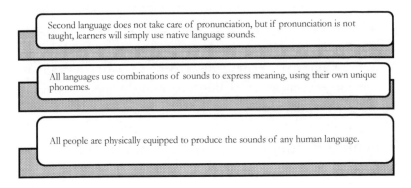

Second language does not take care of pronunciation, but if pronunciation is not taught, learners will simply use native language sounds.

All languages use combinations of sounds to express meaning, using their own unique phonemes.

All people are physically equipped to produce the sounds of any human language.

One main foundation of many new language programs has been to take pronunciation from isolation to become an integral part of communicative language teaching and learning. Meaningful activities, suited to learners' needs and real-life situations, have assumed paramount importance. A variety of communicative techniques to teaching pronunciation have been discussed by many researchers, such as Celce-Murcia and Goodwin (1991), Kenworthy (1987), Naiman (1987), Pica (1984), among others. There is an overall consensus among these researchers that segmental and suprasegmental elements of spoken language should be taught in language classes. According to Morley (1991), speaking activities can be adapted for special pronunciation focus. This implicates that segmentals and suprasegmentals can be learned and practiced in contextualized speaking activities. In addition, there are many publications and materials on teaching pronunciation available (e.g., Baker, 2010; Hewings, 2004; Rogerson-Revell, 2011). They are tailored to address specialized communication needs such as those of international teaching assistants and various academic programs, for instance.

A communicative framework for field-specific pronunciation teaching has been offered by Imber and Park (1991), which can be applied to a wide range of ESP settings. Growing attention has been given to creating a comfortable learning climate in order to encourage classroom interaction using intelligible pronunciation. Morley (1991) claims that "classroom interactions need to be enjoyable and supportive with a focus on both strengths and weakness, where even the most unintelligible students can loose their self-consciousness and embarrassment about sounding funny as they work to improve the sound features of their oral communication" (p. 504). On the other hand, pronunciation teachers, as coaches, play the role of monitoring and guiding adjustments of spoken language at the micro-level of speech production and the macro-level of speech performance.

There has been a growing emphasis on oral communication in order to enable learners to become effective, confident, and fully participating users of English. Much of the research on pronunciation has had the goals of "expanding the horizons of pronunciation learning and teaching, redefining basic concepts and constructing communicative approaches featuring creative classroom and self-study instructional activities" (Morley, 1991, p. 512). Nonetheless, the teaching of pronunciation has long been viewed as offering learners drills and exercises in isolation from the other language skills. A pronunciation-based syllabus can be planned to provide a variety of speaking and listening activities. As summarized by Morley (1991), three instructional modes move from dependent practice with a given model to a guided practice with self-initiated and rehearsed speech to independent practice with self-generated content. Imitative speaking practice that includes contextualized content is viewed as a short-term component within a rehearsed or extemporaneous practice. A great number and variety of activities have been discussed: pair work, group work, presentation, dialogue, audio-lingual analysis of specific speech production and/or speech performance features. Such activities can be very effective with constructive critiques towards integration of modified speech patterns into naturally occurring creative speech, in both partially planned and unplanned talks.

Listening-speaking connections:

- Unheard sounds cannot be produced.
- Sounds originate in the brain before being produced.
- Only the exact sound-image can produce the accurate sound.
- New sounds need time to be mastered.

Principles for teaching pronunciation:

- Pronunciation mastery is possible, but decreases with age.
- Older learners profit more from formal instruction than younger ones.

What to teach:

- segmental features --- vowels, consonants, diphthongs
- suprasegmental features --- word stress, intonation, pattern, rhythm
- "weak forms" --- schwa /i/$_\rightarrow$ /ə/
- aspiration --- initial voiceless stops in stressed position
- specific problems --- related to L1 interference

Pronunciation correction:

- use self- and peer-correction
- choose carefully what to correct
- use visual support --- diagramming a simple sketch of vocal organs and places of sound articulation
- set goals: accuracy, fluency, and intelligibility
- let learners judge a sample of recorded pronunciations

In CLT, teaching pronunciation to advanced ESL learners needs to focus on elements that enhance oral communication (e.g., stress, rhythm, intonation ... etc.) (Brown, 2001; Derwing & Rossiter,

2003; Jones, 1997). English rhythm and intonation have more major roles in oral communication than individual sounds (Wong, 1987). Training ESL learners in using English stress can help them sound more native-like. A pronunciation lesson ought to provide a variety of listening and speaking practice (Morley, 1991). A lesson plan for teaching pronunciation to high-level ESL learners follows.

Practicing stress and rhythm
- *Level*: advanced
- *Aim*: To improve pronunciation by focusing on the stress-timed nature of spoken English.
- *Time*: 1 period (1 hour)
- *Materials*: tape player, a recording of sample authentic conversations with short turn-takings, scripts of the conversations
- *Activities and procedures*:

I. *Listening to authentic conversations.*

1) The teacher has students listen to samples of authentic conversations,
2) As they listen, the students take notes of key or important words (stress) and notice how English rhythm is used (rhythm).
3) The teacher elicits the students' responses and comments about English stress and rhythm as to why and how they are used.
4) The teacher provides the students with necessary feedback and/or explanations.

II. *Oral repetition*:

1) The students listen a second time to the conversations while paying attention to stress and rhythm.

89

2) The teacher pauses the recording at the end of each turn-taking and has the students repeatedly imitate the stress and rhythm they have heard.
3) The teacher elicits repetitions from individual students.

III. *Oral practice in pairs*:

1) The teacher distributes the scripts of the conversations to the students.
2) The teacher has each pair perform each conversation using clear stress and intonation.

IV. *Follow-up*: role-plays

1) The teacher assigns different roles to each pair of the students (e.g., a doctor and a patient).
2) The teacher asks the students to prepare conversations.
3) The teacher has each pair role-play their conversation using clear stress and intonation.
4) The teacher elicits the students' comments regarding their classmates' performance.

This pronunciation lesson conforms to the assumptions of CLT as it exhibits the following characteristics:

1. *Authentic material and contextualization*: The recording of authentic conversations to have the students listen to how English stress and rhythm are used in real-life situations. Inductive learning and contextualization are important aspects of CLT that can improve pronunciation (Hadley, 2001). Such a focus on these suprasegmental features through a listening activity can substantially improve the learners' pronunciation (Elliot, 1997)
2. *Oral communication*: The students' responses or comments are elicited after the listening activity, during the oral

repetition activity, and after the follow-up activity. The students are asked to role-play conversations in pairs and so interact with one another. Repeating sentences or utterances after a native-speaker model can improve the learners' pronunciation (Elliot, 1997)

3. *Learner-centered aspect*: The students carry out most of the class interaction and they make up the conversations they will use in the follow-up activity. The follow-up activity is a variation of what Wong (1987) calls "fluency workshop" activities.

4. *Communicative activities*: The students are engaged in pair and role-play activities during the oral practice and the follow-up tasks. These activities help create an enjoyable and supportive learning experience for weak or shy students (Morley, 1991), and are by their nature conducive to the development of communicative competence (Hadley, 2001).

Therefore, the lesson above conforms to the basic principles of CLT that seek to promote language learning (Richards & Rodgers, 1986):

1. *The communication principle*: The activities used involve communication.

2. *The task principle*: The activities used involve the completion of real-world tasks.

3. *The meaningfulness principle*: The learners are engaged in meaningful and authentic language use.

Teaching Simple Past versus Present Perfect Tenses

The distinction between the simple past and present perfect tenses poses an obvious difficulty to many E2L learners. This section illustrates the differences between the two tenses in terms of form, meaning, and usage, and explains how E2L teachers can help their students tackle this issue.

I. **Why is the distinction between the past and perfect tenses important to teach to EFL learners?**

1) Whether to use present perfect or simple past represents an area of difficulty to EFL learners whose L1s do not mark the perfect aspect (e.g., Arabic).

2) The differences between English and another language in marking the perfect aspect make up areas of difficulties for the speakers of the latter language who are learning English (e.g., Japanese) (Labadi, 1990).

3) Marking the perfect aspect in English involves the use of two separate elements (i.e., has/have + V-ed/-en), which complicates its use for EFL learners (Yule, 1998).

4) EFL learners try to use just one element of the perfect aspect marker, which results in their making mistakes (Yule, 1998).

II. **How can the distinction between the past and perfect tenses be taught?**

1. *Form*:
Simple past: simple ➔ the past form of the verb (V+ -ed/-en)
Present perfect: compound ➔ the auxiliary verb (has/have) + the past participle form of the verb (V+ -ed/-en)

2. *Meaning* and *Usage:*

Simple Past	Present Perfect
 NOW X	NOW XXXXX (an indefinite time before now)
✓ Describes an action that happened and completed at a definite time in the past. *Examples:* ✓ Otaku *ate* his breakfast <u>at 8:00 o'clock</u>. ✓ Raven *visited* her friend <u>last weekend</u>. ✓ Randi *went* shopping <u>yesterday</u>. ✓ Emily *got* married <u>in 2001</u>.	▪ Describes an action that happened at an indefinite time before now. *Example:* ✓ Heinz *has eaten* his breakfast. ▪ Describes an action that began in the past and just completed. *Example:* ✓ ustin *has* <u>just</u> *finished* his homework. ▪ Describes a completed activity whose impact is felt in the present. *Example:* ✓ They *have arrived.* (meaning: a short time ago; here they are). ▪ Describes an action that began at a definite or indefinite time within a period leading up to the present. *Examples:* ✓ Zukav and I *have known* each other <u>since 2004</u>. ✓ Filip and I *have known* each other <u>for three years</u>. ✓ Andreas and I *have known* each other <u>for ages</u>.

III. Research-based teaching suggestions and recommendations:

1) Provide learners with frequent and clear examples to help them notice and perceive the distinct elements of the two tense forms (Yule, 1998).

2) Present the two tenses side by side along with plenty of practice while following a discourse-based approach (Celce-Murcia, 2002).

3) Encourage learners while working on exercises to pay attention to the meanings of the sentences to be better able to decide which tense to use (Ellis, 2003).

4) Follow a systematic approach in teaching the differences among tenses by moving from simple to complex tenses, describing their meanings to learners (Willis, 2003).

IV. Exercises on the simple past and present perfect tenses:

I. *Fill in the blanks with the correct form of the verb in parentheses and explain why.*

1) I ………….. (finish) my homework.

2) Finn ………….. (graduate) from high school last year.

3) Lyn had a high fever last Thursday so she ………….. (take) some aspirin.

4) A: Would you like something to eat?
   B: No, I ………….. (have) my lunch.

II. *Complete the sentences in the passage with the correct forms of the verbs from the list.*

happen – have – be – know – meet – tell – see – ask

Zukav and I *have known* each other since 2004. Unfortunately, I ……………... (not) him for a few days. At the party last weekend, I ……………... my friends about him, but it seemed nobody ……………... anything about what ……………... to him. Yesterday, I ……………... his

father and I .... him about Zukav. He ....
me that Zukav .... to leave the town so hurriedly
to see his grandmother. She .... sick for a couple
of months. [Adapted from: Brown, C. & Brown, P. (2006)]

III. *First, show what is the tense used in each sentence. Then, switch the tenses between present perfect (PP) and simple past (SP) and make all necessary changes.*

1) Jesse has made a nice dish to take out.
   PP SP...............................

2) Garry waited for you until two o'clock.
   PP SP ....

3) Xavier has built his house since 2005.
   PP SP ....

4) Peta passed her math exam last semester.
   PP SP ....

IV. *On-line exercises*:

- The present perfect tense and the simple past tense:
  http://web2.uvcs.uvic.ca/elc/studyzone/410/grammar/ppvpast.htm
- Present perfect or past simple:
  http://www.englishgrammarsecrets.com/presentperfect orpastsimple/menu.php
- Past simple & present perfect:
  http://www.englisch-hilfen.de/en/exercises/tenses/simple_past_present_ perfect.htm

Mohammed S. Assiri

Contrastive Rhetoric and Teaching Advanced Writing

Different languages have different writing discourses (Kaplan, 1966). Kaplan's (1966) article was the first in the field of ESL that focused on the rhetoric of writing. He claims that logic and rhetoric are culture specific. Logic, assumed to be the basis of rhetoric, evolves out of culture, and so is not universal. Rhetoric is not universal either as it varies from culture to culture, and even from time to time within a given culture. He maintains that logic and rhetoric are interdependent as well as culture specific. The cultural component of communication has become the subject of study in a hybrid field called contrastive rhetoric.

Kaplan (1966) analyzed the organization of paragraphs of more than 600 ESL students' essays. He found five methods of paragraph development. Anglo-European expository essays follow a linear development. In contrast, paragraph development in Semitic languages is based on a series of parallel coordinate clauses. For instance, people from the Middle East like Arabs try to balance their ideas, and use parallel structures, similar expressions, and repetitions. Essays written in oriental languages like Japanese use an indirect approach such as symbols or metaphors and come to the point only at the end. In Romance languages, also in Russian, essays are permitted a degree of discursiveness and extraneousness that may seem excessive to an English writer. Therefore, Kaplan's (1966) work points out differences in writing styles across cultures.

Contrastive rhetoric maintains that people in different cultures organize their ideas differently. As a direct consequence, the writing system of each language has rhetorical conventions that may interfere with those of another language. Contrastive rhetoric has moved ahead to compare discourse structures across cultures and genres. According to Kaplan (1966), culture-specific patterns of writing organization can influence L2 writing in negative ways. ESL learners ought to be made aware of the rhetorical conventions in English. They should be informed that the structure of English exposition as linear, because a paragraph in English typically begins with a topic sentence supported by examples that are related to the central point.

Criticisms

Kaplan's (1966) contrastive rhetoric has been criticized for several reasons:

- Being too ethnocentric as it privileges the writing system of English.
- Examining L2 texts at the surface level only and ignoring variables pertinent to educational and developmental processes.
- Dismissing linguistic and cultural differences in writing among related languages, such as Chinese, Thai, and Korean.
- Considering the transfer of writing conventions from L1 to L2 interference.
- An alleged insensitivity to cultural differences.

Moreover, Kaplan's (1966) diagram and his hypothesis have been interpreted quite too simply. Novices may understand the contrastive rhetoric hypothesis to mean that all writers of a particular language compose following the same organizational pattern. It is even more unfortunate that Kaplan's (1966) diagram suggests that a writing pattern reflects a thinking pattern. Thus, for example, since the Chinese write in circles, they must have a style of circular thinking. Many researchers have strongly asserted that the diagram is too simple a model for the representation of a theory of contrastive rhetoric.

Strengths

Although it is often criticized for being too simplistic and for assuming that English rhetorical model is "straight", Kaplan's (1966) theory is invaluable because it points out the nature of the rhetorical differences among writing systems of distinct languages. Contrastive rhetoric examines difference and similarities in ESL writing across language and cultures. Therefore, it considers texts not merely as static elements but as functional products of dynamic cultural contexts. Contrastive rhetoric has had an appreciable impact on our understanding of cultural differences in writing, and will continuously shape our teaching of ESL writing.

Suggestions for teaching ESL writing

Some researchers suggest that ESL writers need writing instructions because they have not developed writing patterns of English. Students have internalized patterns of discourse prevalent in their cultures, and they try to transfer these patterns to the ESL writing settings. Because students are probably unaware of the rhetorical constraints affecting their writing, some conscious knowledge of contrastive rhetoric may help them. Students can be asked to reflect on some of the requirements of their own rhetorical traditions, which can broaden native-speaking students' awareness of writing differences among cultures. This may do well against the insularity of perspective that some native speakers may suffer from. Contrastive rhetoric researchers have proposed various teaching techniques in order to help students raise their awareness of English rhetorical conventions.

Teaching techniques

A number of researchers suggested that writing teachers can have their students:

- become aware of the cultural differences in regard to specific assumptions about the audience (Kaplan, 1988);
- identify topic structures in authentic texts and narrow down a topic to match the writer's knowledge of the world (Grabe & Kaplan, 1989);
- rearrange scrambled paragraphs and fill out an outline following given topic sentences (Kaplan, 1972);
- imitate models, do controlled exercises, fill in missing sentences, and compose by following an outline (Kaplan, 1967);
- explain chronological and logical sequences, make bullet-point outlines, and examine formats for various academic assignments (Reid, 1984);
- pay attention to the lexical and morphological structures of edited texts and discuss rhetorical differences between English academic prose and that of students' L1 (Reid, 1989);
- provide topic sentences and write argumentative paragraphs to support topic sentences or provide argumentative paragraphs and write their topic sentences.

Pedagogical suggestions were driven from an empirical study of native-speaking readers' expectations about the sentence following a topic sentence (Reid, 1996), including the discussion of its use and contribution, the development of the skills necessary to predict it, and the identification of any problems associated with it. In general, the proponents of the contrastive rhetoric hypotheses recommend making rhetorical differences explicit, raising students' awareness of such differences, and acculturating students through language exercises using concrete models that meet audience expectations. ESL students ought to be made aware of the different writing styles that people from different cultures may bring with them. Nonetheless, L2 writers need to adjust their writing structures to fit the L2 situation. Of course, this does not mean that L2 writers must give up their L1, because they still need to apply their L1 norms in L2 writing. What they need to do is to learn to write in an appropriate style in order to enable their readers to understand.

Arguments for ESL teachers

- Familiarity with contrastive rhetoric studies helps teachers understand the difficulties that ESL students may have with writing and the sources of such difficulties.
- It also helps teachers realize when students' problems with writing arise, for example, when applying previously learned writing strategies to new writing tasks.
- The insights into the rhetoric of the other cultures that emerge from studies of contrastive rhetoric indicate to teachers that the particular choices ESL students tend to make in their writings are not random, but may result from their L1 rhetorical constraints.
- Teachers should be wary that teaching contrastive patterns does not necessarily lead to improved writing, but it does allow students to view certain writing problems they may have as evidence of their participation in other discourse communities.

New trend

The new directions of contrastive rhetoric have opposed some of the criticisms with theoretical underpinnings in both linguistic and rhetoric (Connor, 1996). The new directions involve innovative views of culture, literacy, and critical pedagogy, and have a major impact on the research agenda of contrastive rhetoric. Writing in such genres as letters, resumes, and job applications by people who represent disparate languages and cultural backgrounds is becoming a reality. It has been found that L2 writers transfer patterns, styles, expectations, and contexts from their L1s to L2. Different reader expectations cause misunderstanding; and so, there is an increasing need for intercultural communication and understanding (Mauranen, 2001).

From this viewpoint, it can be argued that contrastive rhetoric largely adopted the notion of "receive culture" in the past, because of a set of patterns and rules shared by a particular community. Traditional contrastive rhetoric often viewed ESL students as members of separate, identified cultural groups. However, although contrastive rhetoric often defined national cultures in the "received" mode, researchers have certainly not interpreted all differences in L2 writing as stemming from interference with L1 language or culture. Instead, they have considered such differences as the outcome of multiple sources including L1, national culture, L1 educational background, disciplinary culture, genre characteristics, and mismatched expectations between readers and writers. Contrastive rhetoric is thus in a position similar to that of intercultural pragmatics. In this regard, Sarangi (1994) suggests the term of "intercultural" to refer to migrants' fluid identities. He recommends that we take into account language proficiency, native culture, and interlocutor's mutual accommodation. In a study of how cultural background shapes writing, Petrić (2005) observed that writers who shared the same native language and culture exhibited similarities in composing essays in English, especially the frequent use and positioning of thesis statement as well as its structural and lexical components.

Use of Media in EL2 Classrooms

Visual and audiovisual media play an important role in English language teaching and learning (Celce-Murcia, 1979). EL learners can benefit from aural and visual programs in English, especially in EFL settings, as in China. Because these programs involve authentic materials, they motivate learners to learn not only the target language but also its culture. Besides, they can be easily accessed or made available. Media generally relates the English language classroom to the outside world, thus providing multiple input sources about the culture of the English-speaking people (Brinton, 2001). The various ways in which media are used in intercultural communication affect the teaching and learning of language modalities like writing and speaking (Thatcher, 2004).

A typical media lesson has the following stages:

1) *The information and motivation stage*: The teacher introduces the topic and presents relevant background information.

2) *The input stage*: The teacher ensures the learners' comprehension of the item(s) presented.

3) *The focus stage*: The learners are guided to practice and manipulate the item(s).

4) *The transfer stage*: The learners offer comments or share related experiences.

5) *The feedback stage*: The learners share feedback or perform self-assessment.

Media types and their uses

TV programs provide a readily accessible source of language in context as used by native speakers. The combination of sound and image in TV programs characterizes audiovisual media in the narrow sense of the word. Thus, the use of such media allows for a considerable degree of contextualization (i.e., demonstration of authentic language use in real-life situations). Language learning can be promoted by the use of media especially if the content presented by this media interests the learners and stimulates their participation. According to Fazey and Johnston (cited in Burt, 1999), TV provides audio and visual stimuli, and as such, it is accessible for learners who cannot read or write well. TV helps learners see body language and facial expressions (or gestures) while they hear the stress, rhythm, and intonation of the language (Bello, 1999). Recorded TV programs or videos can be used for presentation, repetition, listening, speaking, dictation, spelling, and writing, as well as in the assessment and testing of language skills. Just like L1 learners, L2 learners should have the opportunities to use the language for fun. Children and adults alike can receive considerable enjoyment from indulging in such frivolity.

By means of media, many "chunks" of useful language can be incorporated into individual's linguistic repertoire at almost any age or level of proficiency. The use of prosodic elements, redundancy, and sometimes thoughtless repetition can produce lower anxiety and greater ego. The message can be rich and multileveled and can initiate discussions that challenge even the most proficient learners among the group. Media can provide students with tools for communication, especially at the beginning levels. Through these genres, learners can internalize routines and patterns with or without consciously committing them to memory. Learners do not need to understand the meanings of all the words used in the content of these media; instead, they can infer their meanings using contextual clues. The level of the students is extremely important. For novice/beginners, they may feel hard to understand the authentic language. Therefore, they need very short (1-2 minutes) action-oriented segments in which there is visual support of meaning. One of the main disadvantages of this type of material, however, is that it gets outdated rapidly because of technical, political, and cultural developments.

<u>*Example*</u>: Dr. Phil

- *Audience*: Intermediate/advanced EFL learners
- *Teaching objective*: To help students develop their listening comprehension of authentic situations, introduce new vocabulary, and provide problem-solving situations.

- *Media*: Dr. Phil: A daily one-hour TV series in which Dr. Phil helps people solve their personal and social problems.
- *Skills*: Listening, vocabulary, speaking
- *Time*: 1 class period (1 hour)
- *Procedures*:

  1) The teacher introduces Dr. Phil program and talks about it briefly: Who Dr. Phil is, what he does, what the program is all about … etc.
  2) The students view one segment or a selected case in the program.
  3) The teacher elicits and explains the new vocabulary and structures used in the segment.
  4) The students view the whole segment a second time.
  5) The students consider the problem discussed and note Dr. Phil's thoughts and his guests' reactions.
  6) The students offer their personal comments and/or relevant experiences, judge Dr. Phil's thoughts and his guests' reactions, and suggest alternative solutions.
  7) The students provide their feedback in connection with the activity or perform self-assessment.

Another form of media is radio, which almost shares all the benefits associated with the use of TV in language learning. What radio lacks in terms of visual features, it makes up for by employing auditory features, including pitch, rhythm, and intonation.

Example: news

- *Audience*: Elementary EFL learners
- *Teaching objective*: To help students develop their listening comprehension of authentic information, learn new vocabulary, and practice note-taking.
- *Media*: CNN Radio News
- *Skills*: listening, vocabulary, speaking

- *Time*: 1 class period (1 hour)
- *Procedures*:

   1) The teacher introduces CNN Radio News and talk about it briefly: What CNN stands for, what it is for, what categories of news or stories it broadcasts: politics, health, technology, business, travel, entertainment, sports ... etc.
   2) The teacher has the students listen to the news and elicits the new vocabulary from them after listening.
   3) The students listen a second time and list down news categories in order.
   4) The students compare their responses to one another in pairs.
   5) The teacher elicits the correct responses from the students.

Examples of on-line media and their uses:

- ➤ *The Internet*: Have students look for information on a certain topic. Or, have students find EFL resources and use them online.
- ➤ *Email*: Have students exchange text messages with native speakers or with one another.
- ➤ *Twitter*: Have student post recent or new events or occasions and react to these posts.
- ➤ *Ads*: Learners can try to answer "what is being advertised?" Teachers can design some activities like fill in the blanks with key words.

For video clips, there certain tips a teacher should follow:

- Make sure the clip is relevant to the students' proficiency level.
- Ensure that the clip does not to violate any religious matters or cultural norms.

- Base your selection of clips on instructional objectives.
- Vary clips in terms of their foci and potential learning tasks.
- Go from simple to complex, global to specific, and from known to unknown.

An observation of a Composition Class

This section reports on a case study involving an observation of a college-level class. The class is a lower-division, undergraduate course in composition skills, offered over a two-month period (June and July).

Situational factors

The course draws on the critical reading and writing skills learned in a previous lower-division course. It aims to prepare students with new skills for subsequent upper-level courses. The instructor employs three main teaching strategies that include lecturing, discussion, and demonstration. She also makes use of digital technology in content presentation and class activities. There are 18 students enrolled in this course, including fifteen freshmen, two sophomores, and one junior. The students took a prerequisite course, in which they developed the reading and writing skills required for the current course. The course is offered in a normal classroom setting equipped with a blackboard, PC, digital projector, in addition to other peripherals that enable the use of a variety of media. The instructor mentioned that the students are often asked to bring their laptops to class in order to use the internet for additional resources and materials.

Learning goals

In general, the course aims to help students develop research skills that involve how to search, locate, and utilize documentary information to write technical reports. Such skills are important in the fulfillment of the requirements of their academic programs and scholarly research. As for the specific goals of the observed class, the students were expected to practice using the skills of analyzing visual and auditory features of selected movie excerpts. This way the students could become fully aware of the terminology used in these excerpts in preparation for the final exam.

Forms of significant learning

Based on course syllabus and class observation, the observer noticed that certain forms of significant learning were adequately made part of the course design whereas others can be described in connection to the observed class. Therefore, the learning *how-to- learn* aspect demonstrated itself in that the students could learn and develop the necessary research skills they need in their subsequent courses and future research. The course activities and tasks required the students to be responsible for their learning. This was accomplished by having the students do part of the coursework outside the class and reflect on their learning experiences. The students were also engaged in tasks that required them to search, locate, and use documentary information in writing. The students could also express their opinions and views; and so, they can be said to have inquired and constructed knowledge. With the aim of promoting foundational knowledge presented through the class content, the students were asked to bring their laptops to class. This allowed them to use the internet for inquiry and practice using authentic resources and materials. In addition, the students were engaged in a variety of assignments, including article readings and essay writings.

In addition, caring was noticed in that almost every time the instructor presented new information, she soon asked at least one question whose answer called for students' relating the information learned to their real-life experiences. For example, when the instructor described "montage" as one style of movie editing, she asked students to give examples of types of movies that use this style of editing. Human dimension characterized the way students expressed themselves when reflecting on what they felt about the use of certain visual and auditory features in selected video excerpts. In so doing, students lived this integration of seeing what features were used and reflecting on the effects of such features. The instructor had students see five movie excerpts, and so offered them many opportunities to apply their learning.

Planning for feedback and assessment

The instructor uses different forms of assessment that include class participation, peer reviews of major essays, written assignments in the form of short essays, frequent quizzes, reading responses, and a final exam. Each form of assessment is clearly described in the syllabus in terms of what it involves, what criteria are used to score it, and how much weight of points it deserves. During the class session that was observed, the instructor asked questions every now and then, praised correct responses, and offered immediate corrective feedback when necessary.

The observation

The observed class was a morning session. The instructor intended to have students practice analyzing visual and auditory features of movie scenes in preparation for the final exam. The instructor used teaching techniques such as lecturing, discussion, and demonstration. At the same time, she asked relevant questions and elicited answers from the students. One major concern the instructor has is that her students do not like the course as they consider it irrelevant to their academic majors. They also see themselves following the same procedures every class session. The instructor believes that, as a result, most students do not make any effort to interact and participate in class sessions.

Another concern the instructor has is that when students view movies, they do not focus on the features and effects used as much as on the content of the movies. Accordingly, the instructor and the observer agreed that the class observation would focus on specific behaviors that included the extent to which students: 1) are engaged in the overall class atmosphere, 2) interact and participate, and 3) pay attention to the movie scenes and analyze the visual and auditory features used in these scenes. That is to say, the technique the observer used was mainly focused note-taking of the given behaviors.

The instructor started the class by pointing out the whole purpose of the class, that is, to study and analyze film editing. Then, the instructor and the students previewed a set of instructions and directions the students will see on the final exam. Next, the instructor described three styles of film editing using the blackboard. First, she made a drawing of the first style, and then, demonstrated the third style. Along with the description of each editing style, the instructor asked questions about the kinds of movies that use it. Next, the instructor moved on to the discussion of two types of lighting used in moviemaking. She used the blackboard to illustrate each, and at the same time asked the students about the kinds of movies that use each type and the effects their use makes upon viewers.

After that, the instructor showed the students five excerpts of movies that differed from one another in terms of editing and lighting styles. When each movie was over, the instructor asked the students about the visual and auditory features as well as the lighting styles used in the movie. Her questions were also about the effects that the use of such elements has on viewers. Last, the instructor concluded the class meeting by asking the students to prepare for a quiz to be taken in the next class. After the class, the instructor and the observer met in order for the observer to point out the major aspects of the class performance. This phase was primarily a collaborative dialogue since the instructor has qualifying experience in terms of the theory and practice of teaching and learning as well as teaching observation. (The next section offers a discussion that focuses on the content of the post-observation dialogue).

Analysis of the observation

During the post-observation dialogue, the observer made mention of the positive aspects of the instructor's performance, which can be summarized as follows. The instructor gave students a good introduction by pointing out the main goal of the class session, which very well served to draw students' attention to what to focus on during the class. She also employed different teaching techniques such as the use of the blackboard to describe the three editing styles, the illustration of one editing style by drawing, and the demonstration of how the third editing style works. In addition, the instructor made good effort to engage her students by posing at least one question every time she had explained a component of the content. However, there was almost always one student who would answer these questions. The instructor discussed "montage" more than the other two editing styles because, as she said, this editing style makes up the major part of the final exam.

On the other hand, before the students viewed each one of the movie excerpts, the instructor talked about the content of the excerpt. This somehow drew the students' focus to the content of the excerpt rather than the features used in it. For example, just before she showed movie excerpt number 4, the instructor said that this excerpt "is the best scene of all time", which caused the students not to attend to the use of lighting and some other visual features used in the excerpt. Nevertheless, the students overall seemed less interested and so less involved in the class atmosphere and discussion than they were supposed to be. In response to this note, the instructor mentioned that it posed an overwhelming difficulty for her to get this group of students to participate and interact. That is why she tended to use questions as a solution.

Faculty support plan

Bearing on the major problem that the instructor is experiencing with her student; that is, the limited interest and interaction in the course, the following plan of support was proposed. It is worth noting that this plan comprises three steps to be taken in order as seen necessary to solve this problem.

First, the instructor was advised to seek consultation with other colleagues who have taught or are currently teaching the same course about practical solutions. The instructor's colleagues may be more experienced when it comes to dealing with the major cause of the problem, that is, the fact that the students consider the course irrelevant to their academic majors. It is highly possible that her colleagues may have developed techniques that have helped them cope with the problem under consideration.

Second, on the basis of the collaborative dialogue, it was recommended that the instructor try different ways in order to maximize student interaction and involvement. For example, she may use pair and/or group discussions and infuse into class work a sense of competition among the students. The instructor may also engage her students in reflective dialogue about what they have learned; and thus, one aspect of active learning is put into practice (Fink, 2003). One motivating aspect of reflective dialogue lies in students' getting to know how they exhibit degrees of variation in their perceptions and interpretations of the content elements being discussed (ibid., p. 162).

Third and last, the instructor was advised to try to involve her students in the decision-making process with respect to the kinds of in-class tasks and activities. This attempt is in line with the modern view of the teacher and learner roles in that the teacher acts as a facilitator of learning and the learner as an active and self-directing participant in the learning process (Brookfield, 1985).

This can better be achieved through the learners' use of their critical reflection about their learning experiences, which can help them both understand what they are learning (Fink, 2003) and extend it beyond the class boundaries. Another important aspect of involving students in the choice of learning activities lies in raising their feelings of confidence, importance, and purpose. This is necessary if the teacher strives to promote significant learning as it implies that caring, human dimension, and self-directed learning are well attended to (ibid., p. 146). Such a goal can be achieved by having students reflect on their learning experiences periodically in class conferences or written journals (ibid., 110).

Chapter 3

EL2 Learning Skills and Strategies

- ☐ BICS versus CALP
- ☐ Language Learning and Use Strategies
- ☐ Strategies for Reading Comprehension
- ☐ Strategies for Listening Comprehension
- ☐ Strategies on Language Tests

Mohammed S. Assiri

BICS versus CALP

Cummins (1979) differentiates between social and academic language learning. He uses the term *Basic Interpersonal Communication Skills* (BICS) to refer to language skills needed in social situations. It is the day-to-day language used to interact with other people. English language learners employ BICS when they are in a cafeteria, on a school bus, at parties, in sports, and on the phone. Social interactions are usually context-embedded. They may also include context-reduced activities (e.g., following directions, writing short notes ... etc.). They are not cognitively demanding. The language requirement is not specialized. Such language skills usually develop within 6 months to 2 years from arrival in the US, for instance.

Cummins (1979) also coins the term *Cognitive Academic Language Proficiency* (CALP) to mean the competency level of language used in academia. This comprises listening, speaking, reading, and writing abilities as they are used in the study of a given subject area. An adequate level of language proficiency is essential for students to succeed in school. Students need time and support to become proficient users of the language used in academic areas. This usually takes from five to seven years. Research by Thomas and Collier (1995) showed that it might take English language learners from seven to ten years to catch up with their native-speaking peers. The learning of academic language is not limited to the content-area vocabulary. It also includes skills such as comparing, classifying, synthesizing, evaluating, inferring ... etc. The tasks in academic language are context-reduced. The language gets low contextual support and the topics may be unfamiliar. Information can be read in a textbook or presented by the teacher. As the learner progresses, the context of academic tasks becomes more reduced. The language also becomes more cognitively demanding. New concepts and ideas are presented to learners.

Cummins (1984) advances his theory, suggesting that there is common underlying proficiency between two languages. The skills, concepts, and ideas that learners have acquired in their L1 can be transferred to L2. Consequently, BICS and CALP complement each other.

Implications

Students who are schooled in a second language must develop proficiency in both interpersonal communication and academic language in L2. The skills of interpersonal communication are easier than those of academic language because they can be acquired through interactions with the L2 speakers both in and out of school. Within two years of exposure to the L2, most learners can become proficient at interpersonal communication about everyday topics. On the other hand, academic L2 skills are learned through education in L2. Mastering academic language is much more difficult than mastering conversational language and takes much longer. In fact, research has indicated that it may take L2 learners from four to ten years to develop academic L2 proficiency equivalent to the level of L2 native-speaking peers. The length of time to develop such proficiency depends not only on the nature of the ESL instruction, but also the amount of prior schooling the learners had in their L1 (Thomas & Collier, 1997). Since the level of conceptual and academic L1 growth influences the development of academic L2, the more education a student has in L1, the easier it will be to develop academic L2.

The BICS and CALP distinction is intended to draw attention to the very different time periods that take immigrant children to acquire conversational fluency compared to grade-appropriate academic proficiency in L2 (Cummins, 2000). Conversational fluency is often acquired to a functional or peer level within roughly two years of exposure to the L2. In contrast, at least five years is required of immigrant children to catch up with their L2 native-speaking peers in terms of the academic aspects. Failure to take account of the distinction has resulted in discriminatory psychological assessment of bilingual students and premature exist from language support programs (e.g., bilingual education) into mainstream classes. In order to plan effective instruction for L2 learners, educators must know the characteristics that distinguish academic language from the language of interpersonal communication. Because interpersonal communication is more dominant than academic language, it develops more rapidly. Students may seem to be very proficient in an L2 even when they have limited proficiency in academic language. Teachers may mistakenly assume that because a student can successfully converse in an L2, she can handle academic work in that language with little or no further language assistance. This misconception may actually result in problems for the students during their course of academic study.

Language Learning and Use Strategies

The term *learner strategies* is used in the literature to refer to both language learning and language use strategies. Since the 1970s, the interest in the study of learner strategies has started hand in hand with the shift of focus from the outcomes of language learning to the mental operations involved in the learning process (Purpura, 1999). One of the most comprehensive definitions states that learning strategies are "specific actions taken by learners to make learning easier, faster, more enjoyable, more self-directed, more effective, and more transferable to new situations" (Oxford, 1990, p. 8).

Extensive research over the last four decades has made it clear that language learners use certain tactics that facilitate their language learning and language use. According to the majority of scholars, learner strategies represent problem-solving techniques (e.g., Smith,

1979), or conscious tactics used by language learners to compensate for the lack of or deficiency in automatic processes (Phakiti, 2006). There is an overall consensus among L2 strategy scholars that when learners resort to strategies, they deliberate their strategy choice and use and so choose those strategies that they have found through their learning and experience to be facilitative of the task they are performing (Hsiao, 2004). Therefore, strategies are conscious and planned choices that language learners make use of in order to aid their dealings through the target language (Cohen & Upton, 2006; Anderson, 1991).

Nonetheless, for some scholars, strategies are actions (i.e., behavioral); for other scholars, strategies are mental processes; and for yet others, strategies can be both behaviors and processes (Ellis, 1995). It seems that this disagreement about whether strategies are observable behaviors or mental processes has to do with whether these strategies are conscious or automatic. However, the view of strategies as behaviors and processes can be qualified on the ground that strategies in the early stages of their use tend to be conscious and deliberate, and as the learner becomes more experienced and proficient such strategies become subconscious and automatic processes or skills (Afflerbach, Pearson, & Paris, 2008; Phakiti, 2006). Language learning strategies and language use strategies are two categories of learner strategies with the purpose of the former being to assist the language acquisition process and the latter to aid the performance of language tasks.

One of the most influential classifications of learning strategies is the one by Oxford (1990), which includes such strategy categories as *cognitive* (used to control the language), *metacognitive* (used to plan, monitor, and evaluate learning), *memory* (used to remember and retrieve linguistic information), *compensation* (used to repair or make up for some deficit), *affective* (used to lessen inhibiting feelings), and *social* (used to collaborate with others in learning) (pp.

37-57, 135-151). From another perspective, Phakiti (2003) points out that learning strategies can be considered traits, since they are part of the long-term memory and are formed with practice, while use strategies are states, as they form part of working memory and so are more associated with the language task being performed.

In an attempt to explore experts' views of learner strategies, Cohen (2005) administered a questionnaire to 23 international scholars concerned with strategy research. A summary of the results suggests that the experts were overall in agreement that learners are conscious when they make their choices of what strategies to use; strategies are used by learners in order or in chorus depending on the nature of the language task they are engaged in; learners' use of strategies relates to such learning styles as being self-autonomous, self-regulated, and self-directed; strategy use is highly dependent upon the characteristics of learners, the nature of the tasks being performed, and the setting where the performance is taking place; and strategies are used by learners to make their learning and use of language more efficient.

Strategies for Reading Comprehension

Reading comprehension has been viewed by reading experts as an interactive and constructive process in which the reader interacts with the text and simultaneously uses a variety of means available to him (e.g., background knowledge and contextual cues) to construct meaning of the text (Dole, Duffy, Roehler, & Pearson, 1991; Alexander & Jetton, 2000; Powers & Wilson Leung, 1995). As was the case in language learning, there has been a shift of focus in the context of reading comprehension from the outcomes to the processes involved in reading (Anderson, 1991). The study of the strategies used in reading comprehension has offered insights about how readers interact with the text with the aim of understanding it and what resources they draw upon towards this goal (Singhal, 2001).

A distinction has been made between reading skills and reading strategies such that reading skills are used synonymously with abilities to mean traits that readers have developed with practice over time, ranging from lower-level abilities (e.g., word-level processing) to higher-level abilities (e.g., text-level processing), while reading strategies represent conscious processes readers utilize to enhance their understanding of a given reading task (e.g., skipping unknown vocabulary) (Aebersold & Field, 1997; Alderson, 2000; Birch, 2002). Readers tend to exhibit considerable variation in how frequently they use reading strategies depending on what they aim through their reading activities; for example, reading for study demands more frequent use of global strategies (e.g., deciding what to read closely) and support strategies (e.g., taking notes while reading) than reading for fun (Mokhtari & Reichard, 2008, p. 95).

Previous research (e.g., Garner & Krauss, 1982; Myers & Paris, 1978; Purpura, 1999) has been revealing about the nature of textual processing that highly proficient readers go through in comparison to low-proficient ones. For example, highly-proficient readers were shown to process textual information at a global level by focusing on the meaning of the text as a whole, using higher-level skills (e.g., understanding main idea, making inferences, synthesizing information) whereas low-proficient readers work with the text at a local level and engage in a decoding process, using lower-level skills (e.g., identifying lexical and syntactic features, making use of various discourse elements). In general, the previous studies of reading strategies with L2 readers at various levels of proficiency in a wide variety of learning contexts point out the crucial role of reading strategies in developing necessary reading skills including comprehension (Alfassi, 2004; Brown & Day, 1983; Mokhtari & Sheorey, 2008; Pressley & Afflerbach, 1995).

The role of metacognition in reading comprehension has been accounted for in terms of metacognitive awareness that involves readers' cognizance of their abilities in relation to the complexity of the reading task, factors pertinent to the difficulty of the reading task (e.g., text familiarity), their repertoire of reading strategies, how the selected strategies are to be used, and the extent to which comprehension is going on (Baker, 2008; Baumann, Jones, & Seifert-Kessell, 1993; Pressley & Gaskins, 2006). This view is consistent with the one that considers "[the] knowledge of text structure ... [and the] awareness of the normal sequencing of information in such structures" as two key strategies of reading comprehension (Storey, 1997, p. 221). Metacognitive awareness and control of reading strategies are crucial to achieve an optimum level of reading comprehension (Mokhtari, Sheorey, & Reichard, 2008).

The relationship between metacognition and comprehension can be described as "reciprocal causation" such that "improvements in metacognition contribute to improvements in comprehension, which, in turn, contribute to further improvements in metacognition" (Baker, 2008, p. 34). In this sense, reading comprehension becomes more "constructively responsive" in which process readers adapt their choice and use of strategies to the demands of the textual information they are dealing with (Pressley & Afflerbach, 1995, p. 2). These perspectives have their origin in L1 reading research; for example, in a number of studies (e.g., Baker & Brown, 1984; Cain, Oakhill, & Bryant, 2004; Roeschl-Heils, Schneider, & van Kraayenoord, 2003), it was found that the extent to which readers made use of their metacognitive awareness of their reading abilities and cognitive strategies determined the effectiveness of their reading performance.

In a study of L1 and L2 readers, Sheorey and Mokhtari (2001) found that the level of metacognitive awareness of reading strategies was strongly positively correlated with the level of reading ability and that high-ability readers surpassed their low-ability counterparts in terms of both frequency and efficacy of reading strategy use.

Metacognitive awareness of reading strategy choice and use was also found to be a sign of developing the necessary level of comprehension and so was a characteristic of skilled L2 readers (e.g., Barnett, 1988; Sheorey & Mokhtari, 2001). Moreover, research on the differences between good and poor readers in the use of reading strategies has shown that good readers tend to be more aware of what strategies to use and when to use them (e.g., Yang, 2002).

On the basis of the information-processing theory, other scholars (e.g., Phakiti, 2008; Purpura, 1999) uphold the view that strategies can be categorized as cognitive strategies (used to understand and utilize the language) such as *comprehending, memory,* and *retrieval*; and, metacognitive strategies (used to act upon and control cognitive strategies) such as *planning, monitoring,* and *evaluating*. The use of these strategies during a reading activity can best be described as "a synchronic situation-related variation between cognitive strategies and metacognitive strategies (Phakiti, 2006, p. 83). Research by Purpura (1998) has confirmed that metacognitive strategies strongly influence and so regulate cognitive strategies during reading. In his study, Phakiti (2006) employed a structural equation modeling approach to analyze the relationships among cognitive strategies, metacognitive strategies, and reading test performance. He found that memory and retrieval strategies aided comprehending strategies, monitoring strategies regulated memory strategies, evaluating strategies acted upon retrieval strategies, and planning strategies influenced cognitive strategies by means of monitoring and evaluating strategies. Also, using structural equation modeling to analyze data based on a reading test with multiple-format tasks, Assiri (2014) found that cognitive strategy use mediated the effect of metacognitive strategy use on test performance.

While the role of cognition and metacognition in shaping human learning experiences has been realized through research in psychology since the mid-1970s, only a decade ago did researchers in the field of language testing and assessment show and express an increasing interest in the study of how cognitive and metacognitive strategies relate and influence test performance. One of the first researchers to study the relationship between cognitive and metacognitive strategy use on reading comprehension tests was Purpura (1997, 1998) who observed, through the use of a structural equation modeling approach, similar factorial structures for the high- and low-proficiency groups of test takers, resulting from the two models of cognitive and metacognitive strategy use and the test performance. Nonetheless, the high-proficiency group exhibited more use of such strategies as *inferencing, linking with prior knowledge, practicing naturalistically, self-evaluating* and *monitoring* while the low-proficiency group used more strategies such as *associating, repeating/rehearsing, summarizing, transferring from L1 to L2, applying rules,* and *assessing the situation* (Purpura, 1998, pp. 352-364). Following the same analytical procedure, Purpura (1999) found that the use of cognitive and metacognitive strategies in general correlated with test performance while memory strategies decelerated it.

Similarly, Phakiti (2003) looked into the differences between successful and less successful test takers in the use of cognitive and metacognitive strategies when responding to a reading test. Phakiti found that the highly successful test takers demonstrated a high degree of awareness of their use of metacognitive strategies in terms of what strategies to use, why they chose these strategies, and how to use them well, which in turn contributed to their performance on the test. He also observed that females and males were almost alike with respect to their cognitive strategy use; however, when interviewed, males expressed more inclination to use metacognitive strategies than females. Moreover, research by Phakiti (2006) and Purpura (1999) indicated that successful test takers used more retrieval than memory strategies, which augmented their use of comprehension strategies. Nevertheless, there is compelling evidence suggesting that highly proficient readers tended to report fewer instances of strategy use, which can be linked to their advanced ability of automatic processing that renders strategy use not available for conscious reporting (Purpura, 1998).

With the advent of electronic mediums of textual information, research started to look at the kinds of strategies readers use when interacting with these mediums, and how these strategies compare with those readers use with print materials (Kymes, 2008). Foltz (1996) points out that unlike print texts where presentation of information often follows a predictable order, information in online mediums is mostly presented in a non-sequential fashion. According to Foltz (1996), this aspect of online information necessitates adequate level of background or topical knowledge to cope with the insufficient orderliness of online presentation. This is what also makes integration of information, both by relating what is new to what is known and by linking information across multiple sources, an essential skill in online reading (Britt & Gabrys, 2001).

Skilled readers have been shown to benefit from using strategies they have developed and mastered with print materials in their reading of online information. In addition, they have shown notable tendencies to develop useful reading strategies specific to online environments (e.g., evaluating how credible and trustworthy the information is) (Bland, 1995). In a comparative study of reading strategies used online and in print, Poole and Mokhtari (2008) found that readers tended to use a set of the same strategies in both environments with some variation in terms of frequency, apply certain strategies more often than others in both formats when they found reading to be challenging, and to use online dictionaries with online reading more often than they use print dictionaries when reading print materials.

It is important here to distinguish between test-taking strategies and reading strategies, as these two categories of strategies show some overlap and so can easily be confused in the context of reading assessment. First, test-taking strategies are not specific to any language skill, although it is true that each language skill has its specific test-taking strategies. However, this does not preclude the fact that some language skills can still share certain test-taking strategies (e.g., a test taker preference to read the questions first on both reading and listening comprehension tests administered in a multiple-choice format). Second, while reading strategies are generally used when readers engage in a reading activity and thus "are related to text comprehension" (Singhal, 2001, p. 1), test-taking strategies are only used when dealing with a test or task which is similar to a test-taking process; that is, the latter are more "driven by the test questions" (Farr, Pritchard, & Smitten, 1990, p. 218).

It is also worth the emphasis here that since there are different types of reading, including reading for test taking, readers tend to utilize different strategies bearing on the goals they try to achieve through the reading activity in which they are engaged (Cordón & Day, 1996). And, because test respondents approach a given reading-test task with the aim of getting it right, they would certainly turn to strategies that involve reading. However, this does not imply that all strategies used on reading tests necessarily relate to the reading process (Allan, 1992), since a considerable number of these strategies are either test-management or test-wiseness strategies or a combination of both. For example, in contrast to non-testing situations, a multiple-choice reading task calls for "a continual, conscious, and linear engagement in problem-solving activities" (Rupp et al., 2006). In practice, Cohen and Upton (2006) observed that their sample of 32 respondents made far more frequent use of test-taking strategies in comparison to reading strategies.

Strategies for Listening Comprehension

In his definition, Vandergrift (1999) stresses that listening comprehension involves active processing of a variety of linguistic elements simultaneously.

Listening comprehension is a complex, active process in which the listener must discriminate between sounds, understand vocabulary and grammatical structures, interpret stress and intonation, retain what was gathered in all of the above, and interpret it within the immediate as well as the larger sociocultural context of the utterance. (p. 168)

Being a dynamic process, listening comprehension necessitates that a learner take an active role. As seen in Vandergrift's definition listening comprehension comprises a number of skills each of which requires strategic training and practice over a period of time. It is in this sense that language learning strategies as aids for active learning have been called for to become part of listening comprehension classes. This section sheds light on strategies to improve listening comprehension.

Listeners typically adapt to the type of linguistic input they are receiving by being aware and effective users of their listening comprehension strategies (Vandergrift, 1999). In a number of studies, metacognitive strategies have been found a distinguishing factor between effective and less effective listeners (Goh, 1998; Vandergrift, 1997a). In other studies, the use of cognitive strategies has set effective listeners apart from their less effective peers (Vandergrift, 2003a). Thompson and Rubin (1996) and Vandergrift (2007a) found from a pretest/posttest experiments that metacognitive strategy instruction helped the learners in the treatment group outperform those learners in the control group. Strategy instruction also improves motivation and affect (Rubin, 1988). A major common finding among these studies and others (e.g., Carrier, 2003; Ross & Rost, 1991) pointed out the effectiveness of strategy instruction and training; specifically, in metacognitive strategies (e.g., Chamot, 2005; Vandergrift, 2004) in improving listening comprehension skills.

There seems to be an overall consensus among researchers that explicit instruction of listening comprehension strategies, especially metacognitive knowledge, enables learners to maintain these strategies and transfer them to other listening contexts (Carrier, 2003). Metacognitive knowledge here entails knowing what strategy to use, when and where to use it, and what the advantages of using such a strategy are (McCormick & Pressley, 1997). In order for teachers to help their students develop metacognitive knowledge, Mendelsohn (1995) recommends the following approach to teaching strategy-based listening:

- Raise learner awareness of the power and value of using strategies.
- Use pre-listening activities to activate learners' background knowledge.
- Make clear to learners what they are going to listen to and why.
- Provide guided listening activities that provide a lot of practice in using a particular strategy (e.g., listening for names or dates).
- Practice the strategy using authentic materials with focus on content and meaning.
- Use post-listening activities to have learners put into use what they have comprehended (e.g., take notes on a lecture to prepare a summary, fill out a form, or write a report).
- Allow for self-evaluation so that learners can assess how accurate and complete their listening has been. (Vandergrift, 2002, p. 558)

An integrated model for teaching listening has been developed by Vandergrift (2004). This model provides listening teachers with a tool they can use to help their students develop their top-down and bottom-up listening processes along with their metacognitive awareness. It comprises the following stages:

1. *Planning or predicting stage:* Students predict what information they will hear using the topic of the listening material and its text type.
2. *First verification stage:* Students listen and confirm their predictions. They also monitor their understanding. Then, they compare their notes with their peers.
3. *Second verification stage:* Students listen selectively to resolve any issues with understanding or agreement with their peers about the listening content. They also work in groups to figure out the main points and the important details of the text.
4. *Final verification stage:* Students listen again while paying special attention to the information they missed before or did not understand using a transcription of the text.
5. *Reflection stage:* Students exchange feedback about how they dealt with the listening activity with the aim of improving their listening performance and doing even better next time.

The usefulness of this model has been empirically supported by two recent studies (Mareschal, 2007; Vandergrift 2007a). Both studies reported enhanced self-regulatory ability, metacognitive knowledge, strategy use, in addition to notable listening success especially for low-proficiency learners (Vandergrift, 2007b).

Teachers of beginning and intermediate level learners should put emphasis on bottom-up and top-down listening processes, along with selective strategy instruction. With advanced learners, teachers ought to offer training in the use of cognitive and metacognitive strategies, for example, elaboration, summarization, and discourse organization (Rost, 2001). Learners become well-acquainted with strategies, if teachers name these strategies, explain why and when they are used, and provide students with a list of these strategies along with brief explanations of how these strategies are used (Chamot, 1999). For the types of listening activities to use, it is recommended that teachers make use of listening tasks that engage students in predicting, inferencing, self-monitoring, evaluating, and problem-solving so as to help them develop their metacognitive knowledge (Coto, 2002; Vandergrift, 2007a). Teachers can also help their students develop their metacognitive awareness by using checklists (see below) (Harris, 2001).

Listening metacognitive awareness checklist

Before listening:

☐ I have checked that I understood the task I have to do.

☐ I have looked carefully at the title and any pictures to see if I can guess what it will be about.

☐ I have tried to remember as many words as I can to do with this topic.

☐ I have thought about what is likely to be said in this situation.

While listening:

☐ I identified if it was a conversation, an advert, a news bulletin etc.

☐ I paid attention to the tone of voice and any background noises for clues.

☐ I used other clues like key words to identify the rough gist.

☐ I used my knowledge of the world to make sensible guesses.

☐ I tried to see if any words were like words in my mother tongue.

☐ I did not panic or stop when there was something I did not understand.

☐ I listened out for the names of people or places.

☐ I tried to hold the difficult sounds in my head and say them over.

☐ I tried to break the stream of sounds down into individual words and write them down to see if they were like words I know.

☐ I did not give up and just make wild guesses.

☐ I listened out for grammar clues like tenses, pronouns.

After listening:

☐ I checked back to see if my first guesses were right and made sense or I needed to think again.

Date: _____ / _____ / 20_____. *In order to improve my performance, next time, I will …*

[Adapted from *French as a Second Language: Formative Assessment Package.* Canadian Association of Second Language Teachers, 176, Gloucester Street, Ottawa, Ontario.]

Depending on the goals of the language program, teachers may want to train their students to use listening comprehension strategies as an aid when engaged in a conversation with an interlocutor. This form of listening is referred to as two-way listening and is known for its specific strategies that teachers can train their students to utilize (Ross). Aiming at these strategies, teachers can follow these steps:

1) Provide students with expressions to clarify meaning and confirm comprehension,

2) Use interactive videos with which listeners can demonstrate the use of different reception strategies, and

3) Model and practice the use of the different expressions and strategies in class. (Vandergrift, 1997b, p. 502)

Most important, teachers should remember that frequent strategy training and practice is vital if these strategies are to be maintained and transferred to other contexts (O'Malley, Chamot, Stewner-Manzanares, Russo, and Kupper, 1985). Here are some listening exercises teachers may find useful in strategy-based listening:

- *Selective listening exercises*: Learners listen to a passage and specifically to the keywords that point to the main idea.
- *T-list*: Learners list the main ideas on the left side of the page and take notes of the supporting details using the right side.
- *Authentic recordings with comprehension questions*: Learners listen and answer a set of comprehension questions one at a time.
- *Inferencing what the next section will be about*: Learners first listen to a section of the listening material and make predictions about the following one.
- *Global listening activities*: Learners listen to a whole segment of the listening material to get the main idea or gist of the given segment.
- *Information-gap activities*: Learners listen to utterances, dialogues, and questions; then, they answer a question requiring a specific piece of information.
- *Real life events*: Learners listen to real world news, commercials, TV shows, radio broadcasts, and then answer a variety of questions (e.g., comprehension, inferencing, prediction ... etc.).
- *Games*: Learners are engaged in games such as association (i.e., learners associate what they are listening to another idea or aspect) and chunking (i.e., learners classify pieces of information into larger chunks). (Coto, 2002, pp.101-103)

As obvious from this discussion, an integrated model of strategy-based listening can be carried out at different stages (i.e., pre-listening, during listening, and post-listening), along with training in the use of metacognitive and cognitive strategies. With this in mind, a typical listening activity may have the following procedures:

1) *Before listening*: The teacher and students plan the activity. The teacher tells students what this activity is about, what they will listen to, what strategies to use and how to use them, and try to elicit students' predictions and relevant ideas.

2) *During listening*: Students listen to the audio material, employ the relevant strategies, and monitor their listening using their predictions and interpretations.

3) *After listening*: The teacher allows students to evaluate their listening and strategy use by eliciting the correct responses from them and how they arrived at these responses, or have them work in pairs or groups and evaluate one another's work.

4) The same activity is carried out a second time following the procedures (1-3).

5) In another similar activity, the same strategies are practiced so that these strategies can be maintained and transferred as McCormick and Pressley (1997) suggested.

The above integrated model is practicable with intermediate and advanced learners whose language abilities allow them for adequate comprehension and strategy use. At the beginning levels, teachers are more likely to experience difficulty having their students become competent users of metacognitive and cognitive strategies. What follows is an outline of metacognitive and cognitive strategies in listening comprehension.

Metacognitive strategies

1. *Planning*: Developing awareness of what needs to be done to accomplish a listening objective, and developing an

appropriate plan of action to overcome difficulties that may interfere with successful completion of a listening task.

1a. *Advance organization*: Clarifying the objectives of an anticipated listening task and/or proposing strategies to handle it.

1b. *Directed attention*: Deciding to attend to the listening task and ignore irrelevant distracters.

1c. *Selective attention*: Deciding to attend to specific aspects of language input or situational details that assist in task completion.

1d. *Self-management*: Understanding the conditions that help one accomplish the listening objectives and ensuring the presence of these conditions.

2. *Monitoring*: Checking, verifying, or correcting one's comprehension or performance in the course of a listening task.

2a. *Comprehension monitoring*: Checking, verifying, or correcting one's understanding at the local level.

2b. *Double-check monitoring*: Checking, verifying, or correcting one's understanding throughout the task.

3. *Evaluation*: Checking the outcomes of one's listening against the measure of comprehensive and accurate understanding.

4. *Problem identification*: Explicitly identifying a central issue in the listening task in need for resolution.

Cognitive strategies

1. *Inferencing*: Using the information in the listening text to guess the meanings of any unfamiliar words or to fill in an information gap.

1a. *Linguistic inferencing*: Using known words to guess the meanings of any unknown words.

1b. *Voice inferencing*: Using tone of voice and/or paralinguistic features to guess the meanings of any unknown words or expressions.

1c. *Extra-linguistic inferencing*: Using background sounds and relationships between speakers in an oral text, material in the response sheet, or concrete situational referents to guess the meanings of any unknown words or expressions.

1d. *Between-parts inferencing*: Using information beyond the local sentential level to guess the meanings of any unknown words or expressions.

2. *Elaboration*: Using prior knowledge or conversational context, and relating it to knowledge gained from the oral text in order to fill in an information gap.

2a. *Personal elaboration*: Referring to one's prior experience.

2b. *World elaboration*: Using knowledge gained from life experience.

2c. *Academic elaboration*: Using knowledge gained in academic situations.

2d. *Questioning elaboration*: Using a combination of relevant questions and knowledge of the world to brainstorm logical possibilities.

2e. *Creative elaboration*: Making up a storyline or adopting a smart perspective.

3. *Imagery*: Using mental or tangible visuals to represent information.

4. *Summarization*: Making a mental or written summary of the information presented in the listening task.

5. *Translation*: Translating ideas from one language to another in a relatively verbatim manner.

6. *Transfer*: Using knowledge of one language (e.g., cognates) to facilitate listening in another language.

7. *Repetition*: Repeating a chunk of language (a word or phrase) in the course of the listening task. (Adapted from Vandergrift, 1997)

Teachers can use the *Metacognitive Awareness Listening Questionnaire*, developed by Vandergrift, Goh, Mareschal and Tafaghodatari (2006), to assess their students' metacognitive awareness and use of strategies. The following statements are adapted from the original questionnaire. Each statement represents a strategy and is followed by a scale from 1 to 6.

1) Listening in English is harder than any other language skill.
2) I find listening comprehension in English a challenge for me.
3) Listening in English does not make me nervous
4) Before I listen, I think of similar texts that I may have listened to.
5) I plan how I am going to listen before I start the listening task.
6) I have a goal in mind as I listen.
7) As I listen, I translate word by word.
8) As I listen, I translate key words.
9) I use the general idea of the listening content to guess the meanings of unfamiliar words.
10) I use any familiar vocabulary to figure out the meanings of the unfamiliar words.
11) I think about what I have understood to check my guesses of word meanings.
12) As I listen, I relate my knowledge about the topic to what I understand.
13) I use my experience to help me understand.
14) When I cannot understand, I give up and stop listening.

15) I try to maximize my concentration when I feel I cannot understand.

16) I retain my attention to the listening content once I feel distracted.

17) I ask myself every now and them if I am satisfied with my level of comprehension.

18) I adjust my interpretation once I feel I am not developing correct understanding.

19) At the end of the listening task, I try to remember how effective my listening has been.

20) I think about what I should do differently next time in order to improve my listening.

Strategies on Language Tests

The last two decades have witnessed a proliferation of research on both language learning and language use strategies. For the most part, this research has looked into the kinds of strategies that language learners use to facilitate their learning and use of the target language. Not until very recently have scholars and researchers (e.g., Cohen, 2006; Cohen & Upton, 2006; Tian, 2000; Yoshizawa, 2002) become increasingly interested in the kinds of strategies the test takers employ when responding to a form of language assessment. This, in turn, has led to ongoing research to explore the nature of these strategies and how they relate to a multitude of factors involved in the two processes of language test-making and -taking.

The kinds of language use strategies employed by learners on the various forms of language assessment are referred to in the literature as test-taking strategies (Cohen, 1998). To be specific, test-taking strategies are techniques that test takers resort to with the aim of getting correct answers on a given test. The successful use of these strategies does not necessarily imply mastery of the testing task at hand. Test respondents very often resort to test-taking strategies to compensate for the lack of information that could aid their response to a given question; for example, they may try to match words in the question to ones in the text, simplify the language of the question or the information needed, or use approximation especially when guessing meanings of vocabulary items (Cohen, 1998).

Similar to language use strategies, test-taking strategies are compensatory in nature; however, whereas the former are used for communicative goals, the latter serve test-taking purposes. The test-taking process of reading comprehension may call upon the use of both test-taking strategies as well as reading strategies; the former are used with the question items whereas the latter are used with the text. In this respect, the use of test-taking strategies far exceeds that of reading strategies since, presumably, test takers' care for answering the question items surpasses their care to fully understand the text. It comes as no surprise that most of the comprehension that test takers attain when responding to a reading test is brought about by their responses to the test questions and not overall understanding of the text. Test-taking strategies are used in order to get correct answers on language tests. Some scholars count test-taking strategies among learner strategies; for example, Cohen (1994a) mentions that test-taking strategies are best viewed as "learner strategies applied to the area of assessment" (p. 119). Nevertheless, test-taking strategies are clearly not limited to language learning since the test taking process itself is not limited to the field of language learning, which means that test takers in other assessment settings in other disciplines can certainly use strategies that can aid their performance on a given test in their fields of study.

Scholars (e.g., Allan, 1992; Cohen, 2006; Phakiti, 2008) have referred to two categories of test-taking strategies: *test-management strategies* and *test-wiseness strategies.* The former call for logical and purposeful response behaviors, are reflective of the underlying competence, and are responsive to the underlying construct being assessed. The latter involve the use of textual and/or technical aspects of the test to get the right answers and are not reflective of the underlying competence nor responsive to the underlying construct being assessed. Other scholars (e.g., Cohen & Upton, 2006) have drawn the distinction between strategies and processes such that "*strategies* are subject to control, more intentional, and used to act upon the processes" whereas "*processes* are general, subconscious or unconscious, and more automatic" (p. 2). Similarly, Phakiti (2008) differentiates between strategic processing and automatic processing, suggesting that the more a language user is conscious and aware of the processing underway the more this processing is strategic rather than automatic. By extension, while there are test-taking strategies that are conscious choices (e.g., when a test taker chooses to read the questions first on a multiple-choice reading test before reading the text), there are test-taking processes that are subconscious operations (e.g., when a high-proficiency test taker attends to the overall meaning using text-level information on a cloze task).

Generally, test-taking strategies are viewed as compensatory since they are typically used by test takers to make up for some deficiency in the language ability necessary to perform the test tasks, in the skill to take the test, or in both. As such, test-taking strategies can be accounted for in terms of the framework of strategic competence as proposed by Bachman and Palmer (1996). According to this framework, test respondents go through four metacognitive processes when reacting to a testing task: *assessment, goal setting, planning,* and *execution.* That is, test takers first assess the goals of the testing task and determine what aspects of knowledge it draws on. Then, they discern what to do in response to the task. After that, they relate the required information in the task to their knowledge and decide about how to act. And finally, they put what they have decided to do and how to do it into action through the actual provision of the answer. The extent to which learners engage in these processes and manage the use of test-taking strategies on a test can distinguish between performances of two test takers, who might be at the same level of language competency (Bachman & Palmer, 1996).

Chapter 4

EL2 Testing and Assessment

- ☐ Key Terms
- ☐ Testing Speaking Skills Using Authentic Materials
- ☐ Assessing the Four Skills at Upper Proficiency Levels
  - ◆ *Listening*
  - ◆ *Speaking*
  - ◆ *Reading*
  - ◆ *Writing*
- ☐ Language Proficiency and Strategy Use on Reading Tasks
- ☐ Test-taking Strategy Use on Reading Comprehension Tests
  - ◆ *Strategy Use and Test Format*
  - ◆ *Strategy Use and Proficiency Level*
  - ◆ *Strategy Use and Test Performance*
  - ◆ *Strategy Use and Test Validation*
- ☐ Training of Test-taking Strategy Use on Reading Tasks
- ☐ Formats of Oral Assessment
- ☐ Student-student Interactions as a Form of Oral Assessment

This chapter centers on a review of theory and research pertinent to the fields of second language testing and assessment. A large part of the chapter is devoted to the area of reading comprehension. This is because the testing and assessment of reading comprehension represents one major area of the author's expertise.

Key Terms

The purpose of this section is to acquaint SL practitioner with widely used terminology in the fields of language testing and assessment:

achievement test. A test showing how well students have learnt the section of a course that has just been taught. Such a test may be called a 'progress test' or an 'attainment test'. A summative test is a form of achievement test.

analytic rating scale. It contains a set of criteria for marking a test. For example, for a writing test it might include criteria relating to discourse, grammar, vocabulary, and task achievement. The raters have to assign marks for each of these criteria.

aptitude test. A test showing how well a student is likely to learn a particular skill. A language aptitude test may contain, for example, subtests of memory, inductive ability, and grammatical understanding.

assessment. An overarching term that covers both 'assessment' and 'testing'. Some people do not like the term 'testing', and refer to most classroom testing as 'assessment'. This is an unnecessary use of the term, but for some people the term 'alternative assessment', which tend to consist of authentic, but often unreliable, tasks, is preferred to the term 'testing'.

test authenticity. Test-task characteristics correspond to those of the target language. Authentic test tasks are of the sort that testees might be expected to perform in real life.

task characteristics. Bachman's (1990) framework of test task characteristics (see Bachman & Palmer, 1996) embodies the characteristics shared by language use tasks and language test tasks: setting (physical circumstances), rubric (structure characteristics), input (the form of material), expected response (language expected), and relationship between input and response (reactivity [interaction involved], scope [range of input], directness [information use]). This provides a mechanism for demonstrating the correspondence to the target langue use tasks, which implies the authenticity of test tasks and the construct validity of score interpretations.

cloze test. A gap-filling task where words are deleted at fixed stages in a text and the candidate has to replace them. For example, a cloze test may have every sixth word deleted. Cloze tests are easy to prepare, but because of the random effect of the deletion of every *nth* word, different cloze tests behave very differently from one another. They should, therefore, undergo item analysis before they are given to test candidates.

composition/essay. A task where candidates have to produce at least a paragraph of their own written language. Such tasks are marked subjectively (see *analytic* and *holistic* rating scales).

computer-adaptive test. A test marked by computer where the computer program selects items for a particular candidate, based on previous item results, so that the items are intended to be of a suitable level of difficulty.

construct validity. This aspect of test validity refers to the degree to which a test or other measure assesses the underlying theoretical construct it is supposed to measure (i.e., the test measures what it is purported to measure).

content validity. An aspect of test validity where specialists decide whether a test, or test items, assesses what the test constructors intend to be assessed.

criterion-referenced test. This term is the opposite of *norm-referenced* test. In a criterion-referenced test, the candidate's performance is compared to predetermined criteria, and not to the performance of other students. For example, a candidate's speaking performance may be compared to a set of speaking criteria. It is common, for objective test papers to be norm-referenced and subjective tests to be criterion-referenced.

c-test. A test where the first half of every second word is removed from a text and the candidate has to restore the missing letters. The candidate may have to read the previous and the succeeding text, in order to be able to replace the missing half-words. This test has many of the same advantages and disadvantages as the cloze test, but is intended to depend less on the candidate's creative imagination.

diagnostic test. A test that diagnoses a student's linguistic strengths and weaknesses. For example, a diagnostic test might reveal that a student has trouble using English articles.

dictation. A test of listening in which the candidate writes down what she hears. This test may assess more than just recognition of spoken words. It may be marked according to the exact words (including the exact punctuation and spelling), the accuracy of certain phrases, or simply according to meaning.

direct test. A test of a student's language skills in a real-life fashion. *Direct test* is the opposite of *indirect test.*

discrimination index. This tells the test constructor how well a particular item discriminates between the strong and the weak students.

discriminability. The extent to which a test distinguishes between strong and weak students.

effective versus ineffective strategy use. Variation in strategy use, including efficacy of strategy use, can explain variability of test performance as evidenced in test scores (Phakiti, 2003). Strategy use can be said to mediate between test-taker characteristics and test performance, and so can optimize the extent to which test performance hinges on test taker characteristics (Yien, 2001). In their study of test-taking strategy use on the TOEFL-iBT reading tasks, Cohen and Upton (2006) point out the possibility of judging aspects of effective versus ineffective strategy use among test takers by examining differences between strategies that contributed to the selection of the right answers and those which did not. Researchers (e.g., Nikolov, 2006) conclude that effective strategy use is determined by strategy compatibility with task or item format and suitability of strategy sequencing and application. Experts in learner strategies (e.g., Neil Anderson, Anna Chamot, Martha Nyikos, Rebecca Oxford, Joan Rubin, Larry Vandergrift) are almost all in agreement that the manner in which strategies are clustered or combined better differentiates between effective and ineffective strategy use than does the focus on independent strategies (Cohen, 2005).

face validity. The views of the 'layman' on the validity of a test.

facility value. This is often calculated at the same time as the discrimination index. It tells the test constructor or researcher how easy an item is for a particular group of students.

formative test. A test used during a course to assess a student's progress. Such a test is generally aimed at producing feedback for the teacher and the student.

gap-filling test. This task is similar to a cloze test, but the test constructor chooses where the gaps in the text should be. The tester can decide what sort of language he is testing and can write or choose the text accordingly. The text gaps can be open-ended, have multiple-choice solutions, or can be accompanied by a bank of possible answers from which the candidate can choose appropriate words or phrases.

holistic rating scale. This term is used in contrast to *analytic rating scale.* The rater gives a single score, rather than an initial variety of scores, for her impression of the language level of the essay or extract of speech, using criteria supplied by the test constructors. The rater may only need to read the script once.

indirect test. A test that tests a skill in an indirect way. An example of such a test would be one where speaking is assessed by a multiple-choice test of the recognition of some of the sounds of the foreign language.

information transfer item. A test task where a candidate has to transfer some information (these tasks are commonly used for testing reading and listening) from one form to another. For example, information in a text may have to be transferred to a table or chart.

inter-rater reliability. The agreement between one rater and another on a candidate's performance.

intra-rater reliability. The consistency with which a single rater assesses one or more samples of spoken or written text. To assess this, the rater would need to rate some scripts more than once.

item analysis. Analysis of the performance of test items, carried out on objectively marked items. For item analysis to be worthwhile, you need about 30 people if chance is not going to play too large a part. For a high stakes test you will need to have at least 100 students in your sample, but 30 students at the same level as those who are going to take the 'live' test will give some idea of how it will perform. This will show up poor items and alert you to problems you might not have thought of, if nothing else.

matching task. A version of a multiple-choice task, where the candidate has to match the items in two lists. There are usually more items in one of the two lists than in the other, so that students cannot get the final answer simply by deduction.

multiple-choice item. A test item where there is a question or statement followed by a range of possible answers. The candidate has to mark the appropriate one or more answers; an answer key is provided for markers. Such items test recognition rather than production, and although they are very easy to mark, they are difficult to construct.

norm-referenced test. This is the opposite of a *criterion-referenced test.* A norm-referenced test is a test in which a candidate's score is compared to the scores of the other students in the group. For such tests it is important, where possible, to carry out an item analysis in which the *facility value* and the *discrimination index* of each item are calculated.

objective test. A test in which the answers have already been decided, so that the candidate's answers can be compared to an answer key. Examples of objective test items are *multiple-choice* and *short answer* questions. Such tests are often easily marked by a computer.

performance test. A form of assessment, for example, an essay or an oral interview, which usually tests a candidate's productive rather than receptive skills.

placement test. A test which assigns to the candidate a level so that he or she can be placed in a particular class or at a certain level.

practicality. Efficiency in terms of effort, time, and money (Hughes, 2003).

predictive validity. The accuracy of a test in deciding the future performance of a candidate. For example, does the test truthfully predict a person's ability to survive in basic Spanish?

proficiency test. A test of the current language level of the candidate. It is distinguished from an *achievement test* by the fact that its candidates may come from a range of different language backgrounds and may have acquired their foreign languages in many different ways.

proficiency. Proficiency refers to language ability that assimilates to or at least considerably approximates that of a native speaker. A language learner is said to be proficient if he has a native-like command and control of the target language. Therefore, there are varying levels of proficiency, and a language learner may exhibit different levels of proficiency across language skills.

rater. A marker of a test; usually a marker of a *subjective test* such as a test of writing or speaking.

reliability. The test provides consistent, replicable information about testees' performance by providing all necessary conditions. And, its characteristics correspond to those of the target language use tasks. Such test tasks offer reliable measures upon which valid inferences ban be based.

short answer question. An objectively scored test item where the student has to produce a short answer, which is compared to an answer key. The fewer words that are allowed in the answer, the easier it is to write an all-inclusive answer key. Another term for this is *open-ended question.*

standard score. A score that has been standardized so that a candidate's reported score means the same thing time after time. For example, British A levels are standardized so that an A grade in one year should be roughly equivalent to an A grade in another year.

subjective test. The opposite of an *objective test.* This test type must be scored subjectively. Most writing and speaking tests are subjective measures, and so are many dictations and translations. Subjective tests are often scored by raters using 'analytic' or 'holistic' rating scales.

summative test. A test given at the end of a course. The term is in contrast to *formative test.*

test format. According to the *Dictionary of language testing* (Davies et al., 2002), test format "refers to the overall design of the test" (p. 200). As such, test format covers such aspects as length of the test, types and numbers of tasks and items, and expected forms of response. Test format represents essential information that test takers should know before they sit for the test. Research has indicated that the nature of the test tasks considerably determines test performance as evidenced in test scores (e.g., Kobayashi, 2002). It has also been confirmed that different test formats tap into distinct reading skills (e.g., Tsagari, 1994).

test performance. Performance on language tests typically correlates with the level of language ability. It is considerably determined by how test taker characteristics (e.g., background knowledge, cognitive style, anxiety ... etc.) and facets of test format act together (Douglas, 2000).

test-taking strategies. Test-taking strategies represent problem-solving techniques or tactics that test takers resort to when trying to answer question items on a given language test or form of assessment. Test-taking strategies comprise test-management and test-wiseness strategies, the former involving the use of construct-relevant response behaviors and the latter employing textual and/or technical aspects of the test that are not construct-relevant. In this sense, a given test-taking strategy is considered contributory or effective so long as its use results in getting the answer to a given question right; if not, this strategy is noncontributory or ineffective.

TOEFL. The TOEFL refers to the worldwide renowned *Test of English as a Foreign Language*, administered by the Educational Testing Service (ETS). The TOEFL measures test takers' ability to use academic English for admission purposes to programs of study at the college or university level in English-speaking countries. The TOEFL has been administered in three mediums: paper, computer, and internet, each of which has relatively distinct modalities and design features. The TOEFL iBT stands for the internet-based TOEFL, which has been in use since 2005. As its name suggests, this latest version of the TOEFL is administered worldwide via the internet. It has four sections that include listening, speaking, reading, and writing, each of which is assigned a score out of 30, with the total score of the test being 120.

translation. A test in which the candidate has to translate either the whole text or parts of it from one language to another.

true/false item. A binary-choice item in which the candidate has to decide whether a given statement is true and false.

validity. The content of a given form of assessment is valid as long as it samples the subject matter and requires assessees to perform the behavior being assessed; operationalizes the construct being measured; and is used to produce positive washback in terms of learners' motivation, subsequent performance, and independent learning. A direct test of performance promotes beneficial backwash (Hughes, 2003); looks right and appears to measure the ability it claims to measure based on assessee's judgment; and shows how students can deal with similar situations in real life (or alternatively, predictive validity).

washback. "… refers to the impact of a test on classroom pedagogy, curriculum development, and educational policy" (Pierce, 1992, p. 687).

[Some terms are adapted from the website of *Centre for languages, linguistics and area studies* (https://www.llas.ac.uk/resources/gpg/1398)]

Testing Speaking Skills using Authentic Materials

Communicative testing must involve how the learner demonstrates his competence in a meaningful situation (performance) (Canale & Swain, 1980). Tests of communicative ability are judged to the extent to which they simulate real-life situations. Role-plays, for example, allow the elicitation of natural production of language functions and speech acts. According to Hughes (2003), a role-play involving an interaction with another classmate can have the following advantages:

- It utilizes language appropriate to exchanges between equals.
- It produces representative performance, as the students feel more confident and less stressed.
- It makes the roles being played sound more natural.

Assumed student background: 10 Arab EFL students at the intermediate level of an intensive language program. They are well familiar with role-plays and the necessary vocabulary.

Procedures:

1) The teacher divides the students into pairs.
2) The teacher assigns each student of a pair a role in a particular situation.
   Example: A friend (Ahmad) invites you (Ali) to a party on an evening when you want to stay at home and watch the last episode of a TV series. Thank your friend and refuse politely.
3) The teacher allows the students some time to get ready to perform the assigned role-plays.
4) Each pair carries out the assigned role-play.
5) The teacher tape-records the role-plays.
6) The teacher assigns a different role to each student of a pair in a different situation.
   Example: You (Ahmad) want your father (Ali) to increase your pocket money. He is resistant to the idea. Try to make him change his mind.
7) The teacher allows the students some time to get ready to perform the assigned role-plays.

8) Each pair carries out the assigned role-play.
9) The teacher tape-records the role-plays.
10) The teacher rates the students' oral performance using the rating criteria recommended below.
11) The teacher requests another teacher to rate the students' oral performance using the same rating criteria the other teacher used.

Rating criteria: The rating of the students' oral performance will be made using an adapted version of the ACTFL Proficiency Guidelines for Speaking (2012). Such criteria can be adapted and suited for the level of the students and the purpose of the test.

ACTFL Proficiency Guidelines for Speaking (2012) at the intermediate level:

Intermediate High: A student at this level

- ➤ can converse with ease and confidence.
- ➤ can successfully exchange the needed information.
- ➤ is very intelligible by native speakers.
- ➤ has few errors.

Intermediate Mid: A student at this level

- ➤ can relatively converse with ease and confidence.
- ➤ can reasonably exchange the needed information.
- ➤ is intelligible by native speakers.
- ➤ has a few errors.

Intermediate Low: A student at this level

- ➤ can converse but with noticeable unease and/or diffidence.
- ➤ can relatively exchange the needed information.
- ➤ is somewhat intelligible by native speakers.
- ➤ has some errors.

Validity and reliability:

- ✓ The test measures what it purports to measure i.e., speaking ability (*construct validity*).
- ✓ The test incorporates a representative sample of spoken language, structures, and vocabulary it is concerned with (*content validity*).
- ✓ The test looks like a measure of speaking ability (*face validity*)
- ✓ The rating of role-plays is related directly to speaking ability (*valid scoring*)
- ✓ The test scores are likely to be similar to those obtained when the same test is used again with the same students (*reliability*).
- ✓ The rater of the test is consistent or would be likely to assign the same score to the same student if the student re-takes the test (*interrater and intrarater reliability*)

Other procedures to ensure validity and reliability:

- ✓ The situations assigned to the students are made similar in complexity.
- ✓ The time allowed for the students to plan for their performance depends on their level and complexity of the situations they are to role-play.
- ✓ The tape-recorded performance will be rated by another colleague (preferably experienced or trained in rating).
- ✓ The two scores assigned to a given student will be averaged if they diverge.
- ✓ The two raters should be experienced in rating or train before rating the students' role-plays.

Assessing the Four Skills at Upper Proficiency Levels

In this section, it is illustrated how the assessment of the four skills (listening, speaking, reading, and writing) can be performed at the two upper levels of an English language program (i.e., intermediate and advanced).

Listening

Level: intermediate
Skill(s) tested: underlined below.
Task: selective (listening to stretches of spoken discourse e.g., short monologues in order <u>to scan for certain information</u> with the aim of demonstrating the ability <u>to comprehend designated information</u> e.g., names, classroom directions, news items, etc.)

Procedures: (Adapted from Hadley, 2001)

1. Students listen to a monologue in which the speaker describes an apartment she has just rented.
2. The speaker gives information about location, price, number and size of rooms, utilities ... etc.
3. Students fill in the information on a chart based on the monologue content.

This form of assessment uses constructed response formats that guarantee adequate levels of validity and reliability (Brown & Hudson, 2002).

Level: advanced
Skill(s) tested: underlined below.
Task: extensive (listening to lengthy spoken discourse e.g., lectures in order <u>to develop a top-down, global understanding</u> by e.g., listening for the gist or the main idea and listening to <u>make inferences</u> (Alderson

& Banerjee, 2002); it may invoke interactive skills e.g., notetaking, questioning, or discussion)

Procedures:

1. Students listen to a 15-minute lecture on *water pollution*.
2. Students take notes while listening.
3. Students respond to multiple-choice question items and open-ended question items that call for making inferences.

This form of assessment involves note-taking in a fashion similar to what occurs in the academic world (Brown & Abeywickrama, 2010).

Speaking

Level: intermediate
Skill(s) tested: underlined below.
Task: *interactive* (producing spoken discourse in response to a spoken prompt in the form of long interactions or conversations involving multiple exchanges and/or multiple participants, used to demonstrate the ability to accomplish communicative functions appropriately according to situation, participants, and goals e.g., role-play)

Procedures: (Adapted from Hadley, 2001)

1. Students are divided into pairs.
2. Each pair is assigned a conversation card about a situation at random e.g., *You are a student (Student 1) looking for a room to rent. Ask the landlord (Student 2) questions about: how he is today, if he has a room to rent, if there is a sink or shower in the room, if there is a telephone, if the room has curtains and a rug, and if the room is expensive.*
3. Each pair is to role-play the assigned situation.
4. Each pair is assigned another conversation card and the students in each pair switch roles.

Role-play has shown to be a successful technique for the elicitation of non-native speakers' oral language (Halleck, 2007). This task illustrates a mode of performance-based assessment, in which the target language is used with high interactivity (Brown & Abeywickrama, 2010). It is considerably natural when eliciting language appropriate for exchanges between equals (Hughes, 2003). Students can converse with each other with creativity and complexity that approach real-world pragmatics (Brown & Abeywickrama, 2010). Practicality manifests itself in that having role-plays among students is more time saving than interviews (Brown & Abeywickrama, 2010).

Level: Advanced

Skill(s) tested: underlined below.

Task: extensive (producing spoken discourse in the form of formal or informal monologues to demonstrate the ability to use adequate speaking skills such as <u>providing a context, communicating information, and offering explanation or description</u> e.g., giving speeches)

Procedures:

1. Students are asked to prepare 10-minute long speeches on topics of interest to them to deliver next class.
2. Each student delivers his/her speech to the class.
3. At the end of each speech, time is allowed to the audience to ask questions or offer comments.

A monologue provides a valid, reliable, and ratable sample of oral discourse (Halleck, 2007). It can take different forms from story-retellings to topical speeches. As an example of a monologue: "You have received an award for serving the community where you live. You want to deliver an acceptance speech. What would you say?" (Halleck, 2007). The fact that the audience are allowed to react to the speech by asking questions or providing comments makes the whole experience authentic and interactive.

Reading

Level: Intermediate

Skill(s) tested: underlined below.

Task: interactive (reading stretches of written discourse of several paragraphs in the form of meaning negotiation and interaction with the text to demonstrate the ability <u>to identify relevant features e.g., grammatical, lexical, symbolic, and discourse in order to understand and retain the information processed</u>)

Procedures:

1. Students are provided with a 300-word impromptu reading along with 10 multiple-choice comprehension questions that call for skimming for the main idea or topic, guessing word meanings from the context, identifying pronoun referents, making inferences, using discourse markers, and scanning for specific details.
2. Students are given 20 minutes to complete the task.

This task engages students in the use and practice of strategies and skills of effective reading (Brown & Abeywickrama, 2010). It also involves a combination of bottom-up and top-down processes.

Level: Advanced

Skill(s) tested: underlined below.

Task: extensive (reading long stretches of written discourse of several paragraphs to more than one page to demonstrate the ability <u>to develop global understanding of a text</u> e.g., essays, articles, reports, short stories ... etc.)

Procedures:

1. Students are provided with a 500-word impromptu text to skim along with 10 open-ended comprehension questions that require such skills as: figuring out the main idea or

topic, figuring out the author's purpose in writing the text, specifying the kind of writing (newspaper article, manual, novel … etc.), specifying the type of writing (expository, technical, narrative … etc.), and telling what he/she has learnt from the text and how the text is useful to his/her (profession, academic needs, interests … etc.).

2. Students are given 5 minutes to skim the text.
3. Students are given 10 minutes to answer the questions

This task assesses higher-order skills or the extent to which students utilize top-down processing (Alderson & Banerjee, 2002). In addition, it represents a performance-based assessment task that involves the provision of open-ended responses (Brown & Abeywickrama, 2010).

Writing

Level: Intermediate

Skill(s) tested: underlined below.

Task: responsive (producing a logically connected written discourse of two or three paragraphs in response to directives or criteria to demonstrate the ability <u>to communicate with coherence and cohesion such relations as main idea, supporting idea, new information, given information, generalization, and exemplification</u> e.g., writing a brief narrative or description, short report, summary, or brief response to a reading)

Procedures: (Adapted from Hadley, 2001)

1. Students are provided with the following directions: *You have just interviewed David, an exchange student from England, about his impressions of the US. Using the notes below, write a résumé of what he has said. Add any necessary words to make a good, interesting paragraph.*
   - likes the university, campus, town very much

- thinks students nice, serious, while some are careless
- town-small, quaint, good stores, lots of theaters
- movies often, see films

2. Students are given 15 minutes to write the résumé.

This task is a form of performance-based assessment in which students express their real-life like experiences (Ferman, 2005).

Level: Advanced

Skill(s) tested: underlined.

Task: responsive/extensive (producing a logically connected written discourse up to the length of an essay in order to demonstrate the ability to <u>achieve a purpose of writing, organize and develop ideas logically, support or illustrate ideas with details, use a variety of syntactic and lexical elements, and show facility and fluency in the use of language</u> e.g., writing about a topic of interest or an impromptu topic)

Procedures:

1. Students are assigned an impromptu topic to write about: *Some people believe that automobiles are useful and necessary. Others believe that automobiles cause problems that affect our well-being. Which position do you support? Give specific reasons or examples for your answer.* Students may be allowed the choice of this topic or another comparable topic (Raimes, 1990).

2. Students are given 40 minutes to compose their responses: 30 minutes to write the essay plus 10 minutes to revise it.

In this form of assessment, a reasonable amount of time is allotted for students to revise their essays. This reflects a real-world aspect of writing. Besides, composition tasks help students develop increasingly complex and creative writings (Lee, 2002).

Mohammed S. Assiri

Language Proficiency and Strategy Use on Reading Tasks

From my brief talks with a number of Arab learners of English language about the TOEFL, it has appeared to me that the majority of them are aware of the importance of strategy use. They believe that certain strategies can aid performance especially on the reading section of the TOEFL, without necessarily having to understand the reading passage. This has been made clear by Cohen (1986) when noting that "test-takers have developed numerous techniques for finding correct answers to reading tests without fully or even partially understanding the text" (p. 132). In a later article, Cohen (1992) suggests that test-taking strategies represent processes that test takers can have control over by selecting from among these processes what they believe would help them tackle a test question. This implies that test-taking strategies are conscious processes. Cohen adds that these strategies can either be a short move (e.g., looking for a clue that links the information in the question to that in the reading text) or a long one (e.g., reading the whole text after reading the questions). The goal of this section is to underline the theory and research that addressed the relationship between proficiency level and test-taking strategy use on reading tasks.

Test respondents very often resort to test-taking strategies to compensate for the lack of information that aids their response to a given question. For example, they may try to avoid or skip words they do not know, simplify the language of the question or the information needed, or use approximation especially when guessing word meanings (Cohen, 1998). Reference to test-taking strategies in the literature involves both *test-management* strategies and *test-wiseness* strategies, with the former being indicative of adequate knowledge and skillful performance and the latter being more compensatory in nature (Cohen & Upton, 2006). It is important here to distinguish between test-taking strategies and reading strategies, as these two categories of strategies show some overlap and so can easily be confused in the context of reading comprehension. First, test-taking strategies are not specific to any language skill, although it is true that each language skill has its specific test-taking strategies. Thus, there are certain test-taking strategies that are shared among a number of language skills (e.g., a test taker prefers to read the questions first on both reading and listening comprehension tests administered in a multiple-choice format). Second, while reading strategies are generally used when readers engage in a reading activity and thus "are related to text comprehension" (Singhal, 2001, p. 1), test-taking strategies are only used when dealing with a test and are thus more "driven by the test questions" (Farr, Prichard, & Smitten, 1990, p. 218).

Because reading test-taking represents a problem-solving situation, high-proficiency test takers employ strategies that increase their chances of getting question items correct to a greater extent when compared to low-level test takers (Nevo, 1989). In this regard, Nevo (1989) suggests that readers' ability to deal with problem-solving situations correlates with their levels of language proficiency, specifically knowledge of grammar and vocabulary. Test takers who are highly proficient also exhibit skillfulness in using text-level comprehension to guide their completion of cloze tasks (Bachman, 1985). Besides the task difficulty, Phakiti (2003) counts the proficiency level as another factor that affects strategy use. He suggests that high-proficiency test takers tend to exhibit more automatic use of such strategies as *checking* and *monitoring* than their low-proficiency counterparts do. What follows is a review of the research that looked into the differential use of test-taking strategies by high- and low-proficiency test-takers.

Homburg and Spaan (1982) studied how readers' word-solving strategies relate to comprehension and reading abilities. A total of 39 respondents who were ESL learners at the three highest levels of their ESL program participated in the study. Reading ranks of the respondents in their classes were provided by their teachers. The researchers used a cloze passage with thirteen underlined nonsense words used instead of the real words. The word-solving strategies needed to infer the meanings of the thirteen nonsense words were determined. The respondents took the cloze test in which they first skimmed the passage, spotted familiar vocabulary, and used real words or descriptions instead of the nonsense words. They were asked to identify each word's part of speech; define it or give its meaning, or provide its synonym; and identify words that helped infer the meaning of the given word. In the last task, they were asked to write a summary of the passage, identifying the main idea. Scoring criteria were followed to grade the completed cloze tests. Significant differences were found among the three levels: Low Intermediate, High Intermediate, and Advanced in terms of identifying parts of speech and looking backward to figure out the nonsense words. It was also found that recognizing the main idea was a noticeable characteristic of respondents who tended to look forward while reading. In addition, those respondents who were high in reading proficiency, according to their teachers' rankings, were the best at word definitions. Interestingly, one conclusion the researchers drew from their study was that the respondents at both high and low levels were almost alike in terms of recognizing the main idea. This indicates that word-solving strategies that helped comprehend the reading texts did not seem to relate to the respondents' levels of proficiency (Homburg & Spaan, 1982).

Gordon (1987) looked into response behaviors among 30 tenth-grade EFL learners when responding to open-ended and multiple-choice reading tasks. The researchers elicited the respondents' response behaviors through the use of think-aloud protocols. The findings from this study suggest that the respondents answered some of the test questions without any indications that they had comprehended the text. Additionally, the respondents who are at a low level of proficiency demonstrated more local-text processing (i.e., by focusing on isolated or fragmented elements of the text) compared to highly proficient respondents who showed more global-text processing (i.e., relating the meaning of intact, individual sentences to the whole text). In relation to this, while the low-proficiency students used strategies such as *matching words in the options to words in the text, copying information from the text,* and *translating word for word,* the high-proficiency students used strategies such as *predicting information.*

Nevo (1989) set out to examine the use of test-taking strategies on a multiple-choice test of reading comprehension among 42 Hebrew tenth-grade learners of French. The subjects responded to a multiple-choice reading test administered first in Hebrew and then in French. While answering the test items, the respondents marked each strategy they used on a strategy checklist on an item-by-item basis. That is, for each question item on the test, the respondents had to mark on the checklist the strategy they used to answer the question. The respondents were allowed 50 minutes to complete the test. The results showed that the respondents used both contributory and non-contributory strategies to answer the test items and that more contributory strategies and fewer non-contributory ones were used when completing the test in Hebrew than in French. Therefore, the respondents' higher proficiency in L1, when compared to L2, enabled them to use more contributory strategies or strategies that led them to provide correct answers.

Mangubhai (1990) used cloze reading procedures along with think-aloud protocols to investigate strategy use among three proficiency levels of young ESL learners. The subjects were six EFL learners in year eleven—2 High, 2 Middle, and 2 Low achievers, according to their scores on a national EFL examination. The procedures involved the use of three cloze passages chosen to be at an appropriate level of difficulty. First, the subjects were trained how

161

to think-aloud. Then, they completed the three cloze tasks and at the same time provided their think-aloud protocols one subject at a time. Based on their scores on the cloze tests and verbalizations of their strategy use, the subjects demonstrated the use of strategies that distinguished between the high and the low levels of proficiency. That is, the high achievers used such strategies as *look at larger context after generating the word, refer to prior knowledge, rephrase the sentences in order to generate the word, evaluate guesses for their correctness,* and *analyze the passage using prior and contextual knowledge in order to generate the word,* whereas the low achievers used such strategies as *look at the immediate context and generate randomly and/or reject words on syntactic or semantic grounds.* Strong positive correlations were observed between the total percentages of successful strategies (i.e., strategies leading to correct answers) the respondents used, their scores, and their levels of proficiency.

Anderson (1991) examined individual differences in the use of test-taking strategies among 28 Spanish-speaking adult ESL learners—nine beginners, ten at the intermediate level, and nine advanced-level students. The respondents were randomly assigned to two groups: One group to take one form of a standardized reading test and another group to take the other form of the same test. The respondents were then asked to take a test of academic reading on an individual basis so that each respondent could think aloud while responding to the test, in either Spanish or English as they wished. The standardized reading test was administered a second time, but with each of the two groups taking the other form of the test they did not take in the first administration. In the second administration, the respondents were asked to think aloud during the test taking in Spanish or English. The two tests were in a multiple-choice format and the administration process was timed. Pauses were made whenever the respondents showed they completed a phase of the test so that they could verbalize their thought processes or strategy use. Based on case studies of three individual respondents, it was found that the high and low scorers did not differ from one another in the kinds of strategies they used, but rather in how effectively they used these strategies individually or in conjunction with other strategies, as well as the ability to assess and monitor strategy use. The researchers also referred to the low scorers' limited repertoire of vocabulary and schema-related knowledge as a potential factor that constrained their strategy use and in turn their performance on the tests.

Purpura (1997, 1998) worked with 1,382 respondents from language centers in three European countries including Czech Republic, Spain, and Turkey. He aimed to examine the relationship between proficiency levels and strategy use on a standardized language ability test. The language ability test is composed of two main sections: reading comprehension with parts on grammar, vocabulary, and passage comprehension, and use of English with parts on word formation, cloze filling, and sentence structure. The respondents first filled out an 80-item cognitive and metacognitive strategy questionnaire. Then, they took the 70-item standardized language test. Using a structural equation modeling, the researcher observed similar factorial structures for the high- and low-proficiency groups resulting from the two models of cognitive and metacognitive strategy use and the test performance. Nonetheless, the low-proficiency group exhibited more use of such metacognitive strategies as *information retrieval, monitoring, self-evaluating,* and *self-testing* than the high-proficiency group who used more of strategies that endorse their comprehension and retention of information (Purpura, 1999).

Yoshizawa (2002) investigated how each of strategy use, proficiency level, and level of language aptitude relates to one another, using structural equation modeling. The researcher had a group of 54 Japanese adult ESL learners. The participants first responded to a questionnaire that elicited the kinds of text-processing strategies they normally use when performing L2 reading tasks. The Language Aptitude Battery for Japanese was used to measure the participants' foreign language aptitude, and the TOEFL Institutional Testing Program to assess their English proficiency. The results of the factor analysis identified three latent variables: (1) comprehension and monitoring strategies, (2) compensatory strategies (including translation and repair), and (3) attention and task assessment strategies. Of particular importance, the participants exhibited progressive strategy use across proficiency levels from low to high.

Phakiti (2003) examined how the use of cognitive and metacognitive strategies relates to performance on an EFL reading test. The researcher had 384 Thai EFL students at the university level take an 85-item reading achievement test in a multiple-choice format. Then, they reported their strategy use on the test by means of a cognitive-metacognitive strategy questionnaire. After that, the researcher selected four highly successful and four low successful test takers based on their scores on the test for retrospective interviews. On the basis of both quantitative and qualitative analyses, it was found that the highly successful test takers demonstrated a high degree of awareness of their metacognitive strategy use in terms of what strategies to use, why they chose these strategies, and how to use them well. The researcher concluded that "[i]ndividual test-takers who are metastrategically competent are more likely to understand how the strategies fit together and how they are related to language tasks or TLU [target language use] domains than those with little of this competence" (p. 49).

Yamashita (2003) sought to determine the extent to which cloze tasks using rational deletion assess the ability of text-level information processing. The researcher had respondents who were 12 Japanese EFL students at the university level. The respondents were selected so as to represent six highly skilled and six low skilled on the basis of their results on a reading test. The respondents completed rational deletion cloze tasks and at the same time verbalized their strategic thoughts. Their verbal report data were then coded and categorized following Bachman's (1985) taxonomy of cloze item types. The results showed that the highly skilled respondents did not spend as much time guessing and inferring the meanings of individual clauses and sentences as did the low skilled ones. Rather, they had a superior tendency to attend to the overall meaning of the text using macro-level strategies.

Nikolov (2006) carried out an exploratory study of test-taking strategy use on reading and writing tasks among 52 young EFL learners. The participants were randomly sampled so as to represent 22 high, 20 intermediate, and 10 low levels. The data were collected using non-mediated think-aloud protocols on an individual basis, while each respondent was taking a language test comprised of reading and writing tasks. Four case studies were conducted with the two top scorers and the two bottom scorers. While there were not quite many consistent patterns of differences between the high and low scorers in strategy use, the findings suggest that the low scorers processed the text at the word level, whereas the high scorers showed more tendency to process the text at the sentence level. The high scorers also benefitted more than the low scorers did from *relating to self* metacognitive strategy by linking the information in the question items to their real-life experiences, in order to check their answers. It was also found that when translating, the high scorers focused on chunks of the text larger than those the low scorers dealt with. Overall, although the high scorers did not show the use of quite as many test-taking strategies, they made more effective use of the strategies they used, when compared to those with low scores.

Cohen and Upton (2006) set out to judge the usefulness of the TOEFL-iBT *reading to learn* tasks in comparison to the *basic comprehension* and *inferencing* tasks. The researchers investigated the use of reading and test-taking strategies among 32 advanced ESL learners. Think-aloud protocols were collected from the participants while responding to reading tests comprising two 600-700 word readings—each with 12-13 question items. A major trend among the participants was using test-management strategies more than test-wiseness strategies, which the researchers attributed to the fact that the respondents did not want to report their use of test-wiseness strategies even if they had actually used them. Among the most frequently used strategies across the three reading tasks were *read the question then read the passage/portion to look for clues to the answer, either before or while considering options*; *consider the options and postpone consideration of the option*; and *discard option(s) based on vocabulary, sentence, paragraph, or passage overall meaning as well as discourse structure* (depending on item type).

Cohen and Upton's (2006) rubrics of test-taking strategies (test-management and test-wiseness) on reading tests encapsulate the strategies that were observed in previous research in addition to those strategies Cohen and Upton (2006) found out through the analysis of verbal reports in their study of test-taking strategies among 32 ESL learners. Rupp et al. (2006) go further to classify the kinds of test-taking strategies used on reading comprehension tests into general strategies that can be applied to any test format, text-related strategies that test takers apply to the text, and item-related strategies that test takers use with the question items.

Assiri (2011) studied how a sample of 25 Arab ESL learners respond to the TOEFL-iBT reading tasks in order to find out what strategies respondents tend to use, investigate if there are differences between high- and low-scorers in strategy use, and determine aspects of effective strategy use among respondents. Data were collected using a procedural integration of stimulated recall, self-observation, and retrospective interview (SRSORI). A pilot study was conducted to evaluate and refine materials and procedures. Data collection was carried out over three stages. First, each participant was oriented to SRSORI and trained in producing verbal reports. Second, the participant responded to two reading sets, and thus was engaged in two SRSORI sessions. And third, the participant was debriefed about his test performance and scores. Data were then transcribed, and results of item analyses were used to decide on episodes for coding. A coding scheme was constructed for each task item by means of inductive coding. Data analysis made use of frequencies to identify patterns of strategy use and qualitative accounts to describe strategy use in relation to such factors as item format, scoring level, and answer correctness.

The major findings of Assiri's (2011) study were as follows. Test takers used strategies depending on item format and difficulty in ways that allowed them to achieve different goals, adapt strategies to various task items, and apply strategies using several textual and technical means. High-test performance and scoring were characterized by superior skills of both comprehension and test-management as well as high levels of strategic awareness and monitoring. Conversely, low-test performance and scoring were associated with poor skills of comprehension and excessive use of test-wiseness. And, test takers sequenced strategies such that certain strategies derived from other strategies, endorsed or facilitated functions of other strategies, or acted in sync with other strategies. Assiri (2011) concluded that strategy use has three facets: purposeful, multi-form, and resourceful. High-test performance and scoring on reading tasks draw on response behaviors and strategies that differ from those associated with low performance and scoring. And, aspects of effective strategy use occur in tandem with logical sequences of strategies.

In summary, there are varying degrees of test-taking strategy choice and use associated with varied levels of proficiency. While there are test-taking strategies that are conscious choices (e.g., when a test taker chooses to read the questions first on a multiple-choice reading test before reading the text), there are test-taking processes that are subconscious operations (e.g., when a high-proficiency test taker attends to the overall meaning using text-level information on a cloze task). The previous studies have identified a number of strategies that distinguish between high- and low- proficiency levels. Such strategies are not limited to test-management strategies, but also include metacognitive and cognitive strategies.

Test-taking Strategy Use on Reading Comprehension Tests

Thought and research on the use of the test-taking strategies on reading comprehension tests have generally followed certain strands that are worth being spotlighted. Accordingly, this section offers an overview of the major themes that characterize these strands.

Strategy Use and Test Format

It is intriguing to know what test-taking strategies might work with one test format, but not with another. In fact, previous research has shown that test-taking strategy use on reading tests is substantially determined by the nature of task types when one considers what strategies to use and how to use them (Anderson, Bachman, Perkins & Cohen, 1991; Nevo, 1989). Nevo (1989) goes further to describe the format aspects of a multiple-choice reading test that can influence strategy use significantly, including the level of text familiarity and task complexity. In her study, which sought to examine the use of test-taking strategies on a multiple-choice test of reading comprehension among 42 Hebrew tenth graders studying French, Nevo (1989) noticed that her respondents' ability to use contributory strategies, or strategies that resulted in correct answers, diminished when they were asked to respond to tests that had unfamiliar texts or difficult question items. For example, the discoursal and pragmatic items, which required test takers to understand the use of the cohesive devices in the texts and so were very challenging, were associated with the use of ineffective strategies on the L2 test. However, this did not apply to all test takers; that is, the use of effective strategies did not always lead to getting the answer correct, which the researcher linked to interfering causes.

Some of the recent studies that looked into task difficulty on reading tests have focused on strategy use among test takers to determine which tasks and question items posed a serious challenge to test takers. For example, Cohen and Upton (2006) observed that the choice of language to report test-taking strategy use among their respondents, while responding to reading tasks on selected practice tests of the TOEFL-iBT, reflected the level of difficulty of the items with which the strategies were associated (for example, one respondent reported that he was *"wrestling with the question intent"* (p. 78) while trying to tackle one of the questions). Other researchers concerned with L1 reading (e.g., Cordón & Day, 1996; Pressley & Afflerbach, 1995) have noted that when readers were provided with an unfamiliar material, they did not only exhibit the use of less effective strategies than that accompanying the use of familiar materials, but also used strategies at low frequencies.

One issue that has triggered extensive research regarding strategy use on reading tests focuses on the extent to which questions on standardized tests are answerable without the texts. For example, Powers and Wilson Leung (1995) had a group of L1 readers answer three sets of reading comprehension questions without the passages, and at the same time mark on a checklist the kinds of strategies they were using. The findings suggested that respondents' scores were higher than the chance level, but not up to the level that matched the respondents' capabilities. Although respondents had difficulty with some questions that were more passage dependent, they mostly employed their ability of verbal reasoning by using the questions as building blocks to develop a mental schema of the text.

In studies where student readers were asked to respond to open-ended questions on reading passages (e.g., Cohen & Aphek, 1979), some respondents were observed to try to find where the answer was most likely to be in the passage and write the whole sentence or context containing the answer in response to each given question. In other studies using multiple-choice reading tasks, there was a notable tendency among respondents, specifically those with low proficiency, to guess the key answers from the options without referring to the text, to match the content of the item stem and options with that of the passage (Allan, 1992; Cohen, 1984; Rupp et al., 2006), or to eliminate what they perceived not to be the key answers among the options (Storey, 1997). Farr and his colleagues' (1990) study was especially insightful in its identification of certain response behaviors on multiple-choice reading tasks. For example, test takers used the questions to guide their dealing with the text in order to identify the key answers. They also used test-taking strategies far more frequently than reading strategies, and showed repeated switching between the questions and the text.

Another study by Anderson et al. (1991) examined response strategies with the aim of validating a TOEFL reading test that used three types of questions: main idea, inferencing, and direct statement. The researchers observed a remarkable consistency among examinees in using patterns of strategies specific to each question type. The researchers noted that question items differed significantly from one another in terms of the kinds of strategies they called for; for example, while inference question items called for more *guessing* and *matching stem with text* strategies, direct statement questions called for examinees' use of *paraphrasing* and *making reference to time allocation* (p. 57). In their study, Rupp et al. (2006) examined response strategies used by a group of 10 ESL readers on three multiple-choice reading tests for academic purposes. Rupp and his colleagues observed that respondents moved from identifying the theme to locating specific details to answer the questions and thus used macro- and micro-level strategies sequentially, used the questions to guide their scanning of the text and locating the key information, used the order of the questions to identify the location of the respective key information in the text, and made use of rational elimination based on prior knowledge or clued-up guessing.

In other studies where cloze tasks were used (e.g., Stemmer, 1991; Storey, 1995), low proficient students were shown to use more micro-level processing when a half of each deletion was given by trying to guess the deleted word using the remnant of it or other local hints. Apparently, these students had a limited ability when it came to understanding the context surrounding the deletion or using macro-level processing. In particular, Stemmer (1991) noted that making inferences was more evident among students taking the cloze test when the number of cohesive devices was low. In a recent study, Assiri (2014) used a structural equation modeling approach to examine effects of metacognitive and cognitive strategies on performance on a reading test composed of four task formats: multiple-choice, true/false, fill-in vocabulary, and constructed response. The data comprised 98 Saudi EFL learners' scores on a reading test and responses to a strategy questionnaire. The findings showed that the use of both metacognitive and cognitive strategies had small to medium effects on performances on the task formats. Most strategy subscales (i.e., *comprehending, memory,* and *retrieval for* cognitive strategies *and planning, monitoring,* and *evaluating* for metacognitive strategies) were directly related to performances on the task formats. Different reading tasks demand versatile uses of metacognitive and cognitive strategies. Thus, speaking of metacognitive strategies, planning strategies enabled test takers to perform well on constructed-response items, monitoring strategies caused test takers to score high on true/false items, and evaluation strategies were especially effective with multiple-choice items. As for cognitive strategies, memory strategies were associated with high performance on multiple-choice and fill-in vocabulary items, retrieval strategies were used on all four task formats; however, comprehension strategies did not have any significant correlations with performance on any of the four task formats.

Everything considered, research points out that the kinds of formats or tasks that appear on reading tests play a crucial role in determining examinees' strategy choice and use, and their overall response behaviors. Thus, those strategies that are typically used on cloze formats are different from those used on multiple-choice formats. Examples of the strategies used on the former include *look backward and forward to figure out the missing word* where those used on the latter include *read the questions, then read the text to locate the critical information.* Format aspects such as text familiarity and task difficulty can also impose certain limits on the choice and use of test-taking strategies such that the less familiar the text or more difficult the task, the fewer strategies are expected to be used by test takers. One implication of the dependency of test-taking strategy use on test format relates to how strategies can enable us to check our tests for validity and authenticity, which is to be discussed next.

Strategy Use and Proficiency Level

Based on an extensive review of research on reading strategies, Singhal (2001) suggests that there is ample evidence that the use of reading strategies is strongly associated with the level of proficiency. He maintains that highly proficient readers use a variety of strategies more frequently and effectively and more knowingly of when and how to use these strategies than less proficient readers. Similarly, Tian (2000) points to the major findings from comparative studies of reading strategy use among varied levels of proficiency, which can be summarized as follows: while proficient readers work towards forming a global understanding of what they read using higher-order processing skills, less proficient readers work on a more local level using lower-order processing skills; proficient readers show high flexibility in their strategy use while less proficient readers tend to be more rigid in this respect; and, highly proficient readers utilize more active and ongoing monitoring while their less proficient counterparts fail to execute an adequate level of monitoring and so are less able to evaluate and fine-tune their strategy use.

Scholars have begun to look at differences between high- and low-proficiency readers in strategy use on reading comprehension tests. Nevo (1989) was among the first scholars to assume that because reading-test taking represents a problem-solving situation, high-proficiency test takers employ strategies that increase their chance of getting a question item correct to a greater extent than low-proficiency test takers. She suggested that readers' ability to deal with problem-solving situations in language use correlates with their levels of language proficiency, specifically knowledge of grammar and vocabulary (Nevo, 1989). Also, Purpura (1999) highlighted the role of language ability in the efficient use of metacognitive strategies on reading comprehension tests.

Besides task difficulty, Phakiti (2003) counted proficiency level as another factor that affects cognitive and metacognitive strategy use. For example, he noticed among his respondents that although both high- and low-proficiency test takers exhibited response behaviors so automatic that they were not aware if they had used metacognitive strategies like *checking* and *monitoring,* the low-proficiency test takers employed these two strategies to a lesser degree. However, questions that have yet to be addressed through more research involve whether high- and low-proficiency readers differ from each other in their use of test-management and -wiseness strategies (Cohen & Upton, 2006; Nikolov, 2006) and, if so, how their differential use of these strategies contributes to disparity in their test performance and scores (Anderson et al., 1991; Purpura, 1998; Phakiti, 2003).

Early research on the differential use of strategies on reading comprehension tests has pointed out that the main difference between

L1 and L2 readers lies in L1 readers' superior ability to make use of intra- and inter- sentential and semantic clues, as measured by means of oral miscue and cloze tasks (e.g., Cziko, 1978, 1980; Douglas, 1981, Hauptman, 1979). This conclusion has been supported by Mangubhai (1991) who further noted that highly proficient readers exhibit resourcefulness that both serves and automatizes their textual and informational processing to a greater extent compared to low proficient readers. Mangubhai (1991) based his view on the results of a study he conducted the year before in which he used cloze reading procedures along with think-aloud protocols to investigate strategy use among three different proficiency levels of young ESL learners. The subjects were six EFL learners in year eleven—two high, two middle, and two low achievers according to their scores on a national EFL examination. The subjects demonstrated differences in their strategy use between the high and the low levels of proficiency in that the high achievers used such strategies as *look at larger context after generating the word, refer to prior knowledge, rephrase the sentences in order to generate the word, evaluate guesses for their correctness,* and *analyze the passage using prior and contextual knowledge in order to generate the word,* whereas the low achievers used such strategies as *look at the immediate context and generate randomly and/or reject words on syntactic or semantic grounds* (Mangubhai, 1990, p. 133). Strong positive correlations were observed between the respondents' levels of proficiency, the total percentages of effective strategies they used, and their scores.

In another study combining open-ended and multiple-choice reading comprehension tasks, Gordon (1987) used think-aloud protocols to look into response behaviors among 30 tenth-grade EFL learners. The findings from this study suggested that the respondents answered some of the test questions without any indications that they had comprehended the text. Additionally, the respondents who were at a low level of proficiency demonstrated more local processing of the text (i.e., focusing on isolated or fragmented elements of the text) where highly proficient respondents showed more global processing (i.e., relating the meaning of intact, individual sentences to the whole text). In relation to this, while the low-proficiency students used strategies such as *matching words in the options to words in the text, copying information from the text,* and *translating word for word,* the high-proficiency students used strategies such as *predicting information* and *making inferences* (as cited in Cohen, 1998, p. 100).

It is very often the case that in reading test-like situations such as cloze tasks, those who are highly proficient exhibit skillfulness in using text-level comprehension to guide their completion of the cloze items (Bachman, 1985), or at least use other problem-solving strategies such as rational guessing when faced with challenging deletions (Cohen, 1984). On the other hand, test takers who are less proficient make heavy use of translation and very localized clues to solve deletions (Cohen, 1984). With respect to translation, Upton (1997) and Upton and Lee-Thompson (2001) have concluded that the use of this strategy is inversely related to the level of proficiency and that while L2 readers at different levels of proficiency can benefit from this strategy, low proficiency readers are prone to resort to mental translation in three cases: to deal with unknown words through guessing and substitution using L1 words, to develop understanding at the text level, and to test hypotheses about understanding and to verify these hypotheses.

The tendency to employ effective strategies was observed to be a characteristic of learners' reading in their L1 in contrast to their reading of L2 texts. In her study, Nevo (1989) sought to examine the use of test-taking strategies on a multiple-choice test of reading comprehension among 42 Hebrew tenth graders studying French. The subjects responded to a multiple-choice reading comprehension test administered first in Hebrew and then in French. While responding to the test items, the respondents were to mark each strategy they used on a strategy checklist on an item-by-item basis.

The results showed that the respondents used both effective and ineffective strategies to respond to the reading test items and that more effective strategies and fewer ineffective ones were used when responding to the test in Hebrew than in French. Therefore, the respondents' higher proficiency in L1 when compared to L2 enabled them to use effective strategies or strategies that led them to provide more correct answers on the test in Hebrew (L1) than on the one in French (L2).

Therefore, it seems that the distinction that Dollerup, Glahn, and Rosenberg-Hansen (1982) proposed between the two modes of taking standardized reading tests as "mainline" versus "fragmented" is justified, seeing that mainline reading involves the test taker's skimming of the text to develop the main idea and then answering the question items on this basis, whereas fragmented reading is characterized by, for example, matching of words in the question items with those in the text (p. 96). Therefore, on tests of reading comprehension, while highly proficient test takers are expected to be mainline readers, less proficient ones follow a more fragmented way of taking the test. This may explain why experienced readers were shown to use fewer strategies on standardized reading tests than those who are less experienced, as in Cordón and Day's (1996) study of L1 readers. Another example comes from a study in which Yamashita (2003) had 12 Japanese EFL students, at the university level, complete a rational deletion cloze test and at the same time verbalize their thoughts. The results showed that the highly skilled respondents did not spend as much time guessing and inferring the meanings of individual clauses and sentences as did the lower skilled respondents. Rather, the highly proficient readers handled the deletions one after another, drawing on information at both the textual and the clausal levels, whereas their lower proficient counterparts switched back and forth among deletions and used mostly clause-level information.

In an attempt to investigate how strategy use, proficiency level, and level of language aptitude relate one to another, Yoshizawa (2002) had a group of 54 Japanese adult ESL learners respond to a questionnaire. The participants were instructed to report the kinds of text-processing strategies they normally use when performing L2 listening and reading tasks. A language aptitude battery was used to measure the respondents' foreign language aptitude and a test from the TOEFL Institutional Testing Program was used to assess their English proficiency. The researcher found that the respondents exhibited progressively more effective strategy use across their proficiency levels from low to high. Moreover, the distinction between the two categories of test-taking strategies as test-management versus test-wiseness strategies seems to be pertinent to the differential strategy use of the two discrete levels of proficiency. In this regard, Cohen and Upton (2006) observed that their respondents, who were asked to perform TOEFL-iBT reading tasks, used predominantly more test-management strategies than test-wiseness strategies. The researchers linked this tendency to the high proficiency level of the test takers. On this basis, one can deduce that test takers who are at a lower level of proficiency would be more likely to use more test-wiseness than test-management strategies.

In short, as one would expect, there are varying degrees of test-taking strategy choice and use associated with varied levels of proficiency. The previous studies of how test-taking strategies and processes relate to L2 proficiency have revealed that high- and low-proficiency test takers approach reading tests in different ways and exhibit varied response behaviors. Moreover, the distinction between the two categories of test-taking strategies as test-management versus test-wiseness strategies seems to be pertinent to the differential strategy use of the two discrete levels of proficiency, in that high-proficiency test takers make more use of test-management strategies than their low-proficiency counterparts whose choices are more limited to test-wiseness strategies. High- and low-proficiency test takers are expected to perform differently on reading tests, which is due in part to their differential use of test-taking strategies. In this regard, high-proficiency test takers are likely to make more effective choice and use of strategies. The following section addresses the question of what aspects determine facilitative versus debilitative effects of strategy use on test performance.

Strategy Use and Test Performance

In their model of communicative language ability, Bachman and Palmer (1996) clearly demonstrated how strategy use, prompted by strategic competence, acts as a mediating component between competence and performance, influences how competence contributes to performance. Whether or not strategy use can make a difference in scores on language tests used to be an issue calling for research into how the use of test-taking strategies shapes test performance. Meanwhile, test constructors relentlessly expressed their refutation to any claims about the possibility of gaining high scores by means of test-taking strategies (Tian, 2000). Unfortunately, the distinction between the two types of test-taking strategies (i.e., test management and test wiseness) has not been adequately addressed in the debate. Presumably, the test-taking process assimilates to a problem-solving situation, in which case the use of strategies to help deal with this process successfully is natural, and so reflects the authenticity of the test.

Problem-solving strategies on tests of reading comprehension can either be test-management strategies or test-wiseness strategies; hence, while the use of the former is a sign of a skilled response behavior, the latter can be indicative of a poor response behavior or an invalid test item, or both (Allan, 1992). On the other hand, while test-management strategies can be mastered through test preparation practices, test-wiseness strategies are more linked to problem-solving abilities of test takers, and so do not lend themselves easily to training or instruction. In contrast to the use of test-management strategies, as Allan (1992, 1995) suggested, the use of test-wiseness strategies is idiosyncratic, and so results in unfair testing and undeserving achievement, assuming that the given test is amenable to test-wiseness (Cohen, 1992).

The issue of how strategy use relates to test performance largely depends on the nature of the test format and tasks. For example, it has been observed across a number of studies of response behaviors on cloze tasks that test takers could still manage to obtain high scores and never had to read the whole text or even understand the main idea of the text (Cohen, 1984). Test takers in other studies of performance on cloze tasks were observed to first use the local clues to solve as many deletions as they could, and then they moved on to forming a general idea about the text and so used more global clues to help them deal with the unsolved deletions (e.g., Kleiman, Cavalcanti, Terzi, & Ratto, 1986). In another study of strategy use on cloze tasks, Homburg and Spaan (1982) reported that their respondents' use of such strategies as identifying parallel elements, discourse chunking, cataphoric reading, and anaphoric reading correlated with their success in identifying the correct completions. It was also found that those who made effective use of cataphoric reading were better able to figure out the main idea of the text than those who did not.

Cohen (1984) also referred to other studies in which test takers were asked to respond to multiple-choice questions in the absence of the reading passages and how these test takers could still manage to score well above the chance level (i.e., 25% with question items with four alternatives). In his study of strategy use on summarization tasks, Cohen (1994b) found that the time some test takers spent going through and applying strategic processing far exceeded the time they spent writing their summaries. And oftentimes, they chose to add whole blocks of the text being summarized to their responses, which made it difficult to decide about the degree to which these test takers actually used their understanding of the text towards constructing their summaries. There is also considerable evidence regarding positive transfer of strategies from L1 to L2 as far as performance on reading tests is concerned. In this regard, Nevo (1989) identified two strategies as the most frequently used ones in both L1 (Hebrew) and L2 (French) among her respondents, including reading the questions first and then looking for the key information in the text and matching clues from the question items to those in the text to locate the key information.

As has been confirmed across studies of strategy use on language tests, test-taking strategies are by and large a function of the testing situation and format; in other words, "[a]s long as the task is part of a test, students are bound to use strategies they would not use under non-testing conditions" (Cohen, 1992, p. 99). Bachman and Palmer's (1996) view of the mediating role of strategic competence between language knowledge and language use is obviously warranted in the context of language testing when we consider how strategies can either facilitate or debilitate performance on language tests. For example, a test taker who chooses to read the questions first on a standardized test of reading has a higher chance of completing the test more quickly and efficiently than one who chooses to read the text first and then proceeds to the questions, assuming that both test takers are at the same level of reading proficiency (Cohen, 1992). Clearly, the use of the first strategy can be said to facilitate test performance, whereas the other strategy may considerably debilitate performance under conditions of timed testing and lack of adequate level of proficiency.

Generally speaking, within the broad field of strategic competence, successful use of strategies demands that strategies be relevant to the nature of the task being performed, strategies be in sync with learner characteristics, and a learner be aware if a strategy is to be used by itself or combined with other strategies and how either form ought to be used (Anderson, 2005). Even those strategies that have been shown to be effective can be more or less so in a given testing situation depending on when and how they are used (Cohen, 1992). Therefore, what Purpura (1998) concluded with regard to how the use of cognitive and metacognitive strategies relates to test performance applies to the case of using test-taking strategies. In other words, the nature of the test task on which a given strategy is used as well as how this strategy is used determine the extent to which this strategy can benefit test performance. Along the same lines, Nikolov (2006) noted that the effective use of test-taking strategies takes into account the degree of compatibility among strategies, the nature of the test task being performed, and command of trends that test takers have developed with the use of these strategies.

The manner in which strategies are used in isolation or in conjunction with other strategies determines their beneficial effect upon test performance and scores (Anderson, 1991). Anderson (1991) based this conclusion on a study in which he looked at individual differences in the use of reading and test-taking strategies among 28 Spanish-speaking adult ESL learners at three different levels of proficiency. Each respondent was asked to take a standardized test of academic reading, in a multiple-choice format, and simultaneously think aloud his or her response behaviors, in either Spanish or English. Based on case studies of three individual respondents, it was found that the high and low scorers did not differ from each other in the kinds of strategies they used. Rather, the two groups of scorers differed in how effectively they used these strategies individually or in conjunction with other strategies, as well as in their ability to assess and monitor strategy use. The researcher referred to the low scorers' limited repertoire of vocabulary and schema-related knowledge as a potential factor that had constrained their strategy use and, in turn, their performance on the test.

In another study confirmatory of the importance of strategic awareness and monitoring during test taking, Phakiti (2003) examined how the use of cognitive and metacognitive strategies by test takers relates to their performance on an EFL reading comprehension test. The researcher had 384 Thai EFL students, at the university level, take an 85-item reading achievement test in a multiple-choice format. Then, the respondents reported their strategy use on the test by answering a cognitive-metacognitive questionnaire. The researcher selected the four highest scorers and the four lowest scorers for retrospective interviews. On the basis of both quantitative and qualitative analyses of the data, it was found that the high scorers demonstrated an elevated degree of awareness of their use of metacognitive strategies in terms of what strategies to use, why they chose these strategies, and how to use them well. The researcher concluded that "[i]ndividual test-takers who are metastrategically competent are more likely to understand how the strategies fit together and how they are related to language tasks or TLU [target language use] domains than those with little of this competence" (p. 49).

Test takers of the TOEFL are commonly encouraged to employ certain test-taking strategies that have been proven useful. The strategies that can be used on the reading section of the test include familiarizing oneself with the test directions before taking it, reading cursorily and taking mental notes of the closest answers, proportioning the allotted time among the number of question items, using any time left to mark the closest answers to question items whose key answers are not known for certain, and marking C or D options if guessing is not promising (Forster, Karn, Suzuki, & Tateyama, 1997, p. 90). Forster et al. (1997) have also highlighted other test-taking strategies when advising test takers to read the questions first and then the passage, postpone answering questions about the main idea or the title of the passage until they have answered the other questions, use elimination of alternatives with questions about excluded facts in order to better discern the key answer, rule out obscure and irrational alternatives, and consider more likely key answers those alternatives that are phrased synonymously with or using the same part of speech as that in the key information in the passage (pp. 120-136). While Forster et al. (1997) were referring specifically to the paper-based format of the TOEFL in giving this account of strategies, their advice is in fact applicable to the computer-based and the internet-based formats of the test. It is obviously the case that on standardized language tests, test takers ought to be familiar with the kinds of test-taking strategies that, as Yien (2001) suggested, can truly mediate between test takers' characteristics including proficiency, and their performance on the test; otherwise, effective strategies would not be characterized as such.

In her study of strategy use on the reading section of the paper-based TOEFL, Tian (2000) worked with a sample of 43 Taiwanese students attending a coaching school. The participants were first asked to take a TOEFL reading practice test and at the same time think aloud their response behaviors. Then, the participants were engaged in a recall task in which they had to write down whatever they could recall from their reading of the test passage. After that, the participants were interviewed as to how they went about preparing for the test and what they thought of the coaching school and the kind of training it offers. A taxonomy of the strategies used was developed, incorporating 42 strategies categorized as technical strategies, reasoning strategies, and self-adjustment strategies. The examinees were divided into three performance levels: high, middle, and low, as determined by their scores on the test.

The results of the study indicated that the high scorers demonstrated substantial use of strategies that focus on global understanding of the passage with the help of the questions. They used the strategies they were trained to use to supplement the kinds of strategies they have developed themselves, and were notably successful in their adapting and personalizing these strategies. On the other hand, the low scorers worked with the test locally by focusing on individual words and isolated constructions, used the trained strategies as their main strategies, and employed these strategies in the same manner they were trained to use them. The high scorers completed the test in less time and exhibited higher ability in comprehension and information retention as measured by the recall task, compared to the low scorers. In general, the high scorers were observed to use fewer strategies than did their low counterparts.

At the level of the three strategy categories, the two performance groups (i.e., high and low scorers) demonstrated variation from each other. In terms of technical strategies, two patterns of variation were apparent. In contrast to the low scorers, the high scorers were found to have developed the ability to start with the passage first and then proceed to the questions and attempt them in the given order, and also the ability to use their understanding of the content of the questions to locate the key information in the text. The two performance groups were different with regard to the level of reasoning they used such that while the low scorers made considerable use of word-based strategies (e.g., matching and association) and micro-level strategies in general, the high scorers were distinctly successful in using macro-level strategies including interpreting and synthesizing the textual information in an effort to get the gist. The use of self-adjustment strategies was more associated with the use of monitoring and as such was a characteristic of the high scorers. Interestingly, the use of elimination strategy was shown to decrease as the performance level increased across the three levels of performance.

All together, the three performance levels reported in the interviews that they often resort to certain test-management strategies, for example, starting with question items first, answering the main idea question after going through the other items, and using word-based strategies and syntactic or semantic clues when confronted with challenging question items. The results of the interviews also revealed what could be one of the major differences among the three performance levels, namely the awareness of how to use test-taking strategies effectively in terms of what strategies to use, when to use them, and how to use them. Such strategic awareness of effective strategy use increases with proficiency level and so augments test performance, as pointed out earlier in other studies (e.g., Anderson, 1991).

Similarly, Nikolov (2006) found that the low scorers among her ESL respondents were more disposed than were high scorers to choose words they were not certain about to complete multiple-matching tasks. This was found through an exploratory study in which Nikolov looked into test-taking strategy use among 12- and 13-year-old EFL learners. A total of 52 participants were randomly sampled so as to represent three levels of proficiency. The data were collected using think-aloud protocols on an individual basis while the respondent was taking a language test comprised of reading and writing tasks. Four case studies were carried out with two top scorers and two bottom scorers, selected on the basis of their scores on the language test. The findings suggested that the two low scorers processed the text at the word level, where the high scorers showed more tendency to process the text at the sentence level and also benefited, more than did the low scorers, from *relating to self* metacognitive strategy by linking the information in the question item to their real-life experiences in order to check their answers. Overall, although the high performers did not show the use of quite as many test-taking strategies, they made more effective use of the strategies they used, when compared to those with low scores.

In the Cohen and Upton (2006) study reviewed earlier, a major strategy trend among the respondents, whom were rated as highly proficient, was the use of more test-management as opposed to test-wiseness strategies. Among the most frequently used strategies across the three reading tasks were *read the question then read the passage/ portion to look for clues to the answer, either before or while considering options*; *consider the options and postpone consideration of the option*; and *discard option(s) based on vocabulary, sentence, paragraph, or passage overall meaning as well as discourse structure* (pp. 46-102). For the most part, these strategies exhibited clear item-type dependency across the three reading tasks.

In his study of test-taking strategy use on the reading section of the TOEFL iBT, reviewed in a previous section, Assiri (2011) found that the manner in which test takers sequenced strategies determined the extent to which their strategy use was effective. Source strategies in strategy sequences possessed both a high level of compatibility with item formats and flexibility of accepting other strategies as attached strategies. Aspects of effective strategy use among test takers can be summarized as follows: a) Certain attached strategies were modified forms of source strategies, b) certain attached strategies endorsed the functions of source strategies, c) source strategies facilitated the functions of attached and subsequent strategies, and d) attached strategies were synchronized with source strategies. Other aspects of effective strategy use were prompted by behaviors of specific strategies in strategy sequences. First, the strategy of option elimination was either synchronized with or used after source strategies in order to reduce the options available for consideration. In three-strategy sequences, the strategy of option elimination assumed either the second position to support the function of a subsequent strategy with BC-*nf*, or the third position to draw on an antecedent strategy with I-*rp*. Second, the strategy of answer confirmation tailed strategy sequences in which it was derived from either a source strategy or an attached strategy, depending on which strategy was critical to the item response. And third, the strategy of deciding on an option tailed strategy sequences in which it served to resolve a state of hesitation between two or more options, as determined by application of an antecedent strategy. It was also found, based on an additional analysis, that the ability to use effective strategy sequences made an important difference between high- and -low scoring groups in favor of the former.

To put it briefly, the previous studies of how test-taking strategy use relates to test performance on reading tasks (e.g., Assiri, 2011; Anderson, 1991; Cohen, 1994b; Nikolov, 2006; Tian, 2000) have shown that the choice and use of test-taking strategies on reading comprehension tests can either facilitate or debilitate test performance depending on whether or not strategies themselves are compatible with the test format, the level of knowledge and awareness of when and how to use a given strategy, and the level of skillfulness in using a given strategy in isolation or in conjunction with other strategies.

Strategy Use and Test Validation

Another intriguing facet to the study of test-taking strategies has to do with how it can inform efforts put into test validation. In fact, exploring test-taking strategy use has been viewed among language testers as one of the most important methods of validating language tests (Cohen & Upton, 2006). The process of test validation serves the purpose of confirming construct validity that stands for the extent to which the test measures the underlying psychological construct or concept, or ability, it purports to measure. Early on, the attempts made to validate language tests benefited from the use of associational or correlational measures that were used to correlate the scores examinees obtained on a certain test with those they had on another, comparable test of the same language skill or ability (Bachman, 1990).

From a strategic standpoint, test validation rests on the question of whether examinees' response behaviors (i.e., test-taking strategies) on a given test conform to the expectations that the test makers have about the test and the purposes for which they designed the test. Language testing experts (e.g., Bachman, 1991) have overemphasized the need to attend to any potential disparity between the test constructors' intentions and test takers' perceptions of the test in the design of the test. Consequently, Bachman (1991) suggests that our study of test-taking strategies for the purpose of test validation provides us with a lens into test performance and reflects the extent to which our test tasks assimilate to real-world uses of language. Test validation can be performed during the pilot phase of test development by having a sample from the target population of examinees take the test and observe their test-taking strategies (Cohen & Upton, 2006). The idea of using test-taking strategies to inform test validation was first initiated in L1 testing and has proven useful in both the refinement and standardization of tests (Cohen, 1984).

The question of what test-taking strategies to use on a given test has to be answered bearing in mind the task or item types that appear on the test (Nevo, 1989). Hence, an incorrect answer to a question item on a test could point out that either the respondent himself failed to answer correctly or the test format influenced the respondent to provide the incorrect answer (Cohen, 1998). Grotjahn (1987), Klein-Braley (1985), and Klein-Braley and Raatz (1984) were among the early researchers who used test-taking strategies as a basis for validating and refining language tests, specifically cloze tasks. The results of their efforts have led to the development of cloze tests that use rational deletion and offer adequate sampling of the language components to be assessed.

In one study, Anderson et al. (1991) attempted to validate a TOEFL reading test in a multiple-choice format by focusing on the relationship between the item types and performances on the test and the test-taking strategies used by their respondents. The researchers found that the question type determined the choice and use of the test-taking strategies to tackle it; for example, wherever respondents were asked to make inferences, some chose to relate and match the content of the question to that of the text. And, wherever a small number of strategies were used, the question items with which such strategies were used were shown to be too easy or too difficult, or less discriminable. Obviously, the number of strategies used with question items can serve to indicate whether these items are adequate as far as their level of difficulty is concerned.

Judgment about the validity of tests is not solely dependent on the behavior of the individual question items on these tests, but on the overall format of these tests as well. In this regard, Tsagari (1994) investigated how the free response format for assessing reading comprehension compares with the multiple-choice format, with a group of ESL learners. On the basis of the examinees' strategy use, Tsagari concluded that the two formats measure reading comprehension differently in that each format calls upon different strategies and so seems to tap into distinct reading abilities. For example, in response to the free response format, students often attempted to locate the key information in the text and use clues to figure out the answer, whereas on the multiple-choice format, students made more use of deductive reasoning and memory.

In a study that aimed to validate a reading test with 13 adult learners of French, Wijgh (1995) observed that test takers' strategy use did not match the test constructors' intentions for the test questions. For example, with question items intended to have test takers scan the text for superficial information, test takers opted for reading the whole text word by word. This led the researcher to suggest as a potential cause that either the test takers were not skilled enough to use appropriate strategies, or the question items themselves failed to call for test takers' strategy use. Abanomey (2002) sought to explore the effect of text authenticity on the use of test-taking strategies. The researcher did not find an effect of text authenticity on the number of test-taking strategies used by respondents as much as on the nature of these strategies. That is, while the authentic texts invoked the use of bottom-up strategies, the inauthentic texts called upon top-down strategies. The researcher ascribed this observation to the fact that inauthentic texts do not possess the kind of textual features (e.g., cohesive devices) that draw on bottom-up strategies.

With the aim of determining what a cloze task truly measures, Storey (1997) had a group of 25 Chinese respondents answer multiple-choice, discourse cloze tests using rational deletion. The researcher noticed that on tests where the deletions involved discourse markers, respondents were prone to detect the line of argumentation and employ the rhetorical organization to supply the deletions. However, where the deletions were cohesive devices, respondents could just rely on local clues to figure out the deletions. The researcher concluded that discourse cloze has the capacity to call upon processing strategies. Such strategies are used at both local and global levels of the text and so are reflective of the kinds of processes involved in reading in non-test-taking conditions.

In two of three recent studies, Lumley and Brown (2004, 2006) looked into the validity of the integrated reading and writing tasks on the Next Generation TOEFL (now TOEFL iBT) with 60 respondents from three language backgrounds. Based on strategy reports collected from the respondents, the researchers were able to identify serious flaws with these tasks in terms of the difficulty among raters of deciding about whether the responses to the writing tasks were in the participants' words or language they copied from the reading texts. In other words, it was not clear how the respondents arrived at their responses to the writing tasks or even how this related to understanding of the reading texts.

Cohen and Upton (2006) attempted to address the question of the extent to which the reading section of the TOEFL iBT truly assesses the kinds of academic reading skills prospective students need to have command of at the university level. The researchers found that test takers dealt with the whole section as demanding of masterful test-taking strategies, and that neither *inferencing* nor the *reading to learn* task types required reading skills distinct from each other. Even so, the researchers concluded that the reading section of the TOEFL iBT adequately measures academic reading skills required at the university level.

In their study of response strategies on multiple-choice reading tests, Rupp et al. (2006) have noticed that whenever test takers were faced with difficult question items, they resorted to logical reasoning on the basis of how a given question item related to the text content; and thus, the test takers were using more lower-order abilities. The respondents also tended to follow the sequence of the questions to get clues as to where the respective key information is located in the text. According to the researchers, these two observations render the taking of multiple-choice reading tests different from reading for a non-testing purpose in terms of strategy use. All things considered, Rupp and his colleagues concluded that

> [Multiple-choice] questions might function well as separable measures of how difficult different aspects of texts are for test-takers or of how well test-takers engage in lower-order component processes rather than as composite measures of higher-order reading comprehension, which they may be sometimes colloquially assumed to be. (p. 468)

Considering that test-taking strategies comprise test-management and test-wiseness techniques, one approach to test validation seeks to ensure that test takers have to rely on the kind of skill or knowledge represented by the test construct to answer the question items more than on test-wiseness. For example, Yang (2000) set out to examine the extent to which test-wiseness impacts performance on the

TOEFL-CBT. First, the researcher had his respondents answer an adaptation of Rogers and Bateson's (1991) Test-wiseness Test and a TOEFL practice test. Based on their scores on the test-wiseness test, two groups were identified—one as test-wise and the other as test-naïve. Then, respondents were asked to report their strategy use with selected items from both the test-wiseness test and the TOEFL-CBT practice test. It was found that test-wiseness could help with at least half of the items from the listening and the reading sections and that test-wise examinees could follow systematic ways in tackling those question items amenable to test-wiseness.

In connection with the above findings, Cohen (2006) suggests that test makers should strive to ensure that their tests are not susceptible to test-wiseness if these tests are to be optimally challenging for examinees. In general, test-wiseness strategies fit in the description that Powers and Wilson Leung (1995) offer when stating that "[s]trategies that raise test scores but bear little, if any, relationship to what the test was designed to measure may diminish the predictive power of a test or dilute the meaning of scores derived from it" (p. 105). This is what also motivated Yamashita (2003) to recommend that test takers' perceptions and opinions about question items be taken into account since test takers are expected to reveal the kinds of strategies that may work for them on given question items, without these strategies being necessarily reflective of the trait or skill being assessed.

Briefly, test validation rests on the question of whether examinees' response strategies on a given test conform to the test maker's expectations or the purposes for which the test was developed. Research has confirmed that the study of test-taking strategy use on reading tests can help us make sure that our tests measure what they are intended to measure, determine how various formats tap into different abilities underlying the main skill of reading comprehension, and ensure that our tests are not susceptible to test-wiseness. This approach has also been found useful in verification of task authenticity; that is, if reading tasks measure the same skills that are part of real-life experiences of reading (e.g., skills of academic reading). One way that can serve as a check of test predictive power is to examine the degree to which high- and low-proficiency groups of test takers differ from each other with respect to their strategy use. Aspects of differential use of strategies by the two proficiency groups on reading tests form the main focus of the next section.

Training of Test-taking Strategy Use on Reading Tasks

A number of researchers (e.g., Anderson, 1991; Nevo, 1989; Nikolov, 2006; Winograd & Hare, 1988) have offered practical implications for test-taking strategy instruction and training. In this respect, Nevo (1989) recommends that teachers work with their students on question formats and items that pose special problems to them. Teachers may want to provide students with ample practice in using strategies that have proven to be helpful, for instance. Nevo (1989) further recommends that learners adhere to test-management strategies that are typically used with certain test formats, including *reading the test instructions and directions carefully, reading the questions and information contained in these questions* (e.g., the options on a multiple-choice test format), and *looking globally at the text rather than focusing on textual chunks or isolated segments.*

Winograd and Hare (1988) encourage teachers to provide as much explanation as necessary to ensure that their students have a grasp of what strategies to use, when and where these strategies can be used, and how to use these strategies and evaluate their use (As cited in Anderson, 1991, p. 470). Nikolov (2006) adopts a conservative approach towards the whole idea of strategy training, suggesting that strategy training does not necessarily benefit all students in the same fashion. Nikolov (2006) might be referring to what the distinction between the two notions of strategy and process seems to imply from the actual implementation of strategy instruction. In other words, teachers can teach and train their students in how to use strategies, but not processes for the reason that the former are conscious and deliberate where the latter are subconscious and unintentional.

It is evident from previous research that the test-taking strategies used on a cloze format are different from those used on a multiple-choice format. Examples of the strategies used on the former include *look backward and forward to figure out the missing word* and *look at larger context after generating the word*, where those used on the latter include *look and process the text globally, predict information, read the question then read the passage/portion to look for clues to the answer, either before or while considering options; consider the options and postpone consideration of the option;* and *discard option(s) based on vocabulary, sentence, paragraph, or passage overall meaning as well as discourse structure* (see Cohen & Upton, 2006). Obviously, these strategies lend themselves to strategy instruction and training as is demonstrated through the following activity.

An illustration of an activity for test-taking strategy instruction

Intended audience: EFL learners at the novice mid-level or higher

Objective: To be able to use three test-taking strategies on multiple-choice reading comprehension tests:

1. read the questions and then read the passage to look for clues to the answer while considering the options,
2. consider the options and postpone consideration of the option, and
3. discard option(s) based on vocabulary, sentence, paragraph, or passage overall meaning.

Materials: 3 multiple-choice reading tasks

Procedures:

Pre-activity (explanation of strategies):

1. The teacher gives the necessary information that students need to know about Strategy 1 above by answering questions such as what the strategy is and when it is used.
2. The teacher performs the first reading task and models for students how Strategy 1 is used to answer the comprehension questions.
3. The teacher repeats Steps 1 and 2 with the other two strategies.

During-activity (practice using strategies):

1. The teacher divides students into pairs, making sure that each weak student works with one of the strong students.
2. The teacher has the students do the second reading task and apply the three strategies, one at a time, to answer the comprehension questions.
3. The teacher elicits feedback from students as to how they went about applying the three strategies and whether they encountered any problems or have any questions.

Post-activity (assessing strategy use):

1. The teacher arranges to sit with each student individually and has the student perform the third reading task and apply the three strategies to answer the comprehension questions.
2. As each student performs the reading task, he/she verbalizes how they apply the three strategies.
3. The teacher provides each student with the needed feedback.
4. The teacher point outs for the whole class any major problems individual students seem to have in common.

In conclusion, test-taking strategy instruction and training can make use of thorough explanations that answer the five questions: what strategies to use; where, when, and why certain strategies should be used; how these strategies can be used; and how to evaluate their use. Teachers are encouraged to acquaint themselves, and in turn their students, with test-taking strategies that have been proven helpful, and offer their students plenty of opportunity to practice using these strategies in situations similar to those of actual test taking.

Formats of Oral Assessment

Language teachers who teach oral skills cannot dispense with the familiarity with a variety of assessment formats. Such familiarity can guide their choice as to what format to employ bearing on the level of their students. One format to assess oral skills that suits a certain level of proficiency may not do those at another level any fairness. There are assessment formats for oral skills that teachers can modify to match their assessment goals.

Role-plays are among the most useful formats used in proficiency-oriented assessment. They represent a naturalistic and motivating alternative to interviews whose use usually informs decisions about job appointments and academic admissions. Interviews are not usually preferred with candidates who tend to exhibit excessive anxiety. Another useful format to use especially with low-level learners is picture-cued conversations in which a pair of students can take turns asking each other about a set of pictures. For example, assuming that the goal of the oral assessment is to measure the extent to which students have mastered job descriptions, the teacher may have two students converse with each other using two pictures; each picture shows a person performing some kind of profession. Each student's task here is to ask his partner what the person in the picture is doing and the partner answers (see the next section for illustrations). From my experience as an ESL instructor who taught oral skills at the beginners' level, I found using picture-cued conversations a very motivating and practical format of oral assessment. More important, it is oriented to communicative language use.

Generally, novice teachers are advised not to use one assessment format or the other of mere preference, but to make sure that the format they use is valid and reliable to use with a given level of learners. In addition, teachers are encouraged to familiarize themselves with the kinds of procedures and steps to follow when using a certain assessment format and take the time planning their assessments.

Student-student Interactions as a Form of Oral Assessment

Teachers usually use their interviews with their students to assess their oral skills. The teacher interviews each student, maybe in the classroom or the hallway. The teacher is the one who asks the questions all the time and the student's task is to answer each question. Thus, in a sense, this interviewing style may not be different from that of a job interview. The kind of conversational communication among speakers in their real world is almost lacking. In this article, another technique for oral assessment that uses student-student interaction is proposed and illustrated.

In student-student interactions, the teacher is the organizer (or mediator). She decides which student can start the interaction and whose turn is next. The interaction can be spontaneous by having the students ask each other a predetermined set of questions. For example,

Ahmad: Hi. How're you?
Ali: Fine, thank you. And you?
Ahmad: I'm fine. What's your name?
Ali: My name is Ali Almuqren. What's your name?
Ahmad: Ahmad Alnamr. How old are you?
Ali: I'm eighteen years old. And you?
Ahmad: I'm seventeen years old. Where're you from?

    Ali: I'm from Taif. Where're you from?
    Ahmad: I'm from Abha. ...

This illustration uses questions about personal information in the EFL context of Saudi Arabia. Of course, other questions can be added to the list of questions as deemed appropriate. Such questions may elicit information for home address, phone number, email, hobbies or interests, daily schedule ... etc. Students may be provided with cards with information prompts especially if the teacher feels they may get nervous or confused.

Another variation of student-student interactions may use handouts that incorporate images and/or prompts. This serves to ensure that students initiate and maintain interaction about specific or domain-related topics. To illustrate, the images may represent everyday activities like eating, washing, studying, playing ... etc.:

Instructions: Use *where* and then the present progressive tense (be + V-ing).

The teacher asks either student to use the first picture to ask the other student.

Badr: Where're you, Khaled?
Khaled: I'm at the sports hall.
Badr: What're you doing?
Khaled: I'm exercising.

The teacher asks the other student who was answering the questions in the first turn to initiate another conversation using the other picture.

Khaled: Where're you, Badr?
Badr: I'm in my bedroom.
Khaled: What're you doing?
Badr: I'm studying.

It is important to note here that this form of oral assessment presumes that students are used to the use of the visual and/or textual information in the handouts to initiate and maintain their interaction. If students are not used to it, they can be offered practice before the assessment date.

Pros and cons

Using student-student interaction, the content and format of oral assessment can be made similar to what students do in their regular classes. The teacher can copy pictures and their captions from the class materials and may try to modify the captions as desired to include them in handouts intended for use in oral assessment. When students are used to this style of turn-taking communication during classes, they are expected to perform well when it is time to put their oral skills to the test. This certainly strengthens the relationship between learning and testing and leads to positive effect of testing on learning (or positive washback). It is obvious that this technique can save teachers and students tremendous amount of time, which would allow them to cover more course material. Teachers can also save a lot of effort and boredom linked to interviewing students on an individual basis. Students may find their face-to-face interaction with their classmates motivating and rewarding.

However, there are certain problems that affect the adequacy of using student-student interactions in oral assessment. First, the fact that students are different in their oral skills may cause stronger students to perform less than expected when interacting with weaker students. In fact, a stronger student may experience lack of understanding what a weaker student is trying to say, because of mistakes in grammar or pronunciation, or both. Nonetheless, there are remedies to these flaws. A stronger student may manage to predict what his weaker counterpart is going to say and respond accordingly, more noticeably when visual and/textual prompts are being used. Otherwise, the teacher may intervene when necessary to recast the weaker student's question or answer. This is to ensure that stronger students are not disadvantaged by the poor communication skills of their partners.

Conclusion

Weighing the pros and cons of student-student interactions, we can safely conclude that we cannot abandon the whole technique because of a couple of problems. The gains of having students interact with each other as part of the assessment of their skills outweigh the pains. This technique is obviously similar to role-plays, but differs in that it is more useful with students at lower levels of language proficiency. Low-level learners may not interact well in the absence of prompts rich in visual and/or textual information. The audience of students who see their classmates as they are interacting with each other can also practice listening to a conversation not totally different from real-world communication.

Chapter 5

Personal Views of EL2 Teaching, Learning, and Testing

- ☐ Philosophy of Language Teaching and Learning
- ☐ Bringing Behaviorism and Nativism Together
- ☐ Paradigm Shift from Empiricism to Rationalism
- ☐ Response to Scholarly Views on the Principle Weaknesses of SLA Research
- ☐ Grammatical Competence as Part of Communicative Competence
- ☐ Native Speakers' Attitudes to Non-native Speakers' Speech
- ☐ Use of Teaching Aids in Pre-reading/-listening Activities and Comprehension
- ☐ Applying Designs of Listening Lessons to Reading Lessons
- ☐ Computer-assisted versus Computer-based Language Learning
- ☐ An Interview with an ESL Learner
- ☐ TESOL Quarterly as a Journal of Second Language Research and Practice

This chapter presents the author's views of aspects pertinent to language learning and testing.

Philosophy of Language Teaching and Learning

- **Language theory**. The *interactionist perspective*: Language acquisition is the result of the interaction between linguistic input from the environment and the innate, mental faculty in the human brain.

- **Goals***:* The goals of language teaching and learning serve both the teacher the learner.
  - *Teacher's general goals:* Teach according to the general and specific objectives of the language program and to the best of his knowledge and experience.
  - *Teacher's specific goals:* Meet the specific objectives of the course he teaches.
  - *Learner's general goals:* Act in accordance with the general and specific objectives of the language program.
  - *Learner's specific goals:* Achieve the specific objectives of the course he is studying.

- **Language learning***:* As a process, it involves the interaction of a variety of factors, and thus its success depends on the extent to which these factors are made supportive to the overall learning process.

- **Content***:*
  - *Aspects of language:* More functional (i.e., have to do with language use).
  - *Perspective on accuracy:* Content should place equal emphasis on both accuracy and fluency.
  - *Evaluation:* Content needs to be evaluated in terms of the extent to which it meets the general and specific objectives of the course of study.

- **Instruction***:*
  - *Materials* need to be relevant to the purpose of the course, contextualized, and authentic.
  - *Techniques* are proficiency-oriented, meaningful, and communicative.
  - *Approach* is eclectic in which the teacher selects what is helpful and useful among different techniques and practices.
  - *The role of the teacher* is a mentor and facilitator of learning.
  - *The role of the student* is an active learner and user of the language.

- **Student-teacher relationship:**
  - *The learning climate* is friendly, mutual, and overall conducive to learning.
  - *Interaction patterns:* Turn-taking is natural involving both student-teacher and student-student interactions with more talk from students.

Bringing Behaviorism and Nativism Together

Since I first knew of the behaviorist and the nativist approaches and how each view explains the process of language acquisition, I have kept wondering until this moment why cannot these two contrasting views be brought together. In other words, why cannot we come up with a theory that explains how language is acquired on the basis of both innate and environmental factors? In my view, a more viable account of language acquisition needs to address at least two sets of factors that pertain to the mental and behavioral domains. Language learning benefits from both the input from the environment and an endowed human-specific ability to acquire a language. Such a mental capacity can be equated with Chomsky's *Language Acquisition Device*. Therefore, a learner receives linguistic input in the form of stimuli from the environment and then her mental processes act upon the input to make it available for language production.

That is to say, I tend to support the interactionist perspective as it lends equal support to the role of both the in-built, genetically determined ability and the input from the surroundings in language acquisition. Although cognitive theory seems to have met this requirement, it clearly assigns a limited role to the environment that represents the immediate source of input. Such a fact renders cognitive theory more on the nativist or rationalist side. I agree with the cognitive approach with regard to the transition of language skills to be learned from controlled to automatic processes. I find this highly applicable to the case of language skills learned in formal settings such as reading and writing. However, the cognitive approach does not explain how language acquisition naturally takes place in the light of controlled versus automatic processing distinction, or the controlled-automatic continuum as Schmidt (1992) suggests. That is, cognitive theory lacks explanatory power when we consider how child language acquisition occurs in comparison to language learning where adults can exert more control over their learning.

In short, I support the formulation of a comprehensive model of language acquisition that takes into account all the aspects and merits of the previous models and refine them in the light of ongoing empirical research. When we have such a model ready, we can start to direct our attention to its practical implications in the field of language acquisition.

Paradigm Shift from Empiricism to Rationalism

Since the early 1940s, the development of language teaching approaches and methods has proceeded hand in hand with the paradigm shift in language acquisition theory from empiricism to rationalism. This has also been in company of the paradigm shift in linguistic theory from structuralism to mentalism. There are some traces of how the theoretical models of linguistics and language acquisition have influenced the assumptions and bases underlying the various teaching approaches and methods, starting specifically from audiolingualism to suggestopedia. On the basis of my aforementioned, proposed combination of the merits of empiricism and rationalism, I feel inclined here to suggest that a combination of techniques and practices from the various approaches and methods of language teaching can prove more useful than adhering to a single approach or method.

Since the early 1970s, there has been a mass movement among language teaching educators towards adopting an eclectic approach by selecting among the various techniques and practices from the various methods and approaches. Some efforts have been directed at customizing a single approach or method to meet local needs (Hadley, 2001). These trends were noticeably practical, especially if we consider the wide variety of language teaching contexts where a single approach or method is certainly not sufficient. Add to the variation of language teaching contexts the variability that exists among language learners in terms of mentality, personality, affect, and perhaps more importantly language competency. All of these factors dictate that we be flexible in our teaching practices by selecting techniques that we have found useful. Obviously, what distinguishes one approach or method from another is what techniques to use, when, and how. And, when we pay due consideration to the teaching context and the class of learners we are dealing with, we will be better able to make adequate choices as to the kinds of teaching techniques to use.

Response to Scholarly Views on the Principle Weaknesses of SLA Research

The purpose of this section is to briefly summarize scholarly views in regard to some principles of SLA research, and then respond and critique these views.

According to the first view, one of the major weaknesses associated with SLA research is that the data collected from contexts in English-speaking countries specifically the UK and the US have been overwhelmingly more than those collected from other contexts (e.g., Africa, Asia, Europe, and Latin America). Moreover, the findings from the latter contexts have been dealt with in such a way so that they do not influence the findings and theories emerging from the former contexts. This view maintains that, on this basis, such terms as native speaker, competence, and fossilization need to be re-evaluated from a bi-/multilingual perspective rather than a monolingual alone. The adoption of such notions in most SLA studies has caused the whole SLA research, due to the monolingual perspective, to be biased. With respect to the notions of native speaker and competence, this view suggests that using Chomsky's view of 'ideal speaker—listener' competence as a yardstick, on the basis of which learner's competence is judged, is a flaw. This is because this Chomskyan view is not actually applicable to actual native speakers in real life situations. It has also rendered evidence from research adopting it uncertain.

This view also suggests that fossilization has been studied in isolation from contexts where an L2 or AL (additional language) serves as a means of socialization. Similarly, considering L2 or AL acquisition to imply ability to use an L2 or AL in a similar way as monolingual native speakers do is a serious misconception. The reason for this is that bi-/multilinguals use their own 'composite competence' to serve their needs of language socialization and interaction. This view argues that research in language socialization has shown that the 'composite competence' is the result of acquiring linguistic competence and socio-cultural competence that interact with each other and, as a result, dictates what and how bi-/multilinguals communicate in an L2 or LA. In this sense, what can be perceived as a fossilized item from the monolingual perspective is rather a sign of a 'composite competence' intended to serve a social, interactive purpose. One reason for this bias is that research evidence from bi-/multilingual contexts is not justifiable from a monolingual perspective. And that, in order for SLA research to be valid and reliable, research from contexts of world Englishes that are by nature bi-/multilingual needs to be involved.

Along the same lines, another view asserts that research data from non-Western, bilingual communities has been rarely considered in the SLA field, and that L2 learners from these contexts are marginalized. This puts findings from SLA research under scrutiny. Because of this bias, specific cultural premises are universalized, irrelevant methods and concerns are uncritically adopted, and generalizations are based on narrow data. Consequently, this view recommends a 'reality check' to evaluate SLA theories with due consideration to the following facts:

- An L2 does not replace an L1; it is used along with it.
- Considerable L2 acquisition occurs in non-native contexts.
- Successful L2 acquisition is attained through formal instruction.
- L2 learners are mostly instrumentally motivated.
- English is not the only L2 learned worldwide.
- International communication is achieved by languages that are not usually the users' L1s.

Similar to the first, the second view maintains that the notion of 'idealized' native speaker's competence is unfounded. This is because this notion is inapplicable to contexts where the language users are non-native and it disregards bilingualism as well as variation among native speakers. The second view refers to the Bloomfieldian duplicative model as another source of this problem because it assumes that an 'ideal bilingual' would be one who has a native-like attainment of both L1 and L2. This view considers this model 'naive', seeing that bilingualism goes well with L1 competence rather than replicating it. According to the second view, the adoption of this model resulted in placing the vast majority of L2 speakers around the world at different stages of interlanguage development. Such claims, according to this view, are based on Selinker's (1972) notion of fossilization.

The proponents of this view believe that SLA models have dichotomized L1 and L2 by suggesting that resorting to L1 is generally a hindrance preventing from a native-like competency in L2. This in turn renders some strategies of using L1 to facilitate the learning of L2 (e.g., code switching or mixing, transfer, and convergence) unsuitable. Such a dichotomy extends to influence how languages interact in multilingual contexts. Transfer, for example, is often 'stigmatized' in that it is seen helpful in some multilingual contexts, but obstructive in some others; consequently, its affective, psycholinguistic, referential, acculturating, and historical roles are disavowed all together. Because SLA models are generally influenced by Western cultural views, their cross-cultural validation research is more a replication than an exploration. The solution is to re-establish SLA theory such that it becomes "more functionally oriented and culturally authentic" with a renewed look at multilinguals as having their own linguistic repertoire in their own rights. Thus, bias does exist in SLA theory and research because no consideration has been given to other contexts and matters other than those of the monolingual perspective.

For the most part, I agree with the two views that little research and few learners have been taken into account when SLA theories and models were formulated. However, should this lead us to question the whole field or distrust current L2 teaching and learning programs? Shall we wait until all studies and all L2 learners from all around the world are taken into account in SLA theories and models? Or, have not any of the SLA theories and models been proven applicable to a number of non-native contexts? The claims that SLA theory and research are totally biased, and so are dubious are simply exaggerated.

I agree with both views about the incongruity of Chomsky's notion of 'idealized speaker-listener' as this model has been criticized for not considering performance variables (Brown, 2007). It is plausible to assume that native speakers' competence is distinct from that of non-native speakers because a lot of variables intervene, affecting non-native speakers' attainment of native-like competence. Some of these variables have to do with the learner himself, and some others can be attributed to the learning environment. Using the term 'composite competence' to describe the type of competence that non-native speakers have is rational since it has its own characteristics that distinguish it from native speakers'. One characteristic is that 'composite competence' is used to serve a purpose of social interaction, among speakers of a community, which may not be otherwise accomplishable. It adequately characterizes the way we should look at L2 learner's competence; that is to say, L2 competence goes well with L1 competence.

Nevertheless, a question can be raised as to whether any situation justifies an ungrammatical or unacceptable usage. My personal belief is that caution needs to be exercised among bi-/multilinguals in non-native contexts because fossilization is more likely to be fertilized. This is due to the fact that speech is less monitored in such contexts. These contexts are more likely to have the type of "positive affective and cognitive feedback" that nutrifies fossilization (Vigil & Oller, 1976). As linguists do, I view that grammaticality and acceptability are the bottom line, or else varieties of English will emerge and so English as a language for international communication will lose its status with time. In fact, it is because of such an influential status and wide spread of English in the world that the English-speaking countries have long been accused of 'linguistic imperialism' (Phillipson, 1992). It is my hope that this trend has not found its way to the growing field of SLA.

I advocate applying fossilization to contexts where an L2 or AL has societal roles for the reason that if a certain utterance is ungrammatical, then we may pose questions: Can it still be acceptable? Can it be used to achieve a certain purpose while the listener is having difficulty making sense of the message? Or, does this mean such situations or contexts are fossilization-free? My suggestion here would be the use of "stabilization" rather than 'fossilization' to indicate a possibility for development (Long, 2003), and to be on the watch of the criticisms launched against the term 'fossilization'. While the second view suggests that fossilization has been used to imply that the majority of L2 speakers are at stages of their interlanguages, I believe that fossilization is not as problematic as the term 'interlanguage' itself. 'Interlanguage' entails an endless stage through which a language learner has to make his way of language learning. Not only is this term mistakenly coined, it is also distressing and despairing to both language learners and teachers.

The claim that an L1 prevents from an L2 native-like proficiency needs to be moderated. The scathing criticism of the Grammar Translation method led to undermining the role of the L1 in the facilitation of the L2 learning. Notably, in the initial stages of L2 learning, learners need to make a reasonable use of their L1 to get along well with the L2. However, as learners proceed, their L1 should gradually be less used. At later stages, however, an L1 can do more of harm to L2 attainment than of a benefit.

As the second view suggests, considerable research conducted in non-native contexts is replication of what has been carried out in native contexts. A possible reason is that researchers in the former contexts, assuming that they have the resources they need or even motives for researching, are tempted to replicate and not to innovate. In fact, a number of factors cause research outside the native contexts to be less considered. Among these factors are sometimes major flaws in the research design or methodology used that render the validity of such research questionable. Moreover, if the tendency in non-native contexts is apparently to replicate research, then we expect considerable amount of this type of research to be left behind. We may also want to consider the meager amount of research done in these contexts when compared to that in native contexts. It is important that we address such potential factors before we charge SLA theory and research with bias. Rather than doing the whole field of SLA a disfavor by questioning its premises, we ought to suggest new directions for theorizing and researching in areas we feel still lacking.

Grammatical Competence as Part of Communicative Competence

There is the controversy as to whether grammatical competence needs to be part of communicative competence, as noted by Canale and Swain (1980). The concept of communicative competence encompasses four components: grammatical, sociolinguistic, discourse, and strategic. The earlier views of communicative competence tended to include grammatical competence as a major component on an equal footing with the other components, if we consider Canale and Swain's (1983) view for instance. However, some other views of communicative competence unjustifiably discounted the status of grammatical competence. For example, Campbell and Wales (1970) considered grammaticality less important than appropriateness as far as language use is concerned. Some scholarly views were so extreme that they looked at communicative competence and grammatical competence as two dichotomous entities. Nonetheless, scholars such as Hymes (1972) and Munby (1978) have attested to the importance of treating grammatical competence as one component of communicative competence. They argued that this has to be the case if communicative competence is to remain a viable framework for language knowledge and use.

In the earlier 1970s, the status of grammar in language classrooms started to diminish because of the negative outcomes in terms of language attainment. It was this attitude towards grammar that has noticeably influenced the view of grammatical competence as well as its relevance to communicative competence. However, from my experience when I was a language learner, when grammatical forms and rules are practiced in meaningful contexts, this considerably contributes to the mastery of both language form and use. One important implication here is that the extent to which language materials present forms and rules in meaningful situations determines the level of language attainment and proficiency. This is also affected by the extent to which teaching practices allow learners to practice these forms and rules in lifelike situations. I remember that a textbook entitled *English Grammar in Use*—Murphy (2012) being its latest edition—was of special interest and help to me in this respect as it truly combines presentation of grammatical forms and practice of how to use these forms in meaningful, real-life situations.

There is ample research evidence that suggests that learning grammar explicitly or with *focus on form* can result in language forms and rules being internalized. In other words, explicit knowledge of grammar can become implicit, which endorses automatic language use. Language learning programs almost all over the globe have continued to offer grammar classes across the various levels of proficiency. As Canale and Swain (1983) maintained, language learners can benefit greatly if grammatical forms and rules are practiced using meaningful contexts and when language teaching and learning become more integrated by incorporating various skills. This is to highlight the importance of giving adequate consideration to grammar in the framework of communicative competence seeing it a necessity for achieving a high level of language proficiency.

213

Native Speakers' Attitudes to Non-native Speakers' Speech

Native speakers' judgment of non-native speech is a function of a number of factors. First, the question of who are the native speakers and who are the non-native speakers needs to be addressed in the form of a detailed description that reflects how each group of speakers differs from the other. Second, the question of what attitudes each group of speakers has towards the other needs to be addressed in light of language attitude studies. Third and last, the question of whether or not the judges in the previous studies are native or non-native speakers also needs to be taken into account; for example, the Spanish non-native raters in Galloway (1980) focused more on the form in their judgment of non-native speech in contrast to the native raters who focused on the message. There are certainly practical implications that we can draw from the previous studies of native speakers' judgment of non-native speech. I postulate that addressing the above-mentioned factors in the design of future studies can result in our findings becoming more reliable and generalizable to other contexts. By extension, we will be better able to draw more consistent implications for classroom practice in these contexts.

Use of Teaching Aids in Pre-reading/-listening Activities and Comprehension

Pre-reading/pr-listening activities can serve at least one of two purposes for a class of learners. First, they can bridge the gap between what the learners already know about a topic and the new information through the activation of the relevant schemata. Second, they can help prepare learners to deal with a new topic or area that is not likely to be part of their prior knowledge. In spite of the advantages of using such advance organizers, teachers ought to be cautious that a number of factors may interfere with the beneficial effects of using these tools. First, learners differ in terms of the extent to which they benefit from the teacher's use of advance organizers depending on their levels of proficiency. Highly proficient learners may profit from the use of textual aids whereas those at lower levels of proficiency tend to make more use of visual aids. Second, there is some evidence that learners do not benefit from the activation of their prior knowledge in the same way because of such factors as individual and cultural differences among them. This, in turn, calls for the teachers' provision of interesting and familiar topics. Third, learners' activation and recall of prior knowledge in relation to existing material depends on the syntactic complexity of such material. The more a text is syntactically complex, the less likely the learners will be able to activate and recall prior knowledge relevant to the topic of the text.

Fourth, teachers need to be attentive to the attitudes that learners may have towards the use of certain advance organizers or the content presented through these aids. This is because ill-chosen materials can considerably retard the activation of the necessary schemata (Hadley, 2001). Fifth and last, it is important that the rhetorical structure of the material to be presented assimilate to what the learners are familiar with when dealing with the same genre. For example, if the rhetorical structure of a story does not follow the pattern learners expect when reading a story, their comprehension of this story is likely to be negatively affected. In a nutshell, advance organizers can certainly be used to facilitate comprehension and so promote learning; however, teachers need to be attentive to the factors listed above. Manifestly, such factors determine the degree to which learners can benefit from the use of advance organizers. Research by Lin and Chen (2006) pointed out that using questions as advance organizers substantially augmented comprehension of texts on content areas among a group of EFL learners.

Applying Designs of Listening Lessons to Reading Lessons

The discussion in this section will center upon describing functions and responses that can be made part of reading lessons in the light of Lund's (1990) description of those functions and responses in the context of listening comprehension. Therefore, the six functions that can be used in reading comprehension instruction are as follows:

- *Identification:* students identify single words, word categories or parts of speech, and language codes in general.
- *Orientation:* students work to recognize the variables represented in the reading such as the topic, situation, participants ... etc.
- *Main idea comprehension:* students try to figure out the main idea of the reading by means of global understanding of the text.
- *Detail comprehension:* students understand the points supporting the main idea, but not necessarily the specific details.
- *Full comprehension:* students understand the points supporting the main idea, including the specific details.
- *Replication:* students work to make a replica of the reading while maintaining the overall purpose and meaning of the text.

By the same token, the nine responses that students can use when responding to reading comprehension tasks include:

- *Doing:* students act physically in response to a certain reading task or activity.
- *Choosing:* students respond to reading tasks that engage them in making choice or selection.
- *Transferring:* students perform another kind of reading activity in order to transfer aspects of their comprehension.

- *Answering:* students answer comprehension questions.
- *Condensing:* students prepare an outline, take notes, or write a summary of what they have read.
- *Extending:* students elaborate or add some details to the text in some way.
- *Duplicating:* students look for indications or signs to verify the accuracy of a replica of the text.
- *Modeling:* students try to replicate the model followed in writing the text.
- *Conversing:* students engage in conversation about the reading.

The connection I have made above, and may be more of an extension, is due in part to the similarity shared by listening and reading skills, being receptive in nature.

Computer-assisted versus Computer-based Language Learning

I tend to support the idea of using computer facilities as assistive tools, and not using them as main tools for language teaching and learning. My position here stems from my acquaintance with a number of drawbacks associated with the use of computer facilities to replace normal classroom practices. It is the teacher's responsibility to ensure that language learning is improved and assisted by the use of computer technology (Hani, 2014). While in preparation programs, student teachers should be acquainted with the necessary knowledge and skills that enable them to make adequate uses of computer technology in their classrooms in the future (Gee, 2013; Lin, Wang & Lin, 2012; Tezci, 2011).

First, human face-to-face interaction is absent in most of, if not all, computer-assisted language learning settings when it is important for language learners to develop necessary skills for using verbal and non-verbal aspects of communication. And, if certain computer programs use some interactive features that are analogous to those of human face-to-face interaction, they are still limited for a simple reason—no one of the participant in the interaction involved is aware of the other. Second, the use of electronic texting can foster in learners the use of informal ways for expressing themselves such as the use of short forms or abbreviations especially when this occurs without their receiving the necessary, spontaneous feedback. Add to this, using electronic texting may result in the absence of pragmatic and sociocultural functions that are important in the target language such as those related to social power and distance (Kern, 1998).

Third, in the use of computer as a medium for language learning there is the absence of the model of the target language use (i.e., the teacher). It is often the case that language learners mainly at the beginning levels view their language teachers as models they need to follow and imitate. This is especially true in the case of the writing skill; for example, beginning-level learners need to see how to hand-write while maintaining the distinct shape of each letter and the norms of writing in the target language. Fourth and last, the use of computer-mediated language learning demands high spending on hardware installation as well as unending technical support. As an example from actual practice, at the intensive language program where I teach, the people in charge spent a lot of money and worked hard to set up computer labs. When using these labs, on numerous occasions I had to send one or two students to another lab because of the shortage in the number of working computers. Besides, I noticed from time to time that some students stopped using their computers, and when I asked why they said they got bored with using the same program every time.

To conclude, as its name suggests, computer-assisted language learning should not replace normal classroom practices; rather, it should be used supplementarily.

An Interview with an ESL Learner

This section reports on an interview conducted with the goal of getting insights into the language learning experience of an ESL learner. My interviewee is a 40-year-old man from Libya. He is married and has two children. His main academic goal of attending a US mid-west university is to pursue his Ph.D. in electrical engineering. He chose to attend a U.S. university because he believes that the U.S. stands at the top of the world with its leading academic programs that emphasize both coursework and research. As for his experiences in the U.S. so far, he has a very good impression about the people here in general. He feels that they show understanding and cooperation to foreigners and tolerance of their potential language deficiency. In general, he likes good habits and personal traits of Americans such as helpfulness, honesty, and punctuality. In his spare time, he likes to play football, go swimming, and do physical exercises. He also likes to read about religion and history and watch TV. His primary interests are to spend as much time as possible with his family and have some time with his friends.

He believes that English can best be learned through an independent effort from the learner that involves mastery of vocabulary in terms of pronunciation and spelling, the use of intensive reading and the practice of reading comprehension skills, and the engagement of oneself into oral interaction with English speakers. In this respect, he puts great emphasis on practice to foster the automaticity of the ESL learned aspects, suggesting that practice makes perfect "practice … practice … practice". He maintains that intensive reading is his most frequently used technique to build up his vocabulary repertoire and compensate for the lack of immediate human interaction in English. His reflection of how English is taught in his home country shows that the teacher-based instruction is the most dominant mode of English education. Besides, the amount of exposure to English at school, mainly middle and secondary schools, was not sufficient for them as learners to achieve a satisfactory level of language proficiency.

One of the major problems they also encountered was that most of their English teachers lacked native-like pronunciation as well as language teaching competency. He asserts that as English learners, they assume part of the responsibility for not achieving higher standards of English proficiency and that was due to the little effort they used to exert out of the class. He mentions that his motivation at these stages was high as he was looking forward to being admitted to a university that requires a high grade in English. At the university, he had to take two courses in English basics for science students. Upon his graduation, he joined a petroleum company back home, where a large number of employees were English native speakers. This compelled him to enroll in an English language program that offers intensive training in reading, grammar, writing, listening, and speaking. Such a language learning experience was so enriching that it paved his way towards a successful completion of the requirements of a master's degree in science at the University of Liverpool in the United Kingdom. He thinks that he has not developed a quite reasonable amount of language learning strategies except for those commonly observed among language learners, including the use of a dictionary upon seeing an unfamiliar word, word repetition through writing and pronunciation, and intensive reading for pleasure.

At the time of the interview, the interviewee as well as a number of his fellow citizens were attending an English language institute that is part of the US mid-west university. They were specifically at the fourth level of their language program. He described his experience at the language program as "good", and his teachers as nice and competent. He and his Libyan classmates like to work together, share learning experiences, and converse in English. When asked about his motivation, he said "it is high", because he is longing for excellence in his English learning and later on his graduate study. He further suggested that he has both types of motivation, that is, instrumental and integrative. He thinks that a language learner should integrate himself into the second language culture and community to practice his aural and oral communication skills.

TESOL Quarterly as a Journal of Second Language Research and Practice

It was first published in 1967.

Why TESOL Quarterly?

- It is a professional, refereed, international journal
- It is tailored to the interests of practitioners in English language teaching and learning.
- It offers a multitude of cross-disciplinary topics in a variety of areas.
- It contributes to bridging theory and practice in English language teaching and learning.
- It also allows for sharing of a myriad of reflections and experiences from diverse contexts around the world (TESOL, 2007).

An overview of TESOL Quarterly:

- TESOL Quarterly, as its name suggests, is published four times a year.
- The editorial board consists of distinguished scholars with opulent expertise in ESL theory, practice, and research. Most of them are teaching faculty in well-known graduate programs in TESL.
- The editorial board serves as an advisory body for *TESOL Quarterly* policy and operations. Each member reviews approximately 10-12 manuscripts per year, recommends additional reviewers, and advises on editorial decisions.

Mohammed S. Assiri

- The target audience is a broad readership that includes practitioners in the fields of English language teaching and learning as well as interested individuals and parties.
- The research methodologies and designs followed in research articles represent both the quantitative and qualitative paradigms: case studies, surveys, ethnographies, corpus-based and discourse analysis studies, experimental and quasi-experimental studies, classroom-based and action research, and responsive evaluations.
- There are typically six sections in the journal, characterizing its submission categories:
  - Articles that present empirical research and analyze original data obtained using sound research methods. At times, this section features reflective articles (or think pieces).
  - Reviews of professional books that provide descriptive and evaluative summaries and brief discussions.
  - Review articles that focus on several publications that fall into a topical category (e.g., pronunciation, literacy training, teaching methodology … etc.).
  - Brief reports and summaries that present preliminary findings or focus on some aspects of a larger study.
  - A forum that publishes four types of articles: commentaries on current trends and practices, responses to published articles and reviews, and brief discussions of research and practice issues.
  - Response articles that critique and react to published works in the journal.

Submission guidelines

In the "For authors" section, TESOL Quarterly encourages submissions of unpublished articles on topics of significance to the target audience. The submitted manuscripts should address the implications and applications of research in such areas as theoretical and applied linguistics, English education, psycholinguistics, first and second language acquisition, and sociolinguistics. Authors are encouraged to adhere to the journal guidelines regarding the accessibility and practicality of their potential submissions as well as manuscript format and length. The journal prefers a writing style and presentation that suit various categories of audiences. Also, all submissions should accord with the requirements of the *Publication Manual of the American Psychological Association (6th ed.).*

My impressions of TESOL Quarterly

I see TESOL Quarterly possess the following qualities:

- A slow and gradual development in the direction of practicality of language teaching and learning.
- A change towards encompassing the major developments in second language theory. The majority of topics discussed in the journal are colored by the most recent theory of second language acquisition, or so-called the constructivist view.
- A considerable number of articles address language aspects and skills (e.g., writing, grammar, accent, speech, pronunciation, reading, listening … etc.). Therefore, these trends in the published topics appear to cast a shadow upon the others, still some other topics are dealt with adequately.
- In general, accumulating theory and research evidence that brings about new theoretical perspectives and research topics.

References

Abanomey, A. (2002). *The effect of texts' authenticity on reading-comprehension test-taking strategies used by adult Saudi learners of English as a foreign language* (Doctoral dissertation). Available from ProQuest Dissertation and Theses database (UMI No. 3069767)

Abello-Contesse, C. (2009). Age and the critical period hypothesis. *ELT Journal: English Language Teachers Journal, 63*(2), 170-172.

Abukhattala, I. (2013). Krashen's five proposals on language learning: Are they valid in Libyan EFL classes? *English Language Teaching, 6*(1), 128-131.

ACTFL. (2012). *ACTFL proficiency guidelines for writing.* Retrieved March 17, 2013 from http://actflproficiencyguidelines2012.org/writing

Aebersold, J. & Field, M. (1997). *From reader to reading teacher: Issues and strategies for second language classrooms.* Cambridge: Cambridge University Press.

Afflerbach, P., Pearson, P., & Paris, S. (2008). Skills and strategies: Their differences, their relationships, and why it matters. In K. Mokhtari & R. Sheorey (Eds.), *Reading strategies of first- and second-language learners: See how they read* (pp. 11-24). Norwood, MA: Christopher-Gordon.

Alderson, J. (2000). *Assessing reading.* Cambridge: Cambridge University Press.

Alderson J., & Banerjee, J. (2002). Language testing and assessment (Part 2). *Language Teaching, 35,* 79-113.

Alexander, P., & Jetton, T. (2000). Learning from text: A multidimensional and developmental perspective. In M. L. Kamil, P. B. Mosenthal, P. D. Pearson, & R. Barr (Eds.),

Handbook of reading research: Vol. III (pp. 285-310). Mahwah, NJ: Lawrence Erlbaum Associates.

Alfassi, M. (2004). Reading to learn: Effects of combined strategy instruction on high school students. *The Journal of Educational Research, 97*(4), 171-184.

Allan, A. (1992). Development and validation of a scale to measure test-wiseness in EFL/ESL reading test takers. *Language Testing, 9*(2), 101-122.

Allan, A. (1995). Begging the questionnaire: Instrument effect on readers' responses to a self-report checklist. *Language Testing, 12*, 133-153.

Anderson, N. (1991). Individual differences in strategy use in second language reading and testing. *Modern Language Journal, 75*(4), 460-472.

Anderson, N. (2005). L2 learning strategies. In E. Hinkel (Ed.), *Handbook of research in second language teaching and learning* (pp. 757-771). Mahwah, NJ: Lawrence Erlbaum.

Anderson, N., Bachman, L., Perkins, K., & Cohen, A. (1991). An exploratory study into the construct validity of a reading comprehension test: Triangulation of data sources. *Language Testing, 8*(1), 41-66.

Anderson, R., Pichert, J., & Shirey, L. (1983). Effects of the reader's schema at different points in time. *Journal of Educational Psychology, 75*, 271-279.

Anderson, R., Reynolds, R., Schallert, D., & Goetz, E. (1977). Frameworks for comprehending discourse. *American Educational Research Journal 14*(4), 367-381.

Asher, J. (1969). The total physical response approach to second language learning. *Modern Language Journal, 53*(1), 3-17.

Asher, J. (1972). Children's first language as a model of second language learning. *Modern Language Journal, 56*, 133-139.

Aslanian, Y. (1985). Investigating the reading problem of ESL students: An alternative. *ELT Journal, 39*(1), 20-27.

Assiri, M. S. (2011). *Test-taking strategy use on the reading section of the TOEFL iBT: A study of Arab ESL learners* (Doctoral dissertation). Available from ProQuest dissertation and theses database. (Document ID 3474513)

Assiri, M. S. (2014). Metacognitive and cognitive strategy use and performance on a reading test with multiple-format tasks. *Arab World English Journal, 5*(4), 187-202.

Assiri, M. S. (2015). Development of a rating scale for elementary EFL writing. *International Journal of Social, Management, Economics and Business Engineering, 9*(1), 91 - 99.

Bachman, L. (1985). Performance on cloze tests with fixed-ratio and rational deletions. *TESOL Quarterly, 19*(3), 535-556.

Bachman, L. (1990). *Fundamental considerations in language testing.* Oxford, England: Oxford University Press.

Bachman, L. (1991). What does language testing have to offer? *TESOL Quarterly, 25,* 671-704.

Bachman, L., & Palmer, A. (1996). *Language testing in practice.* Oxford, England: Oxford University Press.

Baker, A. (2010). *Ship or sheep?: An intermediate pronunciation course.* Cambridge: Cambridge University Press.

Baker, L. (2008). Metacognitive development in reading: Contributors and consequences. In K. Mokhtari & R. Sheorey (Eds.), *Reading strategies of first- and second-language learners: See how they read* (pp. 25-42). Norwood, MA: Christopher-Gordon.

Baker, L., & Brown, A. (1984). Metacognitive skills and reading. In D. Pearson (Ed.), *Handbook of reading research* (pp. 353-394). New York: Longman.

Barnett, M. (1988). Reading through context: How real and perceived strategy use affects L2 Comprehension. *Modern Language Journal, 72,* 150-162.

Baumann, J., Jones, L., & Seifert-Kessell, N. (1993). Using think alouds to enhance children's comprehension monitoring abilities. *The Reading Teacher, 47*(3), 184-193.

Belcher, D. (2004). Trends in teaching English for specific purposes. *Annual Review of Applied Linguistics, 24*, 165-186.

Bello, T. (1999). New avenues to choosing and using videos. *TESOL Matters, 9*(4), 1-20.

Birch, B. (2002). *English L2 reading: Getting to the bottom.* Mahwah, NJ: Erlbaum.

Birdsong, D. (1999). *Second language acquisition and the critical period hypothesis.* Mahwah, NJ: Lawrence Erlbaum Associates Publishers.

Bland, J. (1995). *How adult readers navigate through expository text in a hypermedia environment to construct meaning* (Doctoral dissertation). Available from ProQuest Dissertations and Theses database. (UMI No. 9612595)

Bongaerts, T. (1999). Ultimate attainment in L2 pronunciation: The case of very advanced late L2 learners. In D. Birdson (Ed.), *Second language acquisition and the critical period hypothesis* (pp. 133-159). Mahwah, NJ: Erlbaum.

Brinton, D. (2001). The use of media in language teaching. In Celce-Murcia, M. (Ed.), *Teaching English as a second or foreign language* (pp. 459-475). Boston, MA: Heinle & Heinle.

Britt, M., & Gabrys, G. (2001).Teaching advanced literacy skills for the World Wide Web. In C. Wolfe (Ed.), *Learning and teaching on the World Wide Web* (pp. 73-90). San Diego, CA: Academic Press.

Brookfield, S. (1985). Self-directed learning: a critical review of research. In S. Brookfield (Ed.). *Self-directed learning: From theory to practice* (pp. 5-16). San Francisco, CA: Jossey-Bass.

Brown, H. (1994). *Principles of language learning and teaching.* (3rd ed.) Prentice Hall.

Brown, H. (2000). *Principles of language learning and teaching* (4th ed.). White Plains: Pearson Education.

Brown, H. (2001). *Teaching by principles: An interactive approach to language.* New York: Longman.

Brown, H. (2007). *Principles of language learning and teaching* (5th ed.). White Plains, NY: Longman.

Brown, H., & Abeywickrama, P. (2010). *Language assessment: Principles and classroom practices.* White Plains, NY: Pearson Education.

Brown, A., & Day, J. (1983). Macro-rules for summarizing texts: The development of expertise. *Journal of Verbal Learning and Verbal Behavior, 22*(1), 1-14.

Brown, C., & Brown, P. (2006). *English grammar secrets.* Retrieved April, 12, 2008, from http://www.englishgrammarsecrets.com/presentperfectorpastsimple/exercise3.html

Brown, J., & Hudson, T. (2002). *Criterion-referenced language testing.* Cambridge: Cambridge University Press.

Brumfit, C. (1984). *Communicative methodology in language teaching.* Cambridge: Cambridge University Press.

Brumfit, C., & Johnson, K. (1979). *The communicative approach to language teaching.* Oxford: Oxford Community Press.

Burt, M. (1999). *Using video with adult English language learners.* Retrieved April, 12, 2011, from http://www.cal.org/caela/esl%5Fresources/digests/video.html

Cain, K., Oakhill, J., & Bryant, P. (2004). Children's reading comprehension ability: Concurrent prediction by working memory, verbal ability, and component skills. *Journal of Educational Psychology, 96,* 31-42.

Campbell, R., & Wales, R. (1970). The study of language acquisition. In J. Lyon (Ed.), *New horizons in linguistics* (pp. 242-260). Harmondsworth: Penguin.

Canale, M., & Swain, M. (1980). Theoretical bases of communicative approaches to second language teaching and testing. *Applied Linguistics, 1*(1), 1-47.

Carrell, P. (1988a). Some causes of text-boundedness and schema interference in ESL reading. In P. Carrell, J. Devine, & D. Eskey (Eds.), *Interactive approaches to second language* reading (pp. 101-113). Cambridge: Cambridge University Press.

Carrell, P. (1988b). Interactive Text Processing: Implications for ESL/ Second Language Reading Classrooms. In P. Carrell, J. Devine, & D. Eskey (Eds.), *Interactive approaches to second language reading* (pp. 239-259). Cambridge: Cambridge University Press.

Carrell, P. & Eisterhold. J. (1983). Schema theory and ESL reading pedagogy. *TESOL Quarterly, 17*(4), 553-573.

Carrell, P., Devine, J., & Eskey, D. (1988). *Interactive approaches to second language reading.* Cambridge: Cambridge University Press.

Carrier, K. (2003). Improving high school English language learners' second language listening through strategy instruction. *Bilingual Research Journal 27.*3, 383–408.

Carroll, S., & Swain, M. (1993). Explicit and implicit negative feedback. *Studies in Second Language Acquisition, 15*(3), 357-386.

Casanave, C. (2004). *Controversies in second language writing: Dilemmas and decisions in research and instruction.* Ann Arbor, MI: The University of Michigan Press.

Celce-Murcia, M. (1991). Grammar pedagogy in second and foreign language teaching. *TESOL Quarterly, 25*(3), 459-480.

Celce-Murcia, M. (1992). Formal grammar instruction: An educator comments. *TESOL Quarterly, 26*, 406-409.

Celce-Murcia, M. (2002). Why it makes sense to teach grammar in context and through discourse. In E. Hinkel & S. Fotos (Eds.), *New perspectives on grammar teaching in second language classrooms.* (pp. 119-133). Mahwah, NJ, US: Lawrence Erlbaum Associates Publishers.

Celce-Murcia, M., & Goodwin, J. (1991). Teaching pronunciation. In Celce-Murcia M. (Ed.) *Teaching English as a Second Language.* Newbury House: New York.

Celce-Murcia, M., & McIntosh, L. (1979). *Teaching English as a Second or Foreign Language.* Rowley, MA: Newbury House.

Chamot, A. (1999). *Learning strategy instruction in the English classroom.* Retrieved November 17, 2007 from http:// www.Jalt-publications.org/tlt/article/1999/ Chamot/

Chamot, A. (2005). Language learning strategy instruction: Current issues and research. *Annual Review of Applied Linguistics 25*, 98–111.

Chen, H. (1998). The performance of junior college students studying English through cooperative learning. *Proceedings of the Seventh International Symposium on English Teaching* (pp. 231-240). Taipei: Crane.

Clark, M. & Silberstein, S. (1977). Toward a realization of psycholinguistic principles in the ESL reading class. *Language Learning, 27*(1), 48-65.

Cohen, A. (1984). On taking language tests: What the students report. *Language Testing, 1*(1), 70-81.

Cohen, A. (1986). Mentalistic measures in reading strategy research: Some recent findings. *The ESP Journal, 5*(2), 131-145.

Cohen, A. (1992). Test-taking strategies on language tests. *Journal of English and Foreign Languages, 10-11*, 90-105.

Cohen, A. (1994a). *Assessing language ability in the classroom* (2nd ed.). Boston, MA: Newbury House/Heinle & Heinle.

Cohen, A. (1994b). English for academic purposes in Brazil: The use of summary tasks. In C. Hill & K. Parry (Eds.), *From testing to assessment: English as an international language* (pp. 174-204). London, UK: Longman.

Cohen, A. (1998). Strategies and processes in test taking and SLA. In L. F. Bachman & A. D. Cohen (Eds.), *Interfaces between second language acquisition and language testing research* (pp. 90-111). Cambridge: Cambridge University Press.

Cohen, A. (2000). Exploring strategies in test taking: Fine-tuning verbal reports from respondents. In G. Ekbatani & H. Pierson (Eds.), *Learner-directed assessment in ESL* (pp. 131-145). Mahwah, NJ: Erlbaum.

Cohen, A. (2005). *Coming to terms with language learner strategies: What do strategy experts think about the terminology and where would they direct their research?* Working Paper No. 12.

Research Paper Series. Auckland, NZ: Centre for Research in International Education, AIS St. Helens. Retrieved May 23, 2009, from http://www.crie.org.nz/research_paper/Andrew%20Cohen%20WP12.pdf

Cohen, A. (2006). The coming of age of research on test-taking strategies. *Language Assessment Quarterly, 3,* 307-331.

Cohen, A., & Aphek, E. (1979). *Easifying second language learning.* Jerusalem, Israel: The Jacob Hiatt Institute.

Cohen, A., & Upton, T. (2006). *Strategies in responding to the New TOEFL reading tasks* (TOEFL Monograph Series Report No. 33). Princeton, NJ: Educational Testing Service. Retrieved from http://www.ets.org/Media/Research/pdf/RR-06-06.pdf.

Connor, U. (1996). *Contrastive rhetoric: Cross-cultural aspects of second-language writing.* Cambridge: Cambridge University Press.

Conroy, P. (1999). Total physical response: An instructional strategy for second-language learners who are visually impaired. *Journal of Visual Impairment and Blindness, 93*(5), 315-318.

Corder, S. (1967). The significance of learners' errors. *International Review of Applied Linguistics, 5,* 161–170.

Corder, S. (1971). Idiosyncratic dialects and error analysis. *International Review of Applied Linguistics, 9,* 147-160.

Corder, S. (1973). *Introducing Applied Linguistics.* Harmondsworth: Penguin.

Corder, S. (1978). Language-learner language. In J. C. Richards (Ed.), *Understanding second and foreign language learning* (pp. 71-92). Rowley, MA: Newbury House.

Cordón, L., & Day, J. (1996). Strategy use on standardized reading comprehension tests. *Journal of Educational Psychology, 88*(2), 288-295.

Coto, R. (2002). Improving listening comprehension in a second language through the use of learning strategies. *Revista Káñina, 26*(1), 97-105.

Cummins, J. (1979). Cognitive/academic language proficiency, linguistic interdependence, the optimum age question and some other matters. *Working Papers on Bilingualism, No. 19*, 121-129.

Cummins, J. (1984) *Bilingual Education and Special Education: Issues in Assessment and Pedagogy.* San Diego, CA: College Hill.

Cummins, J. (2000). *Language, power and pedagogy: Bilingual children in the crossfire.* Clevedon, UK: Multilingual Matters.

Cziko, G. (1978). Differences in first- and second-language reading: The use of syntactic, semantic and discourse constraints. *The Candian Modern Language Review, 34*, 473-489.

Cziko, G. A. (1980). Language competence and reading strategies: A Comparison of first- and second-language oral reading errors. *Language Learning, 30*, 101-116.

Davies, A., Brown, A., Elder, C., Hill, K., Lumley, T., & McNamara, T. (2002). *Dictionary of language testing.* Cambridge, UK: Cambridge University Press.

DeKeyser, R. (1995). Learning second language grammar rules: An experiment with a miniature linguistic system. *Studies in Second Language Acquisition, 17*, 379-410.

DeKeyser, R. (2003). Implicit and explicit learning. In C. Doughty & M. Long (eds.), *Handbook of second language acquisition* (pp., 313-348). Oxford: Blackwell.

Derwing, T., & Rossiter, M. (2003). The effect of pronunciation instruction on the accuracy, fluency and complexity of L2 accented speech. *Applied Language Learning, 13*, 1–17.

Dole, J., Duffy, G., Roehler, L., & Pearson, P. (1991). Moving from the old to the new: Research in reading comprehension instruction. *Review of Educational Research, 61*, 239-264.

Dollerup, C., Glahn, E., & Hansen, C. (1982). Reading strategies and test-solving techniques in an EFL reading comprehension test: A preliminary report. *Journal of Applied Language Study, 1*(1), 93-99.

Doughty, C., & Williams, J. (1998). Pedagogical choices in focus on form. In C. Doughty & J. Williams (eds.), *Focus on form in classroom second language acquisition* (pp. 197–263). Cambridge: Cambridge University Press.

Douglas, D. (1981). An exploratory study of bilingual reading proficiency. In S. Hudelson (Ed.), *Learning to read in different languages* (pp. 33-102). Washington, DC: Center for Applied Linguistics.

Douglas, D. (2000). *Assessing language for specific purposes.* Cambridge: Cambridge University Press.

Edge, J. (1994). *Mistakes and correction.* London: Longman.

Elliot, R. (1997). On the teaching and acquisition of pronunciation within a communicative approach. *Hispania, 80,* 95-108.

Ellis, R. (1995). *The study of second language acquisition.* Oxford: Oxford University Press..

Ellis, R. (1997). *Second Language Acquisition.* Oxford: Oxford University Press.

Ellis, R. (2001). Investigating form-focused instruction. *Language Learning, 51,* 1-46.

Ellis, R. (2002a). Does form-focused instruction affect the acquisition of implicit knowledge? A review of the research. *Studies in Second Language Acquisition, 24*(2), 223-236.

Ellis, R. (2002b). The place of grammar instruction in the second/ foreign curriculum. In E. Hinkel and S. Fotos (Eds.), *New perspectives on grammar teaching in second language classrooms* (pp. 17-34). Mahway, NJ: Lawrence Erlbaum.

Ellis, R. (2003). *Task-based language learning and teaching.* Oxford applied linguistics. Oxford: Oxford University Press.

Ellis, R., Basturkmen, H., & Loewen, S. (2001). Pre-emptive focus on form in the ESL classroom. *TESOL Quarterly, 35,* 407-432.

Farr, R., Pritchard, R., & Smitten, B. (1990). A description of what happens when an examinee takes a multiple-choice reading comprehension test. *Journal of Educational Measurement, 27*(3), 209-226.

Fathman, A., & Whalley, E. (1990). Teacher response to student writing: Focus on form versus content. In B. Kroll (Ed.), *Second language writing* (pp. 178-190). Cambridge, UK: Cambridge University Press.

Ferman, I. (2005). Implementing performance-based assessment in the EFL classroom. *ETAI Forum, 16*(4).

Fink, L. (2003). *Creating significant learning experiences: An integrated approach to designing college courses.* San Francisco, CA: Jossey-Bass.

Flege, J., Munro, M., & MacKay, I. (1995). Effects of age of second-language learning on the production of English consonants. *Speech Communication, 16*(1), 1-26.

Foltz, P. (1996). Comprehension, coherence, and strategies in hypertext and linear text. In J. Rouet, J. Levonen, A. Dillon, & R. Spiro (Eds.), *Hypertext and cognition* (pp. 109-136). Mahwah, NJ: Lawrence Erlbaum Associates.

Forster, D., Karn, R., Suzuki, S. & Tateyama, T. (1997). *Strategies 1: Building TOEIC/TOEFL test-taking skills.* Tokyo: Aratake Publishing Co., Ltd.

Frodesen, J. (2001). Grammar in writing. In M. Celce-Murcia (Ed.), *Teaching English as a second or foreign language* (pp. 233-248). Boston, MA: Heinle & Heinle.

Galloway, V. (1980). Perceptions of the communicative efforts of American students of Spanish. *Modern Language Journal, 64*(4), 428-433.

Garner, R., & Krauss, K. (1982). Good and poor comprehender differences in knowing and regulating reading behaviors. *Educational Research Quarterly, 6*, 5-12.

Gass, S., & Selinker, L. (2001). *Second language acquisition: An introductory course.* Mahwah, NJ: Lawrence Erlbaum Associates.

Gee, J. (2013). *Language and learning in the digital age.* New York, NY: Routledge.

Goh, C. (1998). How ESL learners with different listening abilities use comprehension strategies and tactics. *Language Teaching Research 2*, pp. 124–147.

Goodman, K. (1998). The reading process. In P. Carrell, J. Devine, & D. Eskey (Eds.), *Interactive approaches to second language reading* (pp. 11-21). Cambridge: Cambridge University Press.

Gordon, C. (1987). *The effect of testing method on achievement in reading comprehension tests in English as a foreign language* (Master thesis). Tel Aviv, Israel: Tel Aviv University.

Grabe, W. (1988). Reassessing the word interactive. In P. L. Carrell, J. Devine, & D. E. Eskey (Eds.), *Interactive approaches to second language reading* (pp. 56-70). Cambridge: Cambridge University press.

Grabe, W., & Kaplan, R. (1989). Writing in a second language: Contrastive rhetoric. In D. M. Johnson & D. H. Roen (Eds.), *Richness in writing: Empowering ESL students* (pp. 263–283). New York, London: Longman

Grabe, W., & Kaplan, R. (1996). *Theory and practice of writing: An applied linguistic perspective.* Essex: Longman.

Grotjahn, R. (1987). How to construct and evaluate a C-Test: A discussion of some problems and some statistical analyses. In R. Grotjahn, C. Klein-Braley, & D. K. Stevenson (Eds.), *Taking their measure: The validity and validation of language tests* (pp. 219-254). Bochum, Germany: Brockmeyer.

Gulzar, M., Gulnaz, F., & Ijaz, A. (2014). Utility of Krashen's five hypotheses in the Saudi context of foreign language acquisition/learning. *English Language Teaching, 7*(8), 134-138.

Hadley, A. (2001). *Teaching language in context.* Boston, MA: Heinle and Heinle.

Halleck, G. (2007). Data generation through role-play: Assessing oral proficiency. *Simulation & Gaming, 38*(1), 91-106.

Hani, N. (2014). Benefits and barriers of computer assisted language learning and teaching in the Arab world: Jordan as a model. *Theory and Practice in Language Studies, 4*(8), 1609-1615.

Harris, V. (2001). *Helping Learners Learn: Exploring strategy instruction in language classrooms across Europe.* Strasbourg: Council of Europe.

Hauptman, P. (1979). A comparison of first and second language reading strategies among English-speaking university students. *Interlanguage Studies Bulletin, 4,* 173-201.

Hayes, D. (2009). Non-native English-speaking teachers, context and English language teaching. *System, 37*(1), 1-11.

Hedgcock, J., & Lefkowitz, N. (1994). Feedback on feedback: Assessing learner receptivity in second language writing. *Journal of Second Language Writing, 3,* 141–163.

Hendrickson, J. (1976). *The effects of error correction treatments upon adequate and accurate communication in the written compositions of adult learners of English as a second language.* Unpublished dissertation, Ohio State University.

Hendrickson, J. (1980). The treatment of error in written work. *Modern Language Journal, 64,* 216-221.

Herschensohn, J., Stevenson, J., & Waltmunson, J. (2005). Children's acquisition of L2 Spanish morphosyntax in an immersion setting. *IRAL: International Review of Applied Linguistics in Language Teaching, 43*(3), 193-217.

Hewings, M. (2004). *Pronunciation practice activities: A resource book for teaching English pronunciation.* Cambridge: Cambridge University Press.

Higgs, T., & Clifford, R. (1982). The push toward communication. In T. V. Higgs (Ed.), *Curriculum, competence, and the foreign language teacher* (pp. 57-79). Lincolnwood, IL: National Textbook Co.

Hillocks, G. (1986). Synthesis of research on teaching writing. *Educational Relationship, 44*(8), 71-82.

Hinkel, E. (2002). Grammar teaching in writing classes: Tenses and cohesion. In E. Hinkel & S. Fotos (Eds.), *New perspectives* on grammar teaching in second language classrooms (pp.181–198). Mahwah, NJ: Erlbaum.

Homburg, T., & Spaan, M. (1982) ESL reading proficiency assessment: testing strategies. In M. Hines and W. Rutherford (Eds.), *On TESOL '81* (pp. 25-33). TESOL, Washington.

Hood, P. (1994). Communicative grammar: a practical problem-solving approach? *Language Learning Journal, 9*(1), 28-31.

Housen, A., & Pierrard, M. (2005). Investigating instructed second language acquisition. In A. Housen, & M.Pierrard (Eds.), *Investigations in instructed second language acquisition* (pp. 1-27). Germany: Mouton de Gruyter.

Housen, A., Pierrard, M. & Van Daele, S. (2005). Structure Complexity and the Efficacy of Explicit Grammar Instruction. In A. Housen & M. Pierrard (Eds.), *Investigations in instructed second language acquisition* (pp. 235-269). Berlin: Mouton de Gruyter.

Hsiao, T-Y. (2004). Testing a social psychological model of strategy use with students of English as a foreign language. *Psychological Reports, 95,* 1059-1071.

Hudson, T. (1988). The effects of induced schemata on the 'short circuit' in L2 reading: Non-decoding factors in L2 reading performance. In P. Carrell, J. Devine, & D. Eskey (Eds.), *Interactive approaches to second language reading* (pp. 183-205). Cambridge: Cambridge University Press.

Hughes, A. (2003). *Testing for language teachers.* Cambridge: Cambridge University Press.

Hurst, B., Scales, K., Frecks, E., & Lewis, K. (2011). Sign up for reading: Students read aloud to the class. *The Reading Teacher, 64*(6), 439-443.

Hymes, D. (1967). Models of the interaction of language and social setting. *Journal of Social Issues, 23*(2), 8-38.

Hymes, D. (1972). On Communicative Competence. In Pride, J., & Holmes, J. (Eds.), *Sociolinguistics* (pp. 269-293). Baltimore, MD: Penguin Books Ltd.

Imber, B., & Parker, M. (1991). *Milieu-specific pronunciation*. Paper presented at the 26ᵗʰ Annual TESOL Convention, New York.

Ioup, G., Boustagui, E., El Tigi, M., & Moselle, M. (1994). Reexamining the critical period hypothesis: A case study of successful adult SLA in a naturalistic environment. *Studies in Second Language Acquisition, 16*(1), 73-98.

Johns, A. (1997). *Text, role, and context: Developing academic literacies*. Cambridge: Cambridge University Press.

Johnson, J., & Newport, E. (1989). Critical period effects in second language learning: The influence of maturational state on the acquisition of English as a second language. *Cognitive Psychology, 21*(1), 60-99.

Jones, R. (1997). Beyond "Listen and Repeat": Pronunciation teaching materials and theories of second language acquisition. *System, 25*(1), 103-112.

Kaufmann, L. (1993). *"Please correct me if I'm wrong"*. Unpublished paper presented at the 10ᵗʰ AILA Congress, Amsterdam.

Kalivoda, T., Morain, G., & Elkins, R. (1971). The audio-motor unit: A listening comprehension strategy that works. *Foreign Language Annals, 4*(4), 392-400.

Kaplan, R. (1966). Cultural thought patterns in inter-cultural education. *Language Learning, 16*, 1-20.

Kaplan, R. (1967). Contrastive rhetoric and the teaching of composition. *TESOL Quarterly, 1*, 10–16.

Kaplan, R. (1972). *The anatomy of rhetoric: Prolegomena to a functional theory of rhetoric*. Philadelphia, PA: Center for Curriculum Development.

Kaplan, R. (1988). Contrastive rhetoric and second language learning: Notes towards a theory of contrastive rhetoric. In A. C. Purves (Ed.), *Writing across languages and cultures* (pp. 275–304). Newbury Park, CA: Sage Publications.

Karen, L., Eleonore, S., Wolfgang, G., Inge, K., & Marko, W. (2011). Language comprehension versus language production:

Age effects on fMRI activation. *Brain and Language, 119*(1), 6-15.

Kenworthy, J. (1987). *Teaching English pronunciation.* Essex: Longman.

Kern, R. (1998). Technology, social interaction and FL literacy. In J. Muyskens (Ed.), *New ways of learning and teaching: Focus on technology and foreign language education* (pp.57-92). Boston, MA: Heinle & Heinle Publishers.

Kleiman, A., Cavalcanti, M., Terzi, S., & Ratto, I. (1986). *Perception of the lexicon and its discourse function: Some conditioning factors.* Universidade Estadual de Campinas, Campinas, Brazil.

Klein-Braley, C. (1985). A close-up on the C-Test: A study in the construct validation of authentic tests. *Language Testing, 2,* 76-104.

Klein-Braley, C. & Raatz, U. (1984). A survey of research on the C-Test. *Language Testing, 1,* 134-146.

Kobayashi, M. (2002). Method effects on reading comprehension test performance: Text organization and response format. *Language Testing, 19*(2), 193-220.

Krashen, S. (1982). *Second language acquisition and second language learning.* Oxford: Pergamon Press.

Krashen, S. (1992). Formal grammar instruction: An educator comments. *TESOL Quarterly, 26,* 409-411.

Krashen, S. (1993). The effects of formal grammar teaching: Still peripheral. *TESOL Quarterly, 27,* 722-725.

Kumaravadivelu, B. (2001). Towards a post-method pedagogy. *TESOL Quarterly, 35*(4), 537-559.

Kymes, A. (2008). Reconceptualizing reading strategy use in online environments. In K. Mokhtari & R. Sheorey (Eds.), *Reading strategies of first-and second-language learners: See how they read* (pp. 185-196). Norwood, MA: Christopher-Gordon.

Labadi, Y. (1990). *A contrastive study of tense and aspect in English and Japanese: Pedagogical implications.* Ph.D. dissertation, The

University of Texas at Austin, United States -- Texas. Retrieved April 11, 2008, from ProQuest Digital Dissertations database.

Lado, R. (1957). *Linguistics across cultures: Applied linguistics for language teachers.* University of Michigan Press: Ann Arbor.

Lee, I. (2002). Helping students develop coherence in writing. *English Teaching Forum, 40*(3), 32-39.

Lenneberg, E. (1967). *Biological foundations of language.* New York: Wiley.

Lennon, P. (1991). Error: Some problems of definition, identification, and distinction. *Applied Linguistics, 12,*180-195.

Lewis, M., & Reinders, P. (2007). *Using student-centered methods with teacher-centered students.* Toronto, Canada: Pippin Publishing.

Li, C. (2013). The influence of Krashen's input hypothesis on teaching college English listening in China. *Studies in Literature and Language, 6*(3), 49-52.

Lightbown, P. (1991). What have we here? Some observations on the influence of instruction on L2 learning. In R. Phillipson, E. Kellerman, M. Sharwood Smith, & M. Swain (Eds.), *Foreign/ second language pedagogy research* (pp. 197- 212). Clevedon, England: Multilingual Matters.

Lightbown, P., & Pienemann, M. (1993). Comments on Stephen D. Krashen's "Teaching Issues: Formal Grammar Instruction." *TESOL Quarterly, 27*(4), 717-721.

Lin, H., & Chen, T. (2006). Decreasing cognitive load for novice EFL learners: Effects of question and descriptive advance organizers in facilitating EFL learners' comprehension of an animation-based content lesson. *System, 34*(3), 416-431.

Lin, M., Wang, P., & Lin, I. (2012). Pedagogy technology: A two-dimensional model for teachers' ICT integration. *British Journal of Educational Technology, 43,* 97-108.

Long, D. (1989). Second language listening comprehension: A schema-theoretic perspective. *The Modern Language Journal, 73,* 32-40.

Long, M. (1985). Input and second language acquisition theory. In S. Gass & C. Madden(Eds.), *Input in second language acquisition* (pp. 377–393). Rowley, MA: Newbury House.

Long, M. (1991). Focus on form: A design feature in language teaching methodology. In K. de Bot, R. Ginsberg, & C. Kramsch (Eds.), *Foreign language research in cross-cultural perspective* (pp. 39-52). Amsterdam: John Benjamins.

Long, M. (1996). The role of the linguistic environment in second language acquisition. In W. C. Ritchie & T. K. Bhatia (Eds.), *Handbook of language acquisition, vol. 2: Second language acquisition* (pp. 413-468). New York: Academic Press.

Long, M. (2003). Stabilization and fossilization in interlanguage development. In C. Doughty & M. Long (Eds.), *The handbook of second language acquisition* (pp. 487-535). Malden, MA: Blackwell Publishing.

Long, M. (2012). Current trends in SLA research and directions for future development. *Chinese Journal of Applied Linguistics, 35*(2), 135-152.

Long, M., & Robinson, P. (1998). Focus on form: Theory, research, and practice. In C. Doughty & J. Williams (Eds), *Focus on form in classroom second language acquisition* (pp. 15-41). New York: Cambridge University Press.

Lumley, T., & Brown, A. (2004). Test-taker and rater perspectives on integrated reading and writing tasks in the Next Generation TOEFL. *Language Testing Update, 35*, 75-79.

Lumley, T., & Brown, A. (2006). *Test taker response to integrated reading/writing tasks in TOEFL: Evidence from writers, texts, and raters.* (Final Report to ETS). Melbourne: Language Testing Research Centre, University of Melbourne.

Lund, R. (1990). A taxonomy for teaching second language listening. *Foreign Language Annals, 23*, 105-115.

Lyster, R. (2004). Research on form-focused instruction in immersion classrooms: Implications for theory and practice. *Journal of French Language Studies, 14*(3), 321-341.

Lyster, R., & Ranta, L. (1997). Corrective feedback and learner uptake. *Studies in Second Language Acquisition, 19*(01), 37-66.

Macaro, E., & Masterman, E. (2006). Does intensive explicit grammar instruction make all the difference? *Language Teaching Research, 10*(3), 297-327.

Mangubhai, F. (1990). Towards a taxonomy of strategies used by ESL readers of varying proficiencies while doing cloze exercises. *Australian Journal of Reading, 13*(2). 128-139.

Mangubhai, F. (1990). Towards a taxonomy of strategies used by ESL readers of varying proficiencies while doing cloze exercises. *Australian Journal of Reading, 13*(2). 128-139. Belford Park, Australia: Australian Reading Association.

Mangubhai, F. (1991). The processing behaviors of adult second language learners and their relationship to second language proficiency. *Applied Linguistics, 12*, 268-298.

Mareschal, C. (2007). *Student perceptions of a self-regulatory approach to second language listening comprehension development.* Ph.D. dissertation, University of Ottawa.

Marinova-Todd, S., Marshall, D., & Snow, C. (2000). Three misconceptions about age and L2 learning. *TESOL Quarterly, 34*(1), 9-34.

Mauranen, A. (2001). Descriptions or explanations? Some methodological issues in contrastive rhetoric. In M. Hewings (Ed.), *Academic writing in context* (pp. 43-54). Birmingham, UK: University of Birmingham Press.

McCarthy, M. (1991). *Discourse analysis for language teachers.* Cambridge: Cambridge University Press.

McCormick, C., & Pressley, M. (1997). *Educational psychology: Learning, instruction, assessment.* New York: Longman.

Medgyes, P. (1992). Native or non-native: Who's worth more? *ELT Journal, (46)*4, 340–349.

Moore, Z. (1996). *Foreign language teacher education: Multiple perspectives.* Lanham, MD: University Press of America.

Myers, M., & Paris, S. (1978). Children's metacognitive knowledge about reading. *Journal of Educational Psychology, 70*, 680-690.

Mendelsohn, D. (1995). Listening comprehension: disturbing realities and attainable dreams. *English Teachers' Journal (Israel) 48.* Ministry of Education and Culture, Jerusalem, Israel.

Mokhtari, K., & Reichard, C. (2008). The impact of reading purpose on the use of reading strategies. In K. Mokhtari & R. Sheorey (Eds.), *Reading strategies of first-and second-language learners: See how they read* (pp. 85-97). Norwood, MA: Christopher-Gordon.

Mokhtari, K., & Sheorey, R. (2008). *Reading strategies of first- and second-language learners: See how they read.* Norwood, MA: Christopher-Gordon.

Mokhtari, K., Sheorey, R., & Reichard, C. (2008). Measuring the reading strategies of first- and second-language readers. In K. Mokhtari & R. Sheorey (Eds.), *Reading strategies of first- and second-language learners: See how they read* (pp. 43-65). Norwood, MA: Christopher-Gordon.

Morley, J. (1991). The pronunciation component of teaching English to speakers of other languages. *TESOL Quarterly, 25*, 481–520.

Munby, J. (1978). *Communicative syllabus design.* Cambridge, UK: Cambridge University Press.

Murphy, R. (2012). *English grammar in use: A self-study reference and practice book for intermediate students of English with answers.* Cambridge: Cambridge University Press.

Naiman, N. (1987). Teaching pronunciation communicatively. *TESL Talk, 17*(1), 141-147.

Nevo, N. (1989). Test-taking strategies on a multiple-choice test of reading comprehension. *Language Testing, 6*(2), 199-215.

Nikolov, M. (2006). Test-taking strategies of 12-13-year-old Hungarian learners of EFL: Why whales have migraine. *Language Learning, 57*(1), 1-51.

Norman, J. (2003). *Creativity is important.* The Orange County Register.

Norris, J., & Ortega, L. (2000). Effectiveness of L2 instruction: A research synthesis and quantitative meta-analysis. *Language Learning, 50*(3), 417-528.

Nunan, D. (1985). Content familiarity and the perception of textual relationships in second language reading. *RELC Journal, 16,* 43-50.

Nunan, D. (2000). *Language teaching methodology: A textbook for teachers.* Hong Kong: Open University of Hong Kong Press.

O'Malley, J., & Chamot, A., Stewner-Manzanares, G., Kupper, L., & Russo, R. (1985). Learning strategies used by beginning and intermediate ESL students. *Language Learning, 35,* 21–46.

Olson, L., & Samuels, S. (1973). The relationship between age and accuracy of foreign language pronunciation. *The Journal of Educational Research, 66,* 263-268.

Oxford, R. (1990). *Language learning strategies: what every teacher should know.* Boston: Heinle & Heinle.

Patkowski, M. (1980). The sensitive period for the acquisition of syntax in a second language. *Language Learning, 30,* 449–472.

Patkowski, M. (2003). Laterality effects in multilinguals during speech production under the concurrent task paradigm: Another test of the age of acquisition hypothesis. *IRAL: International Review of Applied Linguistics in Language Teaching, 41*(3), 175-200.

Petrić, B. (2005). Contrastive rhetoric in the writing classroom: A case study. *English for Specific Purposes, 24*(2), 213-228.

Phakiti, A. (2003). A closer look at the relationship of cognitive and metacognitive strategy use to EFL reading achievement test performance. *Language Testing, 20*(1), 26-56.

Phakiti, A. (2006). Modeling cognitive and metacognitive strategies and their relationships to EFL reading test performance. *Melbourne Papers in Language Testing, 11*(1), 53–95.

Phakiti, A. (2008). Strategic competence as a third-order factor. *Language Assessment Quarterly, 5*(1), 20-42.

Pica, T. (1984). Pronunciation activities with an accent on communication. *English Teaching Forum,* July, 2-6.

Pica, T., Doughty, C., & Young, R. (1986). Making input comprehensible: Do interactional modifications help? *ITL Review of Applied Linguistics, 72*, 1-25.

Phillipson, R. (1992). *Linguistic Imperialism.* Oxford: Oxford University Press.

Poole, A., & Mokhtari, K. (2008). ESL students' use of reading strategies when reading online and in print. In K. Mokhtari & R. Sheorey (Eds.), *Reading strategies of first-and second-language learners: See how they read* (pp. 197-213). Norwood, MA: Christopher-Gordon.

Powers, D., & Wilson Leung, S. (1995). Answering the new SAT reading comprehension questions without the passages. *Journal of Educational Measurement, 32*(2), 105-129.

Prabhu, N. (1987). *Second language pedagogy.* Oxford: Oxford University Press.

Pressley, M., & Afflerbach, P. (1995). *Verbal protocols of reading: The nature of constructively responsive reading.* Hillsdale, NJ: Lawrence Erlbaum Associates Inc.

Pressley, M., & Gaskins, I. (2006). Metacognitively competent reading comprehension is constructively responsive reading: How can such reading be developed in students? *Metacognition and Learning, 1*(1), 99-113.

Purpura, J. (1997). An analysis of the relationships between test takers' cognitive and metacognitive strategy use and second language test performance. *Language Learning, 47*(2), 289-325.

Purpura, J. (1998). Investigating the effects of strategy use and second language test performance with high- and low-ability test takers: A structural equation modeling approach. *Language Testing, 15*(3), 333-379.

Purpura, J. (1998). Investigating the effects of strategy use and second language test performance with high- and low-ability test takers: A structural equation modeling approach. *Language Testing, 15*(3), 333-379.

Purpura, J. (1999). *Strategy use and second language test performance: A structural equation modeling approach.* Cambridge: Cambridge University Press.

Raimes, A. (1990). The TOEFL test of written English: Causes for concern. *TESOL Quarterly, 24*(3), 427-442.

Rasinski, T. (2006). Reading fluency instruction: Moving beyond accuracy, automaticity, and prosody. *The Reading Teacher, 59*(7), 704-706.

Reid, J. (1984). ESL composition: The linear product of American thought. *College Composition and Communication, 35*, 449–452.

Reid, J. (1989). English as second language composition in higher education: The expectations of the academic audience. In D. M. Johnson & D. H. Roen (Eds.), *Richness in writing: Empowering ESL students* (pp. 220–234). New York, NY: Longman.

Reid, J. (1993). *Teaching ESL writing.* Englewood Cliffs, NJ: Prentice Hall Regents.

Reid, J. (1996). U.S. academic readers, ESL writers, and second sentences. *Journal of Second Language Writing, 5*, 129–161.

Reyes, M. (1992). Challenging venerable assumptions: Literacy instruction for linguistically different students. *Harvard Educational Review, 62*, 427-444.

Richards, J. & Rodgers, T. (1986). *Approaches and Methods in Language Teaching.* Cambridge University Press.

Rivers, W. (1964). *The psychologist and the foreign language teacher.* Chicago, IL: University of Chicago Press.

Roeschl-Heils, A., Schneider, W., & van Kraayenoord, C. (2003). Reading literacy, metacognition and motivation: A follow-up study of German students in Grades 7 and 8. *European Journal of Psychology of Education, 18*, 75-86.

Rogers, W., & Bateson, D. (1991). The influence of test-wiseness on performance of high school seniors on school leaving examinations. *Applied Measurement in Education, 4*(2), 159-183.

Rogerson-Revell, P. (2011). *English phonology and pronunciation teaching.* London: Continuum.

Ross, S., & Rost, M. (1991). Learner Use of Strategies in Interaction. Typology and Teachability. *Language Learning, 41*, 235-273.

Rost, M. (2001). *Teaching and researching listening.* London: Longman.

Rubin, J. (1988). *Improving foreign language listening comprehension.* ERIC Clearinghouse on Languages and Linguistics. Washington, DC: US Department of Education.

Rupp, A., Ferne, T., & Choi, H. (2006). How assessing reading comprehension with multiple-choice questions shapes the construct: A cognitive processing perspective. *Language Testing, 23*(4), 441-474.

Sarangi, S. (1994). Intercultural or not? Beyond celebration of cultural differences in miscommunication analysis. *Pragmatics, 4*(3), 409-427.

Scarcella, R. (1996). Secondary education and second language research: ESL students in the 1990's. *The CATESOL Journal, 9*, 129–152.

Schachter, J. (1988). Second language acquisition and its relationship to universal grammar. *Applied Linguistics, 9*(3), 219-235.

Schmidt, R. (1990). The role of consciousness in second language learning. *Applied Linguistics, 11*, 129-158.

Schmidt, R. (1992). Psychological mechanisms underlying second language fluency. *Studies in Second Language Acquisition, 14* (3), 357-385.

Schmidt, R. (1994). Deconstructing consciousness in search of useful definitions for applied linguistics. *AILA Review, 11*, 11-26.

Scovel, T. (2000). A critical review of the critical period research. *Annual Review of Applied Linguistics, 20*, 213-223.

Selinker, L. (1972). Interlanguage. *International Review of Applied Linguistics, 10*, 209-241.

Semke, H. (1984). Effects of the red pen. *Foreign Language Annals, 17*, 195-202.

Sheorey, R., & Mokhtari, K. (2001). Differences in the metacognitive awareness of reading strategies among native and non-native readers. *System, 29*(4), 431-449.

Silva, T. (1993). Toward an understanding of the distinct nature of L2 writing: The ESL research and its implications. *TESOL Quarterly, 27*, 657–677.

Singhal, M. (2001). Reading proficiency, reading strategies, metacognitive awareness and L2 readers. *The Reading Matrix, 1*(1), 1-23.

Singleton, D. (2005). The critical period hypothesis: A coat of many colors. *IRAL: International Review of Applied Linguistics in Language Teaching, 43*(4), 269-285.

Singleton, D. (1989). *Language acquisition: The age factor.* Philadelphia, PA: Multilingual Matters.

Smerdon, B., Cronen, S., Lanahan, L., Anderson, J., Iannotti, N., & Angeles, J. (2000). *Teachers' tools for the 21ˢᵗ century: A report on teachers' use of technology.* Washington, DC: National Center for Education Statistics.

Smith, S. (1979). Strategies, language transfer and the simulation of the second language learner's mental operations. *Language Learning, 29*, 345-361.

Snow, C., & Hoefnagel-Höhle, M. (1978). The critical period for language acquisition: Evidence from second language learning. *Child Development, 49*(4), 1114-1128.

Spada, N. (1997). Form-focused instruction and second language acquisition: A review of classroom and laboratory research. *Language Teaching, 30*, 73–87.

Sreehari, P. (2012). Communicative language teaching: Possibilities and problems. *English Language Teaching, 5*(12), 87-93.

Stemmer, B. (1991). *What's on a C-test taker's mind? Mental processes in C-test taking*. Bochum, Germany: Brockmeyer.

Storey, P. (1995). *Developing and validating a taxonomy of test-taking strategies*. In Proceedings of the conference on Testing and Evaluation in Second Language Education, Hong Kong University of Science and Technology.

Storey, P. (1997). Examining the test-taking process: A cognitive perspective on the discourse cloze test. *Language Testing, 14*(2), 214-231.

Stott, N. (2001). Helping ESL students become better readers: Schema theory applications and limitations. *The Internet TESL Journal, 7*(11). Retrieved February 20, 2012, from http://iteslj.org/Articles/Stott-Schema.html.

Sutherland, K. (1967). The place of dictation in the language classroom. *TESOL Quarterly, 1*(1), 24-29.

Swales, J. (1990). *Genre analysis*. Cambridge: Cambridge University Press.

Swain, M. (1985). Communicative competence: Some roles of comprehensible input and comprehensible output in its development. In S. Gass & C. Madden (Eds), *Input in second language acquisition* (pp. 235-253). Rowley, MA: Newbury House.

Terrell, T. (1991). The role of grammar instruction in a communicative approach. *The Modern Language Journal, 75*, 52-63.

TESOL (2007). *About TESOL Quarterly*. Retrieved November 5, 2007, from http://www.tesol.org/s_tesol/seccss.asp?CID=632&DID=2461

Tezci, E. (2011). Factors that influence pre-service teachers' ICT usage in education. *European Journal of Teacher Education, 34,* 483-499.

Thatcher, B. (2004). Rhetorics and communication media across cultures. *Journal of English for Academic Purposes, 3*(4), 305-320.

Thomas, W., & Collier, V. (1997). School effectiveness for language minority students. Washington, D.C.: National Clearinghouse for Bilingual Education.

Thompson, I. & Rubin, J. (1996). Can strategy instruction improve listening comprehension? *Foreign Language Annals, 29*(3), 331-342.

Tian, S. (2000). *TOEFL reading comprehension: Strategies used by Taiwanese students with coaching-school training* (Doctoral dissertation). Available from ProQuest Dissertations and Theses database. (UMI No. 9976766)

Truscott, J. (1996). The case against grammar correction in L2 writing classes. *Language Learning, 46*(2), 327-369

Tsagari, C. (1994). *Method effect on testing reading comprehension: How far can we go?* (Master's thesis). Available from ERIC database. (ED424768)

Upton, T. (1997). First and second language use in reading comprehension strategies of Japanese ESL students. *TESL-EJ, 3*(1).

Upton, T. & Lee-Thompson, L. (2001).The role of the first language in second language reading. *Studies in Second Language Acquisition, 23*(4), 469-495.

Vandergrift, L. (1997a). The cinderella of communication strategies: Receptive strategies in interactive listening. *Modern Language Journal, 81,* 494-505.

Vandergrift, L. (1997b). The strategies of second language (French) listeners: A descriptive study. *Foreign Language Annals, 30,* 387–409.

Vandergrift, L. (1999). Facilitating Second Language Listening Comprehension: Acquiring Successful Strategies. *ELT Journal, 53*, 168-176.

Vandergrift, L. (2002). 'It was nice to see that our predictions were right': Developing Metacognition in L2 Listening Comprehension. *Canadian Modern Language Review, 58*, 555-575.

Vandergrift, L. (2003a). From prediction through reflection: Guiding students through the process of L2 listening. *The Canadian Modern Language Review, 59*(3), 425–440.

Vandergrift, L. (2004). Listening to learn or learning to listen? *Annual Review of Applied Linguistics, 24*, 3–25.

Vandergrift, L. (2007a). Teaching students how to listen: Effects on listening achievement. Paper presented at the annual meeting of the American Association of Applied Linguistics, Cosa Mesa, CA, USA.

Vandergrift, L. (2007b). Recent developments in second and foreign listening comprehension research. *Language Teaching, 40*, 191-210.

Vandergrift, L., Goh, C., Mareschal, C., & Tafaghodatari, M. (2006). The Metacognitive Awareness Listening Questionnaire (MALQ): Development and validation. *Language Learning 56*, 431–462.

Vigil, N., & Oller, J. (1976). Rule fossilization: A tentative model. *Language Learning, 26*, 281-295.

Walz, J. (1982). *Error correction techniques for the foreign language classroom*. Washington, DC: Center for Applied Linguistics.

White, L., Spada, N., Lightbown, P., & Ranta, L. (1991). Input enhancement and L2 question formation. *Applied Linguistics, 12*, 416–432.

Widdowson, H. (1978). *Teaching language as communication*. Oxford: Oxford University Press.

Widdowson, H. (1986). The untrodden ways. In C. Brumfit & R. Carter (Eds), *Literature and language teaching* (pp.133-139). Oxford: Oxford University Press.

Widdowson, H. G. (1996). Comment: Authenticity and autonomy in ELT. *ELT Journal, 50*(1), 67-68.

Wijgh, I. (1995). A communicative test in analysis: Strategies in reading authentic texts. In A. Cumming & R. Berwick (Eds.), *Validation in language testing* (pp. 154-170). Clevedon: Multilingual Matters.

Wilkins, D. (1976). *Notional syllabuses.* Oxford: Oxford University Press.

Willis, D. (1997). *Second language acquisition.* Birmingham: The University of Birmingham.

Willis, D. (2003). *Rules, patterns and words: Grammar and lexis in English language teaching.* Cambridge language teaching library, Cambridge: Cambridge University Press.

Willis, D. & Willis, J. (2001). Task-based language learning. In R. Carter, & D. Nunan (Eds.), *The Cambridge guide to teaching English to speakers of other languages* (pp. 173-179). Cambridge: Cambridge University Press.

Winograd, P., & Hare, V. (1988). Direct instruction of reading comprehension strategies: The nature of teacher explanation. In C.E. Weinstein, E.T. Goetz, & P. A. Alexander (Eds.), *Learning and study strategies: Issues in assessment, instruction, and evaluation* (pp. 121-139). New York: Academic Press.

Wong, R. (1987). *Teaching pronunciation: Focus on English rhythm and intonation.* New Jersey: Prentice Hall-Regents.

Wright, M. (1999). Grammar in the language classroom: Findings from research. *Language Learning Journal, 19*(1), 33-39.

Yamashita, J. (2003). Processes of taking a gap-filling test: Comparison of skilled and less skilled EFL readers. *Language Testing, 20*(3), 267-293.

Yang, P. (2000). *Effects of test-wiseness upon performance on the Test of English as a Foreign Language* (Doctoral dissertation). Available from ProQuest Dissertations and Theses database. (UMI No. NQ59700)

Yang, Y. (2002). Reassessing readers' comprehension monitoring. *Reading in a Foreign Language, 14,* 18-42.

Yien, L. (2001). Effective test-taking strategies on English tests: Implications from Taiwanese students. *Hong Kong Journal of Applied Linguistics, 6*(2), 22-43.

Yorio, C. (1980). Conventionalized language forms and the development of communicative competence. *TESOL Quarterly, 14*(4), 433-442.

Yoshizawa, K. (2002). *Relationships among strategy use, foreign language aptitude, and second language proficiency: A structural equation modeling approach* (Doctoral dissertation). Available from ProQuest Dissertations and Theses database. (UMI No. 3040378)

Young, D. (1991). Creating a low-anxiety classroom environment: What does language anxiety research suggest? *The Modern Language Journal, 75*(4), 426-439.

Yule, G. (1998). *Explaining English grammar.* Oxford handbooks for language teachers. Oxford: Oxford University Press.

Zhang, Y., & Wang, J. (2012). The elaboration of cultivating learners' English communicative competence in China. *English Language Teaching, 5*(12), 111-120.

Subject Index

Author Index